TRACING YOUR
SURREY ANCESTORS

FAMILY HISTORY FROM PEN & SWORD BOOKS

Birth, Marriage & Death Records
The Family History Web Directory
Tracing British Battalions on the Somme
Tracing Great War Ancestors
Tracing History Through Title Deeds
Tracing Secret Service Ancestors
Tracing the Rifle Volunteers
Tracing Your Air Force Ancestors
Tracing Your Ancestors
Tracing Your Ancestors from 1066 to 1837
Tracing Your Ancestors Through Death Records – Second Edition
Tracing Your Ancestors Through Family Photographs
Tracing Your Ancestors Through Letters and Personal Writings
Tracing Your Ancestors Using DNA
Tracing Your Ancestors Using the Census
Tracing your Ancestors Using the UK Timeline
Tracing Your Ancestors: Cambridgeshire, Essex, Norfolk and Suffolk
Tracing Your Aristocratic Ancestors
Tracing Your Army Ancestors
Tracing Your Army Ancestors – Third Edition
Tracing Your Birmingham Ancestors
Tracing Your Black Country Ancestors
Tracing Your Boer War Ancestors
Tracing Your British Indian Ancestors
Tracing Your Canal Ancestors
Tracing Your Channel Islands Ancestors
Tracing Your Church of England Ancestors
Tracing Your Criminal Ancestors
Tracing Your Docker Ancestors
Tracing Your East Anglian Ancestors
Tracing Your East End Ancestors
Tracing Your Family History on the Internet
Tracing Your Female Ancestors
Tracing Your First World War Ancestors
Tracing Your Freemason, Friendly Society and Trade Union Ancestors
Tracing Your Georgian Ancestors, 1714–1837
Tracing Your Glasgow Ancestors
Tracing Your Great War Ancestors: The Gallipoli Campaign
Tracing Your Great War Ancestors: The Somme
Tracing Your Great War Ancestors: Ypres
Tracing Your Huguenot Ancestors
Tracing Your Insolvent Ancestors
Tracing Your Irish Family History on the Internet
Tracing Your Jewish Ancestors
Tracing Your Jewish Ancestors – Second Edition
Tracing Your Labour Movement Ancestors
Tracing Your Legal Ancestors
Tracing Your Liverpool Ancestors
Tracing Your Liverpool Ancestors – Second Edition
Tracing Your London Ancestors
Tracing Your Medical Ancestors
Tracing Your Merchant Navy Ancestors
Tracing Your Northern Ancestors
Tracing Your Northern Irish Ancestors
Tracing Your Northern Irish Ancestors – Second Edition
Tracing Your Oxfordshire Ancestors
Tracing Your Pauper Ancestors
Tracing Your Police Ancestors
Tracing Your Potteries Ancestors
Tracing Your Pre-Victorian Ancestors
Tracing Your Prisoner of War Ancestors: The First World War
Tracing Your Railway Ancestors
Tracing Your Roman Catholic Ancestors
Tracing Your Royal Marine Ancestors
Tracing Your Rural Ancestors
Tracing Your Scottish Ancestors
Tracing Your Second World War Ancestors
Tracing Your Servant Ancestors
Tracing Your Service Women Ancestors
Tracing Your Shipbuilding Ancestors
Tracing Your Tank Ancestors
Tracing Your Textile Ancestors
Tracing Your Twentieth-Century Ancestors
Tracing Your Welsh Ancestors
Tracing Your West Country Ancestors
Tracing Your Yorkshire Ancestors
Writing Your Family History
Your Irish Ancestors

Tracing Your Surrey Ancestors

A Guide for Family Historians

SARAH PETTYFER

Pen & Sword
FAMILY HISTORY

First published in Great Britain in 2025 by
PEN AND SWORD FAMILY HISTORY
An imprint of
Pen & Sword Books Ltd
Yorkshire – Philadelphia

Copyright © Sarah Pettyfer 2025

ISBN 978 1 03611 010 9

The right of Sarah Pettyfer to be identified as Author of this work has been asserted by her in accordance with the Copyright, Designs and Patents Act 1988.

A CIP catalogue record for this book is available from the British Library.

All rights reserved. No part of this book may be reproduced, transmitted, downloaded, decompiled or reverse engineered in any form or by any means, electronic or mechanical including photocopying, recording or by any information storage and retrieval system, without permission from the Publisher in writing. NO AI TRAINING: Without in any way limiting the Author's and Publisher's exclusive rights under copyright, any use of this publication to "train" generative artificial intelligence (AI) technologies to generate text is expressly prohibited. The Author and Publisher reserve all rights to license uses of this work for generative AI training and development of machine learning language models.

Typeset by Mac Style
Printed in the UK by CPI Group (UK) Ltd, Croydon, CR0 4YY.

The Publisher's authorised representative in the EU for product safety is Authorised Rep Compliance Ltd., Ground Floor, 71 Lower Baggot Street, Dublin D02 P593, Ireland. www.arccompliance.com

For a complete list of Pen & Sword titles please contact

PEN & SWORD BOOKS LIMITED
47 Church Street, Barnsley, South Yorkshire, S70 2AS, England
E-mail: enquiries@pen-and-sword.co.uk
Website: www.pen-and-sword.co.uk
or
PEN AND SWORD BOOKS
1950 Lawrence Road, Havertown, PA 19083, USA
E-mail: uspen-and-sword@casematepublishers.com
Website: www.penandswordbooks.com

CONTENTS

Preface and Acknowledgements — vii
Abbreviations — ix
Introduction: A Brief History of the County of Surrey — x

Chapter 1 Traditional Trades and Occupations — 1
　　　　　　Agriculture — 1
　　　　　　Trades and craftsmen — 3
　　　　　　Mills — 3

Chapter 2 Getting Started — 15
　　　　　　A. General Registration Office Records (GRO) — 15
　　　　　　B. Census returns — 19
　　　　　　C. Parish registers and Bishop's Transcripts — 23
　　　　　　D. Monumental Inscriptions — 32
　　　　　　E. Wills and Probate — 35

Chapter 3 Taking your Online Research Further — 48
　　　　　　A. Newspapers — 48
　　　　　　B. Directories — 53
　　　　　　C. Poll books and electoral registers. — 55
　　　　　　D. Land Tax records. — 58
　　　　　　E. Tithe records. — 61
　　　　　　F. Inland Revenue valuation records – Lloyd
　　　　　　　　George Domesday Survey — 62
　　　　　　G. Useful indexes available from the Surrey
　　　　　　　　History Centre website — 64

Chapter 4	**Researching in Local Archives**	65
	A. Parish chest records – beyond the registers	65
	B. Quarter Sessions, Petty Sessions and associated records.	84
	C. Land ownership and occupation	96
	D. Manors and manorial records	110
	E. Surrey schools	119
	F. Apprenticeship indentures and associated records	124
	G. Locally held military, militia and defence records	130
	H. Mental health asylums	135
	I. Nonconformity	142
	J. Ecclesiastical court records (excluding probate)	148
	K. Heraldry	152
	L. Miscellany	153
Chapter 5	**Records at The National Archives**	155
	A. Civil court records	155
	B. Assize courts	158
	C. Land records	163
	D. Tax records	166
Chapter 6	**Directory of Archives, Libraries and Societies**	171
Notes		174
Bibliography		176
Index		179

PREFACE AND ACKNOWLEDGEMENTS

Surrey, with its rich history, once encompassed several areas that now form part of the London boroughs south of the River Thames. This historical backdrop, coupled with numerous boundary changes over the years, adds layers of complexity to genealogical research in the region. Tracing Surrey ancestors requires navigating through various repositories and understanding the historical context that influenced record-keeping practices.

This book is designed to be a comprehensive guide for anyone embarking on the journey to uncover their Surrey ancestry. It provides essential background information on the history of Surrey, highlighting the significant boundary changes that have occurred and their impact on where records are held today. These changes can often cause confusion for researchers, and this book aims to clarify these complexities by guiding you to the most likely places where relevant records can be found.

The primary objective of this book is to introduce readers to the sources and resources available for tracing Surrey ancestors. It offers a thorough overview of the various archival repositories and online databases, detailing which records are held where and any finding aids that may assist in your research. While no book can claim to be a definitive guide, due to the ever-expanding catalogues of digitised records, this guide aims to be as comprehensive as possible, providing a clear roadmap for researchers.

Whether you are just beginning your genealogical journey or are a seasoned researcher seeking specific insights into Surrey's past, this book is intended to be your guide. Our hope is that it will equip you with the tools and knowledge needed to navigate the often-complex landscape of Surrey's genealogical records.

This book would not have been possible without the hard work and research undertaken by those who have compiled the many research aids and guides, archives and organisations detailed throughout, including (but not limited to):

- Surrey History Centre
- The London Archive
- The National Archives
- Hampshire Record Office
- Cliff Webb
- West Surrey Family History Society
- East Surrey Family History Society

My grateful thanks in particular go to the staff at Surrey History Centre for their encouragement and support. All extracts of records are reproduced by permission of Surrey History Centre unless otherwise stated.

My grateful thanks also go to the Bray family and the More-Molyneux family for allowing the publication of extracts from the manorial records held among their vast family collections at Surrey History Centre.

Unless otherwise stated, photographs have been taken by me.

ABBREVIATIONS

ESFHS – East Surrey Family History Society
HRO – Hampshire Record Office
TLA – The London Archive
QS – Quarter Sessions
RBA – Royal Berkshire Archives
SHC – Surrey History Centre
TNA – The National Archives
WSFHS – West Surrey Family History Society

Introduction

A BRIEF HISTORY OF THE COUNTY OF SURREY

Surrey has been described as 'the residential appendage of an overgrown monster of a city',[1] having been the rural retreat of the monarchy and many wealthy London gentry since before the time of Henry VIII. The county does not appear to have ever really had its own identity or centre, with London ever encroaching on its boundaries.

Most of the ancient boundaries of Surrey are characterised by indistinct features, created no doubt by the various occupiers and battles over the land through the ages. With the city of London having originally been founded by the Romans on the northern banks of the River Thames, until the late nineteenth century the county of Surrey was bounded by the River Thames and the county of Middlesex to the north, the counties of Berkshire and Hampshire to the west, the county of Kent to the east and the county of Sussex[2] to the south.

Relatively little is known about the history of Surrey. Roman remains have been found, but it seems Ancient Surrey, during Roman times, was largely an agricultural area through which the Romans passed rather than settled in large numbers; no large Roman encampments have been found. Southwark was most probably the largest Roman town in Surrey where two Roman roads, Watling Street (linking London and Dover) and Stane Street (linking London and Chichester) met. Roman remains have also been found at Staines (in Middlesex until 1965), where the Romans would have crossed the Thames towards London. The High Street at Staines was formed from an island where the Colne met the Thames, and where a small Roman town developed with bridges over the many tributaries from those rivers carrying the London to Silchester highway.

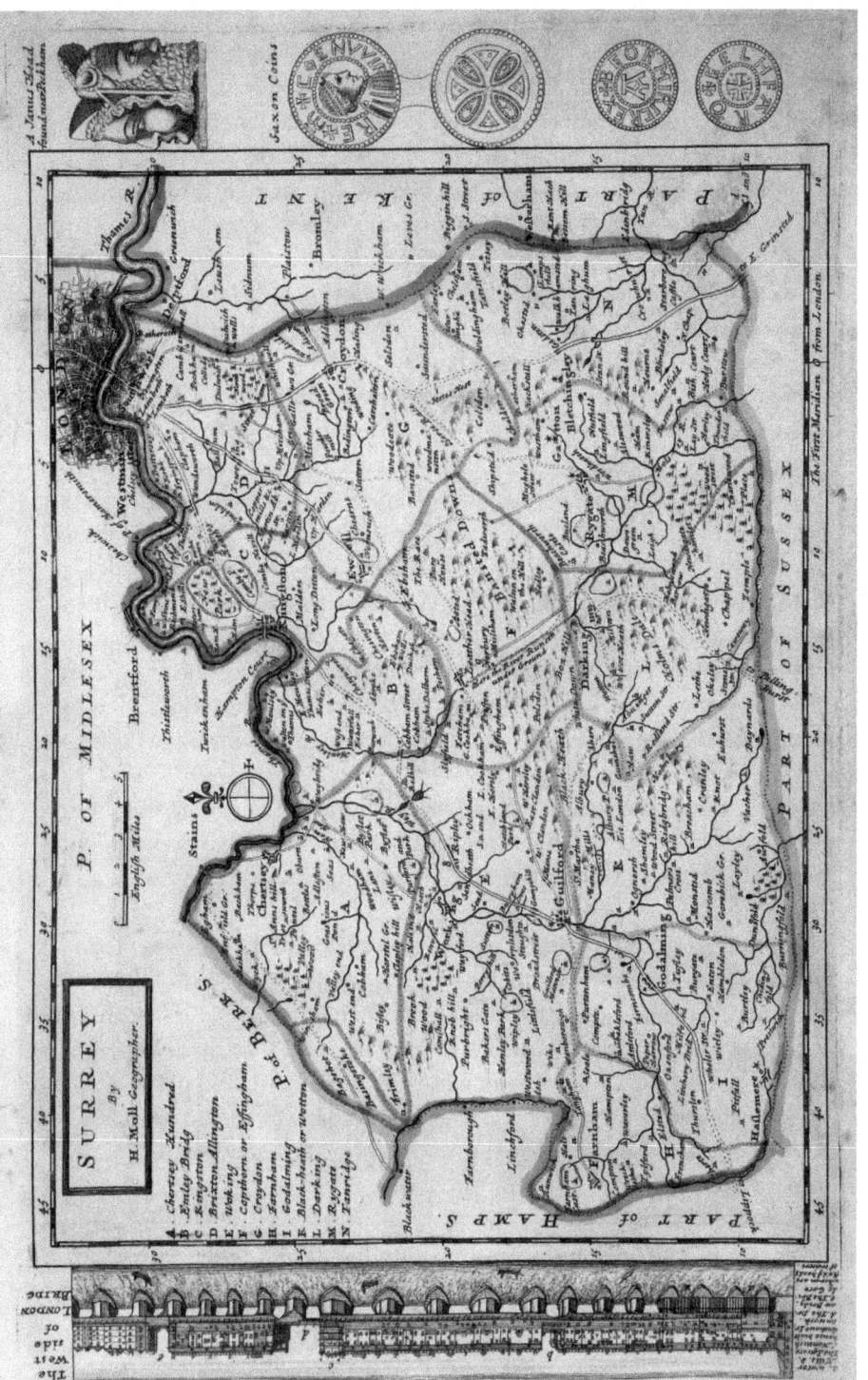

Ancient map of Surrey parish boundaries reproduced by permission of ARCHI UK.

Some records do survive from Anglo-Saxon Surrey with its earliest entry in the *Anglo-Saxon Chronicles* dating from AD 675[3] when, following the founding of St Peter Chertsey Benedictine Abbey in AD 666 under King Egbert, dwellings were granted to support 200 men at Cirotesige (Chertsey) and five dwellings 'in a place called Thorpe'.

Land was also granted by Cedwalla at Farnham in AD 688[4] for a monastery, while the Manor of Chertsey Abbey was confirmed in AD 727[5] as having being granted by Fritheuuald, the *Subrefulus* of Surrey (meaning petty prince or vassal ruler) in 675, to include land at Muelseie (Molesey), Piterichesham (Petersham), Totinge cum Stretham (Tooting and Streatham), Micham (Mitcham), Suþton (Sutton), Æuuelton (Carshalton), Bedintone (Beddington), Whatindaon (Waddington), Curedesdone (Coulsdon), Mestham (Merstham), Chepstede cum Chalvedune (Chipstead with Chaldon), Benstede cum suþemeresfelda) (Banstead with Suthemeresfelda (Canon's Farm in Banstead)), þeddewurþe (Tadworth), Ebesham (Epsom), Euuell cum Cotintone (Ewell with Cuddington), Cegeham cum porcorum pascuis in þanewald (Cheam with swine-pasture in the Weald), Bocham cum Effingeham (Bookham with Effingham), Coveham cum Pontinton (Cobham with Pointers), Essere (Esher), Clenedone et in altera Clenedone (East and West Clandon) Aldeburi (Albury), Comptone (Compton), Henlea (Henley Park), Winchefeld (Winchfield), Byflete cum Weibrugge (Byfleet with Weybridge).

During the seventh century, Surrey, or Suthrige[6] meaning southern region as it was known at the time, did not exist as a separate kingdom but was a battleground between the kingdoms of Mercia, Wessex and Kent.

At the time of the founding of St Peter Chertsey Benedictine Abbey in AD 666, King Egbert was the ruler of the kingdom of Kent; however, Fritheuuald was a vassal ruler under Wulfhere, the first Christian ruler of the kingdom of Mercia, while by AD 688 Cedwalla, who made the grant to establish an abbey at Farnham, was ruler of the kingdom of Wessex.

Because Surrey is a landlocked county, the area was spared the coastal raiding of the Danish Vikings in the ninth century until an extraordinarily large invasion in AD 851 when,

> came three hundred and fifty ships into the mouth of the Thames; the crew of which went upon land, and stormed Canterbury and London; putting to flight Bertulf, king of the Mercians, with his army; and then marched southward over the Thames into Surrey. Here Ethelwulf and his son Ethelbald, at the head of the West-Saxon

army, fought with them at Aclea [Ockley near Dorking], and made the greatest slaughter of the heathen army that we have ever heard reported to this present day. There also they obtained the victory.[7]

Over the next twenty years, Southern England endured further battles against the Danes. In AD 853 the Saxons combined the Kent and Surrey army. Further rampages by the Danes across the south followed over the next twenty years although confined to East Anglia and Kent. In AD 871 there were a total of nine battles in the kingdom of Wessex including at Reading (in Berkshire) and Basing (Basingstoke) (in Hampshire) in which King Ethered lost his life and was succeeded by his brother Alfred. The Viking army retreated to London at the end of the year for the winter; however, it is likely that King Alfred paid the Danes in silver to leave, the Danes retaining control of the kingdoms of Mercia, Northumbria and East Anglia in the AD 880s.

This period also saw Alfred gradually extend his kingdom, reoccupying London in AD 886. When his eldest son, Edward, led an army to the Danes in AD 893 at Farnham, the safety of Surrey and Wessex were secured for the rest the Alfred's reign. His defeats over the Danes and his consolidation of the territories he gained, brought both Alfred and his successors power over the other Anglo-Saxon kings.

It was King Alfred (AD 871–899) who divided the country into burhs (boroughs) and shires (counties) and it is then that the county of Surrey was formed. In his will,[8] dated late AD 880s, Alfred bequeathed several places in Surrey including Godalming, Leatherhead, Guildford, Eashing and Sutton.

In the tenth century, Kingston (upon Thames) appears to have been a centre of importance with evidence of seven Anglo-Saxon kings being crowned there:[9] Edward the Elder (AD 899), Æthelstan (AD 925), Edmund I (AD 939), Eadred (AD 946), Eadwig (AD 955), Edward the Martyr (AD 975) and Æthelred the Unready (AD 979).

When William the Conqueror landed at Hastings in East Sussex in 1066, his men travelled west and north through Surrey, Hampshire, Berkshire and Oxfordshire crossing the River Thames at Wallingford, Oxfordshire to approach London from the north. It must be remembered that the River Thames was once much wider than it is today, particularly through London. Following the Roman settlement on the northern bank known as Londinium, the use of the river and the land surrounding was increased during the Middle Ages, mostly by farmers reclaiming the marshland and building protective embankments. In 2015, during construction work in the grounds of Parliament, a stone wall dating

'Guildford Castle' by Reading Tom is licensed under CC BY 2.0. T.

from around 1300 was unearthed, which is believed to be a stone river wall standing about 3 metres high. The oldest discovery, believed to date from before the thirteenth century, were the timber beams of a waterfront structure.

The Domesday Book[10] of 1086–7 states that Guildford was held by William the Conqueror consisting of '75 closes [parcels] in which dwell 175 men' but the castle, which he had ordered be built at Guildford shortly after the invasion, is not mentioned so perhaps was not complete by this time.

There were also a further five closes or parcels of land held by William. William had developed the feudal system and established the royal demesne whereby all land was owned by William and in return for fighting and providing knights, he granted large tranches of land to his barons as tenants-in-chief or demesne lords. In return for service, the barons then granted land within their holdings to their knights which they held as mesne lord. Large tranches were also retained by, or granted to, religious leaders, such as the archbishops, bishops and abbots.

According to the Domesday Book, there were thirty-five demesne lords and five mesne lords in Surrey across fourteen 'Hundreds', a 'Hundred' being an administrative area which had enough land to sustain approximately 100 households headed by an ealder or senior official. One hundred and forty villages are named with a population of around 4,600 heads of households suggesting an average of 32 households per village, the total number of heads of households in England at that time being 268,984.

The land comprised about 1,010 acres of plough land, 1,715 acres of meadows and 3,775 acres of woodlands. These figures demonstrate that Surrey was dominated by forests and in fact remains today England's most wooded county with over a fifth of the area covered by woodland.[11] These woodlands were such that Henry II (reigned 1154–1189) attempted to bring the entire county under the forest laws introduced by William the Conqueror, which protected animals such as deer from being hunted by anyone except the king or those to whom the king granted permission.

In the north of the county, the land of the London Basin is a mix of clay, silt, sand and gravel, forming heathland in the boroughs of Runnymede, Surrey Heath, Elmbridge and Woking. Below that is a ridge of chalk forming the North Downs, while Southern Surrey forms part of the Weald valley between the North and South Downs where Wealden Greensand, a type of sandstone, is the dominant soil.

The Weald was once a much denser forest than that of today, being famous for its oak, birch and beech trees, and extending across Sussex, Surrey and Kent. In Surrey, the Weald reaches its highest point of 294 metres at Leith Hill, the second highest point in south-east England. The South Downs National Park, Kent Downs Area of Outstanding Natural Beauty (AONB) and Surrey Hills AONB protect about half of the Weald.

Other than the River Thames forming the ancient county border to the north, three other important ancient rivers remain: the River Wey, the River Mole and the River Wandle, all tributaries of the Thames; the Wey flows south-west from Weybridge to Guildford and Godalming before splitting to head west into Hampshire and south into West Sussex; the

View of The Surrey Hills.

Mole flows south-east from Hampton Court Palace through Dorking and into West Sussex passing Gatwick airport; and the Wandle flows south from Wandsworth passing through those parts of old Surrey which now form London boroughs, such as Merton, Sutton, Mitcham, Carshalton, Beddington and Croydon. The Tillingbourne was also once an important river flowing from the north of Leith Hill through Friday Street, Abinger Hammer, Gomshall, Shere, Albury, Chilworth and Shalford.

Perhaps the most notable event to occur in Surrey's history is the signing of the Magna Carta by King John at Runnymede in June 1215. Stephan Langton, the then Archbishop of Canterbury, was fundamental in the negotiations which led to the signing of the Magna Carta and is alleged to have been born[12] at Friday Street, Surrey. The hamlet boasted a pub named after him until its closure in March 2020. It is more likely, however, that he was born at Langton by Wragby, Lincolnshire where his father, Henry Langton, was a landowner.

The Baron Wars concerning the rightful claimant to the throne, which followed the signing of the Magna Carta and King John's refusal to accept and abide by it, were centred in Surrey between two rival families: Richard de Clare's family seated at Bletchingley Castle (on the side of the Barons), and William de Warenne's seated at Reigate Castle (on the side of King John). When Louis of France (King Louis VIII as he later became) invaded England in 1216, King John retreated across Surrey to Corfe

Castle in Dorset. The castles of Guildford and Farnham fell to Louis but were retaken in the spring of 1217 by John's son, Henry III, following John's death.

In the fourteenth century, Surrey was not spared the effects of the Black Death (1338) and the Hundred Years War with France. It is impossible to determine the effect on the population of Surrey itself; however, it is commonly believed that between a third to a half of the entire population of England lost their lives to the Black Death. There is nothing to suggest Surrey faired any better. What few records do survive centre around the religious institutions and suggest entire populations fell to the disease. The decimation of the population had a significant impact on the feudal system and has been heralded as the catalyst for the decline of the manorial system when a shortage of labour saw landholders increasingly offer wages and require the paying of rent for smallholdings rather than land being provided in return for services.

The Black Death and the cost of the Hundred Years War resulted in the first introduction of the Poll Tax and the Peasants' Revolt of 1381 when in Surrey, tenants stormed Chertsey Abbey burning records including some of its manorial rolls, with another mob storming Guildford destroying the town's charter. The Poll Tax records reveal the population of men and women in Surrey over the age of 15 (excluding clergy) was 12,622. The actual population (including children, clergy etc.) was therefore likely to be about double that.

The reign of Henry VIII had a significant impact on Surrey and its residents. He built royal palaces at Richmond, Hampton Court, Oatlands (near Weybridge) and Nonsuch (which was unfinished when he died in 1547), and acquired several manors, either by exchange, confiscation or purchase – including Byfleet, Weybridge, Walton (on Thames), Molesey, Esher and Malden – which he declared royal forests. From these residences, Henry VIII enjoyed hunting.

The first round of Henry VIII's dissolution of the monasteries in 1536 saw many of Surrey's religious institutes closed and land sold, including Tandridge Priory, Reigate Priory and Waverley Abbey, followed in 1537 by Chertsey Abbey and in 1538 by Guildford Friary, while Tandridge and Waverley were left to rack and ruin. Reigate Priory was granted to Lord Edmund Howard in whose family it stayed for 140 years before passing through various families and today being Reigate Priory Junior School.

Chertsey Abbey had held several manors, some of which were initially retained by the Crown and later granted to certain families with lands then passing through generations and/or conveyed to others. Guildford Friary was retained by Henry VIII who converted the house into a dwelling as an occasional royal retreat which remained until 1606 when it was partly demolished before being granted to the Earl of Annandale in 1630. In 1794, the Friary was converted into barracks before being pulled down in 1818.

Following Henry VIII's lead, from the sixteenth century Surrey increasingly became a country retreat for the wealthy of London, while Surrey farmers began transporting their fresh produce to be sold to the growing population of London. The growing market led to an increase in agriculture, encroaching into the forests, parks and marginal lands to eke out every profit. These were, however, challenging times for the poor and several almshouses and/or hospitals were built, such as the Whitgift Hospital at Croydon during the reign of Elizabeth I by John Whitgift, and Abbot's Hospital at Guildford founded by George Abbot during the reign of James I.

Wealthy businessmen purchased land. For example, George Evelyn (whose grandson was the diarist, landscape designer and collector, John Evelyn) purchased Wotton Manor in 1579, building Wotton House there in the early seventeenth century; Sir William More built Loseley House from stone reclaimed from the ruins of nearby Waverley Abbey.

One benefactor of the poor in the early seventeenth century was Henry Smith, a wealthy silversmith and alderman of the City of London. When he died in 1627, his will left the bulk of his estate in trust to provide for the poor throughout the parishes of Surrey. The establishment of charities was no doubt welcomed in a century which saw the Great Plague and epidemics such as smallpox, measles and flu spread through the country. Those ancient parts of Surrey, which now form London boroughs, were particularly prone to such diseases, with the growing population of London spreading to these northern regions of Surrey. This is illustrated in the burial records for those parishes in comparison to the more southern rural parishes of Surrey.

The Civil War of the 1640s brought many battles to Surrey; its gentry, on the whole, were Parliamentarians obeying the order of Parliament issued on 20 June 1642 forbidding recruitment of militia in support of the king. Only Captain Quennel of Haslemere attempted to resist that order.

The first battle in Surrey was that at Farnham Castle, which the Royalists took possession of in November 1642. On 1 December that year, the Parliamentarians stormed the castle; the Royalists surrender allowed the Parliamentarians to use the castle as a base for Surrey, Hampshire and Sussex. When the second war began in 1649, battles were fought at Redhill, Ewell, Nonsuch Park, and Surbiton Common.

Following the restoration of Charles II, Surrey thrived once again as a country retreat with its Epsom Salts spa and the clean country air of the North Downs in contrast to the poor air quality in London. Writing in 1804, Manning and Bray[13] stated: 'The air is pure and wholesome: the general face of the Country open, and beautifully varied.'

The wealthy of London continued to purchase land and estates and build large country houses including Tadworth Court near Banstead, built by London merchant Leonard Wessels, and Westbrook at Godalming build by Sir Theophilus Oglethorpe (although its most famous owner is perhaps his son, James, who was the founder of the State of Georgia in the USA). Country houses still standing from this period also include Polesden Lacey at Great Bookham built by Anthony Rous after he purchased the estate in 1630.

At the same time, London continued to expand, with grand brick houses emerging from Camberwell to Clapham and along the southern banks of the River Thames to Richmond and beyond. In the eighteenth century, many more grand country houses were built, and Surrey became renowned for its landscaped gardens and parks. One good example that remains today is Claremont Landscape Garden near Esher, displaying the designs of landscape gardeners such as Charles Bridgeman and Capability Brown.

New mansions were built by large business owners such as the heads of the Castle Shipping Line, Royal Doulton Potteries (originally based in Vauxhall and later in Lambeth), Wedgewood Potteries, Stephen's Inks, Brook Bond Tea, and Price Waterhouse accountants, along with the Lord Chief Justice, High Court judges, doctors, artists, architects and other professionals. The net effect was increasing rents, increasing parish rates and overall Surrey becoming a more expensive place to live.

From the late eighteenth century, another significant change for Surrey was its transport links. Surrey was not well served with roads; most were in poor condition causing farmers, in particular, great difficulties accessing markets in the winter months – there being no regular carrier service. *Britannia Depicta*, an illustrated road atlas of Britain first published in 1720, only recorded four high roads across Surrey: the two old Roman roads; a further road running north to south from London to Arundel; and a further road running across the county from Godalming to Petworth and Chichester.

The late eighteenth and early nineteenth century saw the introduction of turnpike roads, built and managed by turnpike trusts set up by Acts of Parliament, the use of which required the payment of tolls. The A3 today, connecting London with Portsmouth, was one of these turnpike roads. Overall, there were twenty-three turnpike roads built across Surrey.

The nineteenth century brought further transport networks to the county. The county had been served by the Wey navigation canal since 1653 between the River Thames at Weybridge and Guildford and its extension to Godalming was completed in 1764. The Wey and Arun canal was completed in 1816 connecting the Wey navigation canal to the River Arun at Pallingham in West Sussex. The Basingstoke canal was also completed in 1794 connecting the River Thames at Weybridge to Basingstoke, passing through Mytchett, Brookwood, Knaphill and Woking in Surrey.

Surrey also provided an important link when a chain of semaphore stations was built, establishing a permanent communication link between the Admiralty in London and Portsmouth Dockyard, with seven of the fifteen towers being erected in Surrey at Putney Heath (Wimbledon then part of Surrey), Coombe Warren (New Malden then part of Surrey), Coopers Hill (Esher), Chatley Heath (Wisley), Pewley Hill (Guildford), Bannicle Hill (Witley), and Haste Hill (Haslemere). The line was operational from 1822 until railway and electric telegraph were introduced in 1847.

What is believed to have been England's first public railway opened in Surrey in 1802. The Surrey Iron Railway linked Wandsworth and Croydon via Mitcham – all still part of Surrey at the time. This was a horse-drawn toll railway established by Act of Parliament in 1801 transporting coal, building materials, lime, manure, corn and seeds. Its success, however, was short-lived. The building of the London to Croydon canal in 1809 increasingly made the railway less commercially viable. However, the canal itself was also not a success and closed in 1836. Upon the closure of the canal, the London & Croydon Railway Company bought the land and built the London to Croydon railway which opened in 1839. The introduction of this line and the steam engine led to the closure of the Surrey Iron Railway in 1846 when the London to Croydon railway line became part of the London, Brighton and South Coast Railway.

A further steam railway line was built from London in 1838, this time to Southampton, travelling through Esher, Walton-on-Thames, Weybridge and Woking, and throughout the century, more local network lines were opened connecting towns and villages across Surrey and to neighbouring counties creating commuter towns and villages boosting Surrey's population. In 1801, the population of Surrey was 269,043, by 1881 it was 1,436,899.[14] By 1891, due to boundary changes, Surrey's population reduced by almost two-thirds to 521,551.[15]

A steam train travelling on the London and Croydon Railway towards London Bridge. Tinted lithograph by E. Duncan, 1838. Source: Wellcome Collection. Reproduced under CC PDM 1.0.

In 1889, Surrey's ancient boundaries were changed when the Local Government Act 1888 created a new County of London incorporating the Surrey parishes of Battersea, Bermondsey, Camberwell, Clapham, Deptford, Lambeth, Newington, Penge (detached part of the parish of Battersea), Putney, Rotherhithe, Southwark, Streatham, Tooting Graveney, and Wandsworth to form the London boroughs of Lambeth, Southwark and Wandsworth. Further, while Croydon remained within the county of Surrey, a new borough council was created, and Barnes also remained within the county but under a new municipal borough.

Despite the boundary changes, over the next seventy years the population of Surrey once again swelled to 1,731,042[16] in 1961, but further boundary changes meant the recorded population dropped by just over a third to 1,002,889 by 1971.[17]

In 1965, the London boroughs of Croydon, Kingston, Merton, Richmond, Sutton and Wimbledon were created which saw the county of Surrey lose the parishes of Addington, Barnes, Beddington, Carshalton, Cheam, Chessington, Coulsdon, Croydon, Farleigh, Kew, Kingston, Malden, Merton, Mitcham, Morden, Mortlake, Petersham, Richmond, Sanderstead, Sutton, and Wimbledon. Simultaneously, the county of Middlesex was abolished, and Surrey gained a newly created borough of Spelthorne, which included the parishes of Ashford, Laleham, Littleton, Shepperton, Staines, Stanwell and Sunbury. Save for some minor changes in more recent years, these major changes created the modern county and boundaries of Surrey where the population has remained stable with a population of 1,203,108[18] being recorded in 2021.

Surrey today is a commuter county with the recent Covid pandemic and all its restrictions seeing yet another influx of previous London inhabitants moving to relatively cheaper housing with gardens and the open space of the countryside – which Surrey still retains as a result of the Surrey Hills AONB covering more than a quarter of the county across the North Downs.

Chapter 1

TRADITIONAL TRADES AND OCCUPATIONS

Surrey today is not well known for any particular industries but thought of as a commuter county for those working in London. However, like most of England, agriculture was the mainstay occupation throughout history with various industries have developed, thrived and declined over time.

Agriculture
Agriculture was particularly difficult in Surrey due to the varying soil; in the northern regions of the county, arable farming dominated on the easy-to-plough sandy loams, whereas the hard-drying heavy clay with poor drainage in the more southern and Wealden valley regions is difficult to plough and more suited to pasture.

For arable farmers, wheat, barley and oats were the mainstay crops, and prior to the nineteenth century, Surrey was largely a peasant population despite its attraction as a rural extension or countryside retreat for Londoners who brought pockets of wealth to the county. The produce of Surrey's agricultural labourers, therefore, was negligible compared to larger, more productive counties. In Surrey, the more successful agricultural labourers would have been able to produce sufficient crops/cattle to feed their families and sell small amounts at market – most likely selling annually raised calves, with many reliant on ancient rights of grazing animals on common land for this purpose. However, from the later eighteenth century, the London markets were opening to those who could turn their agricultural skills to market gardening and supply fresh fruit and vegetables. Root crops such as parsnips, carrots, turnips and potatoes, proved suitable for cultivation in the soils around Woking and Chertsey, became popular on the London markets.

Surrey's agricultural labourers benefited from the improvements in farming methods and crop rotation introduced in the eighteenth century that increased productivity and reduced the need to leave fields to rest and regenerate. The planting and success of root crops and new varieties of grasses also provided better food for cattle and sheep, enabling farmers to increase their herds and flocks. Banstead became well known for good quality local mutton.

Despite this, animal farming actually became increasingly difficult. The increase in wealthy merchants seeking the benefits of the Surrey air and open spaces led to the enclosure of the more fertile common land extinguishing those ancient rights of grazing on common land.

Enclosure awards were essentially the granting of enclosed larger areas of land rather than having strips of land spread across open fields. The process began in the twelfth century but became widespread from 1750. Open land was allotted to landowners by private Acts of Parliament and later by the Enclosure (aka Inclosure) Acts between 1801 and 1845.

Although the first private Act of Enclosure in Surrey was granted in 1709/10 for enclosing open land in Farnham, the Tudor monarchs had long been claiming and enclosing land to create royal parks, ousting tenants from their homes. For example, in 1526 Henry VIII purchased the Manor of Cuddington near Epsom where in the Domesday Book were recorded twenty-eight households. Henry demolished the manor house, parish church and all its houses, clearing out all who lived there, to build Nonsuch Palace and enclose two parks totalling about 1,600 acres of land. This had a significant impact on those who had been reliant on their grazing rights to eke out a living.

At the start of the nineteenth century, there were an estimated 73,940 acres of unenclosed land (total acreage of the county in 1831 was 474,480) most of which was common and heath land with about 8,000 acres being open field. By 1870, the general Act of Enclosure had reduced this to about 32,000 acres of unenclosed common and heath land.

This was exacerbated in Victorian times by wealthy merchants buying up farms to let at increased rents. Rising land costs and parish rates (to fund road improvements) along with the dramatic fall in grain prices in the agricultural depression of 1873 and 1896 had a major impact on the occupational landscape of Surrey and across the country. Labourers left the land to seek alternative occupations in towns. While the percentage of agricultural workers remained at around 2 per cent of the population of Surrey between 1871 and 1911,[1] due to the rise in the population, the numbers themselves fell by around 44 per cent with the acreage of arable land falling by around 47 per cent in a similar period (193,434 acres in 1872 to 102,364 in 1909).[2] By 1991, fewer than 1 per cent of Surrey's population were farmers and agricultural labourers, representing a further drop of more than 60 per cent from 1911 in the actual numbers of those involved. The increased mechanisation of farming has played a significant role in the reduction in farming not just in Surrey but across the country. The reduction in Surrey, however, can further be attributed to the county's proximity to London, which has placed significant pressure on farmland as the demand for housing, infrastructure and commercial spaces has grown. Many farms have sold land for development because of the high value of real estate, especially since the period after the Second World War.

Trades and craftsmen

Alongside agriculture were, of course, those essential trades and craftsmen using local raw materials available such as timber, clay, iron and water. These trades and craftsmen included blacksmiths and ironmongers, carpenters and coopers, tanners, wheelwrights, cordwainers, drapers, and grocers (to name just a few) and, for many of which, apprenticeship records may be found in local archives (see Chapter 4).

In the nineteenth century, the census returns for Surrey suggest the four main categories of occupations were boot and shoemakers, tailors and dressmakers, bakers, and blacksmiths. However, they also demonstrate a decline in boot and shoemakers after 1841 in contrast with a growth and prominence in tailors and dressmakers, in which at its peak in 1911 there were 13,256 recorded. Bakers were the second most prominent occupation reaching a peak in 1901 of 3,320.

Alongside agriculture and the local artisan craftsmen, other industries, some of which have made their impact on the Surrey landscape, developed and declined over time. These include gunpowder mills, textile industry, paper mills, ironmaking and glassmaking, the remnants of which can still be seen across Surrey today.

Mills

Mills were one of the buildings specifically recorded in the Domesday Book and in Surrey there were a total of 119 water mills recorded, principally along the three main rivers, the Wandle, the Wey and the Mole, and their tributaries. Many of these mills survived for centuries, being adapted for different products over their lifespan, with about 100 water corn mills still being active in Surrey at the end of the nineteenth century.

'Outwood Mill – storm damage' by Ian Capper is licensed and reproduced under CC BY-SA 2.0. T.

Thirteen watermills are recorded along the River Wandle which produced flour, also served as breweries or textile mills at different times, while along the River Wey and its tributaries there were more mills per mile than anywhere else in Great Britain. The largest was at Coxes Lock near Addlestone while the last commercial mill was Botting's Mill at Albury along the Tillingbourne which continued working until 1991.

The Tillingbourne in fact powered twenty-four mills which between 1086 and the twentieth century supported at least twelve industries including corn-milling, gunpowder manufacturing, papermaking, tanning, iron-forging, wiredrawing and more.

Mills were also found along the River Mole at places such as Reigate, Dorking, Fetcham and Merstham, while the River Thames and its tributaries also powered watermills in Surrey at locations such as Mortlake, and Cuddington, the village which was demolished by Henry VIII to make way for Nonsuch Palace.

Surrey also boasts the oldest working Post mill (type of windmill) in England dating from 1665 at Outwood, although it now only works as a tourist attraction. Surrey once had about forty windmills but only six survive: Buckland, Lowerfield Heath, Outwood, Reigate Heath, Tadworth and Wimbledon. Some have been converted to other uses.

Gunpowder

Developed by the Chinese, the production of gunpowder spread across the Middle East and into Europe by the thirteenth century. While its base powder, saltpetre, appears to have been produced in England from the fourteenth century when it was mixed with sulphur for use in the king's guns, it was not until the early sixteenth century that gunpowder as a solitary product was produced in England.

In 1514, Hans Wolf was appointed the king's gunpowder maker at the Tower of London where gunpowder was made until the 1540s when, following the building of Ordnance storehouses and a Royal Dockyard, production was most likely moved – by Thomas Lee who had been appointed the king's gunpowder maker in 1531 – to a new gunpowder mill at Rotherhithe on the south bank of the River Thames. Until the boundary changes of 1889, Rotherhithe was in the county of Surrey.

'The Crenge,' a private gunpowder mill, was opened in 1555 by Henry Reve also at Rotherhithe and this was the start of a 300-year long industry in Surrey with licences by letters patent being granted chiefly to Surrey gunpowder producers.

Thomas Lee was succeeded by his son Francis in 1575 who may also have built the gunpowder mill at Leigh Place in Godstone which was later owned by the Evelyn family of Wotton Manor. The Evelyn family also built gunpowder mills at Tolworth and Wotton.

Until the 1580s, while licences were granted to produce the gunpowder for the Crown, gunpowder generally was a free trade. By the 1580s, the growing threat from Spain led to commissions being granted and monopolies being developed in the production of gunpowder. In 1588,

Chilworth gunpowder mills.

eleven-year licences were granted to George Evelyn, Richard Hills and John Evelyn 'to dig, open and work for saltpetre,' anywhere they liked except in the 'City of London and 2 miles outside it, the northern counties of York, Northumberland, Westmoreland, Cumberland, and the Bishopric of Durham'.³

The Evelyns were also transferred a licence in 1596, originally granted to Thomas and Richard Robinson in 1590, for the rights of gunpowder production in London and Westminster. They, therefore, became a prominent family in gunpowder production, albeit short-lived with Tolworth mill closing around 1606/7 and Wotton before 1625. Wotton was later adapted for use as a wireworks and copper mill.

The Evelyn family continued to run Godstone Mill until 1636, when it was acquired by the East India Company who had established a gunpowder mill at Chilworth, Surrey along the Tillingbourne, leasing the land from the lord of Chilworth Manor, Sir Edward Randyll.

The site of Chilworth mills covers 11 hectares (27 acres) and the remains are now a protected ancient monument managed by Guildford borough council being in the Surrey Hills AONB.

Chilworth mills are thought to have been the largest in the country, employing around 600 people at the height of its production. Workers came from surrounding villages such as Blackheath and were employed not only directly in the production of gunpowder but also in providing supporting trades such as coopers, who made the barrels for storage. The mills changed hands many times in its history until the Chilworth Gunpowder Company was formed in 1885; the mills were eventually closed in 1920.

Gunpowder mills were also established by converting existing mills along the River Wandle at Carshalton in 1650 when Abel Richardson, William Mollins and John Jarvis, in partnership, converted Brazil mills (mills used for producing dyes from brazilwood) and at Wandsworth by Abel Richardson and James Lloyd in 1656. Also along the River Mole at East Molesey were two mills, the Upper Mill and Lower (or Sterte) Mill, which were converted from flour mills by John Samyne in 1649. Smaller mills could also be found, such as one built along the River Wandle in the 1680s by Josiah Dewey near Carshalton.

The mills at Carshalton and Wandsworth were short-lived with Carshalton closing by 1655 due to their inferior product and Wandsworth by the late 1660s due to lack of demand after the Civil War. In 1666, Sterte Mill later reverted to a flour mill while Upper Mill continued its production of gunpowder until 1780, when it closed after a fire caused several explosions and fatalities.

Textiles
Along the River Wey, a clothing industry thrived for about 800 years from the twelfth century when the monks at Waverley Abbey near Farnham, using effective methods of husbandry, were highly successful in rearing sheep. The wool thus produced sparked a clothing industry.

By the sixteenth century, the clothing industry had become so important to the economy along the Wey valley that special laws were introduced to protect and control it. From 1530, the industry became heavily focused in and around Godalming, Guildford and Farnham when these laws made it illegal to produce cloth outside of the market towns.

In Godalming, the clothing industry continued until the end of the twentieth century, converting to framework knitting following the establishment of the Framework Knitters Company in 1657, and from 1788 specialising in fleecy hosiery providing much of the town's wealth.

The village of Wonersh also had a thriving clothing industry between the late fourteenth and early seventeenth century. This was a cottage industry based in three houses, today known as Throwsters, Meed House and The Old House on the south side of The Street, in which 'Kersey', a

Merton Abbey Waterwheel by Fresh on The Net is licensed and reproduced under CC BY 2.0.

coarse woollen cloth, was woven and became known as 'Wonersh Blue', which was traded with the Canary Islands, Western Europe and India.

The woollen industry involved a variety of occupations from shearers, scourers (who cleaned the fleece), carders, staplers, spinners and weavers, fullers and dyers. The shearing and cleaning would be carried out by the sheep farmers; the carders and staplers were responsible for preparing the wool and selling it to the spinners and weavers who were often cottage-industry workers local to the water mills. The clothiers, who would pay the millers to have the cloth fulled (the removal of natural wool grease or lanolin, and any remaining dirt) and dyed, then bought the cloth from the weavers.

Linen was another textile industry to be found along the River Wey. Perhaps not on the same scale as wool but on a more local cottage-industry scale. Flax, a slender, blue-flowered plant with strong woody fibres, was grown along the valley of the River Wey where retting was a common skill. Retting is the process of soaking flax plants in water to separate the soft tissue of the flax from the fibres, which would then be spun by hand to make linen.

Along the River Wandle[4] there were also several established mills engaged in dyeing cloth, including at Wandsworth where the Huguenots who fled France due to persecution after 1684, brought with them their superior skills in several industries, including the cloth dyeing industry. After Huguenots settled in Wandsworth and Mitcham, it is suggested they improved the red dye used in these cloth mills; this became known as Wandsworth Scarlet and is believed to have been used to make the red cardinal hats for the Catholic clergy. Hats made in Wandsworth became an acclaimed product; a necessity for anyone who thought themselves fashionable after about 1690.

There were also a substantial number of local tanneries to be found in the villages and towns in the Wey valley, particularly in the eighteenth and nineteenth centuries, although the history of tanning and tanneries goes back much further.

Tanneries would use hides from locally slaughtered animals to make leather. Tanneries employed a variety of occupations including skinners, who removed the hides, fell-mongers who removed wool from sheepskin, tanners who infused the skins with tannin, curriers who refined the leather to make it supple, and cordwainers who made shoes from leather.

In the sixteenth and seventeenth centuries, tanners were found in Lingfield, in particular the Underhill family at White House Farm, Baldwins Hill (now known as Cromwell Hall). In Crowhurst, Gateland/

Gatland Farm was previously known as Tanners Farm according to a map of Crowhurst dated April 1679 produced by John Gainsford.

From the later seventeenth century, larger-scale tanneries began to open such as that in Bermondsey – in Surrey until the 1889 boundary changes – which has a history of leather-making dating back hundreds of years to at least the fifteenth century. By the 1790s, the tanneries at Bermondsey were producing a third of all leather in the country. Its success was down to a combination of a good water supply, oak trees and plenty of space to keep animals. Leather makers outside London were free from the regulations and restrictions imposed by the city authorities at the time.

A tannery existed at Lingfield, in a building opposite the racecourse, until the end of the nineteenth century, along with a tanyard, drying sheds and mill at the mansion house of Batnors (otherwise Battners) bought by James Farindon in 1684, with the tannery building being rebuilt and developed in about 1840.

A tannery was also established in Mill Lane, Godalming in 1808, along with tanneries near Meadrow and at Westbrook Mill both on the River Wey, and Gomshall along the Tillingbourne river which continued operating until the 1980s.

These tanneries made items essential to the agricultural communities, such as leather bottles and buckets, saddles and harnesses, as well as clothing such as hats, gloves, shoes and boots, jackets, jerkins and breeches. Also connected with tanneries and the leather industry were saddle and harness makers.

Paper

Paper mills were first found in England in Hertford in 1488. The first in Surrey was founded in Godalming during the reign of James I (1603–1625) with a second being established in Guildford at Stoke Mill in 1653 – now the headquarters of the *Surrey Advertiser* newspaper.

Over the next two centuries, numerous paper mills were established along the Wey valley: Bower's (1716–1790), Byfleet (1673–1703), Catteshall, Farncombe (1661–1928), Eashing, Godalming (1658–1889), Westbrook, Godalming (1732–1842), and Woking (1840- 1895); while along the Tillingbourne they included: Albury Park (1790–1810), Chilworth Great (1704–1870), Chilworth Little (1704–1829), Postford Lower, Albury (1809–1875), and Postford Upper, Albury (1809–1830). Many of these served as mills for other products both before and after these periods of use for papermaking.

Traditionally, a coarse brown paper called 'whited-brown paper' was produced in these mills with higher quality paper being imported from Europe. However, the late seventeenth century saw the migration into England of Dutch and French papermakers and the Company of White Paper Makers was established in 1686. The company gained a monopoly to produce writing and printing papers. One notable event was the manufacture of banknote paper in 1793 by Charles Ball who converted the corn mill at Albury Park.

There were also paper mills along the River Mole at Esher and Cobham as well as several paper mills on the Wandle, at Wandsworth, Garrett, two at Merton, Morden, Wallington and Carshalton, where the Ansell family owned and let two sites: Paper Mill and Lower Mill.

Paper was hand produced in individual sheets until the nineteenth century. The Fourdrinier papermaking machine, introduced in England in 1806, produced continuous sheets of paper and thereby increased the production of paper, which led to the closure of the many watermills that could not produce enough power to operate such machines.

The paper mills would not, however, have been large employers. The basic papermaking process required four employees: a beaterman who pulped the rags to 'stuff'; a vatman who produced individual sheets of paper; and a coucherman who was responsible for stacking alternate sheets of the wet paper before it was pressed. There would then be a layer who removed the sheets from the wet press, separated the individual sheets and hung them to dry. Once dry, the sheets would be pressed and polished. These workers may have simply been referred to as paper workers.

Iron industry
Evidence of iron production, both its primary production (the extraction and smelting) and the secondary working (that is working the bloom into iron bars of billets and making final marketable iron products such as would be produced by the local blacksmith), has been found in parts of Surrey dating back to the Iron Age and Roman times.

From the late fourteenth, but particularly in the sixteenth and seventeenth centuries, the Wealden valley of Surrey and Sussex was home to an iron industry of national importance. From the middle of the sixteenth century into the early seventeenth century, ironworks, furnaces and forges were established in the Surrey Weald at Leigh Hammer (finery forge, 1551), Ewood (blast furnace and finery forge, 1553), Vachery (finery forge, Cranleigh, 1557 and blast furnace, Cranleigh, 1587), Abinger Hammer (finery forge, 1557), Woodcock Hammer (finery forge,

Lingfield 1561), Burningfold (blast furnace and finery forge, Dunsfold, 1568), West End (Chiddingfold blast furnace by 1570), Imbhams (blast furnace, Haslemere, 1570), Coldharbour Hammer (finery forge, 1608), Upper finery forge and Lower finery forge (both at Thursley, 1608), Sturt Hammer (finery forge, Haslemere, 1609), and Witley (blast furnace, date unknown).

These ironworks were water powered and the location of the furnaces was therefore restricted by the need for a water supply – thus they were located near large ponds and later the streams of the lower Wealden Greensand. The forges were not so restricted but did need to be within an economical travelling distance of a blast furnace and were often the only alternative place of employment to agriculture.

Ironworks were predominately built by the local landowning families and/or London merchants and leased to established ironmasters.

Furnaces would then employ skilled workers such as the founder and his deputy, who were responsible for maintenance of the furnace; the filler and his deputy, in charge of the furnace; and the moulder, along with labourers to work the furnace. Horse- and ox-drawn wagon drivers, and labourers who dug the ore, would also form the workforce.

Depending on the size of the outfit, forges would employ a finer to refine the iron, a hammerman or blacksmith, and about ten labourers. The wagon drivers and labourers were often agricultural labourers working to supplement their income during times when farm work was limited or out of season, while some of the skilled labour may have been carried out by foreign workers.

The survival of these ironworks was relatively short-lived with all but Burningfold being closed by the end of the seventeenth century. Some works were repurposed. Sturt Hammer was the first in Surrey to become a sickle mill (which is a water mill used for sharpening newly fabricated blades, including scythes, swords, sickles, and knives) by the 1690s. The lower forge at Thursley became a silk crepe mill, Woodcock Hammer became a wire mill, and Imbhams a gun foundry; others were either abandoned, such as those at Cranleigh, or transformed into corn and paper mills.

From the seventeenth century, iron-processing mills were also established along the rivers Thames, Wey and Mole, mainly by the converting of existing mills. These mills were not furnaces or forges but were engaged in the secondary production of iron, producing goods, such as hoops, wires, pots, pans and utensils, largely from imported raw material from Sweden. For example, Esher Mill and Ember Mill at Molesey, both originally corn mills, became brass wire mills in the 1630s;

Byfleet paper mill was converted by Thomas Wethered, in or about 1703 to a hoop and wire mill. Other mills converted to iron-processing mills could be found at Chilworth (part of the old gunpowder mills, 1603), Weybridge (1720), Coxes Lock Mill at Chertsey (1777), Downside Mill at Cobham (1771), Wandsworth Gun foundry (1782), and Grove Mill at Carshalton (after 1864).

Again, many of these mills were relatively short-lived, having been converted back to their original use by the early nineteenth century, particularly those along the rivers Wey and Mole.

Glassmaking

Although there is little trace of the industry today, glassmaking was another industry which thrived in the Surrey Weald with a history going back to the fourteenth century in the parishes of Kirdford, Chiddingfold and Hambledon. Although the core of the industry in the sixteenth century was just over the border at Wisborough Green, West Sussex, by the latter part of the century there were glass works at Alfold and Ewhurst. These areas prospered in glassmaking due to the sandy ground and plentiful firewood for the furnaces from local woodlands.

In these early periods, glassmaking was an artisan craft carried out by local farmers to supplement their income; it was only after the Huguenot refugees brought with them their glassmaking skills from France that the industry rapidly expanded.

Of special mention is the glassmaker Jean Carre, a Huguenot refugee who was granted a licence by Queen Elizabeth I to produce glass for windows at Fernfold on the Surrey–Sussex border and at Alfold, employing his glassworkers from Normandy and the Lorraine Valley.

While the foreign owners of glassmaking furnaces, which caused a nuisance to local inhabitants, were unpopular, the decline of the industry in Surrey is most likely attributable to King James I prohibiting the burning of wood for glassmaking in 1615, claiming the use of wood for glassmaking was uneconomical and could be better used in other more profitable industries.

Brick works, kilns and clay pits

The last industry worthy of mention is that of brickmaking, a more modern industry than those already explored because permanent brickworks did not start to emerge until the end of the sixteenth century. Brickmaking was originally a seasonal occupation, often combined with other occupations such as farming, because the clay/earth was extracted in the autumn after harvesting when it was easier to dig up than in the drier sunnier months, and the brickmaking commencing in late spring after lambing and sowing was complete. The clay was formed into brick shapes and left to dry in the open air until after harvest time when the dried bricks were baked in the kilns.

Until the nineteenth century, brickmaking was usually a local industry for local buildings employing a small number of labourers. For example, one of the earliest brickworks was Wilderwick Brickworks at Dormansland, near Lingfield which, in 1851, employed four men plus the master brick maker. Other brickworks also existed in Dormansland – at Moor Lane and Clinton Terrace – and by the later nineteenth century at Bakers Lane.

The nineteenth century and the advent of the railway bringing in larger quantities of coal to rather than wood fire the kilns, enabled the brick-making industry to prosper. During the nineteenth century, further brickworks were established at Lingfield Common Road, Coldharbour, Crowhurst, and South Godstone. By 1902, the sites at Crowhurst were owned by the London & Brighton Tile and Terracotta Company which, by 1935, had become the Dorking United Brick Company Ltd and in 1958 was bought by Redland Bricks until its closure in 1979.

In the 1921 census, twenty-one brick makers were recorded at Woking and many others worked clay pits at Chobham. However, the 1920s building trade depression saw many of those pits close. The last to close was in Woking along the Lower Guildford Road in 1942.

Many brickworks have since been preserved as wildlife reserves, places of special interest or preservation areas such as those at Newdigate, Clock House Brickworks at Capel and Limpsfield Common at Oxted which is now owned and managed by the National Trust. According to Limpsfield Parish Council, red bricks, tiles and probably grey stock bricks were manufactured here with a clay pit still being found on the golf course in Brick Kiln Lane.

Some original sites have been left derelict, such as those at Ewhurst, although a modern brick-making company, Wienerberger Bricks Works, continues to thrive at Walliswood, Ockley just outside Ewhurst.

Chapter 2

GETTING STARTED

A. General Registration Office Records (GRO)

The records of the GRO are the civil registration records of birth, deaths and marriages introduced by the 'Act for Registering Births, Deaths and Marriages in England' 1836 often referred to as the Civil Registration Act 1836. The Act came into effect on 1 July 1837 after which births, deaths and marriages were to be registered in their local registration district office. For this purpose, England and Wales were originally divided into 619 registration districts (reorganised in 1851 into 623 districts) each supervised by a Superintendent Registrar and were based on the recently introduced Poor Law Unions (see Chapter 3). Registration districts were divided into sub-districts each under the charge of a locally appointed registrar.

Births and deaths

Births and deaths would be registered in the local registration office from where the registrar would send copies to the district superintendent registrar. They in turn, would send copies to the Registrar General at the GRO in London where the entries were then indexed. It is these indexes which provide the means for locating and ordering a copy of an entry and/or certificate. It is important to understand this process because at each stage there is margin for error, mis-transcription, misinterpretation and loss of entries when the Registrar General compiled the indexes, particularly in the earlier years when records were handwritten.

It must be noted there were no penalties for failing to register a birth or death. Prior to 1874, the onus was on the registrar to investigate what events had taken place and register them. While deaths and marriages were relatively easy to find out, births may not have been. The effect was that registration of births did not truly become compulsory until legislation was introduced in 1874 placing the onus on parents to register a birth; penalties were introduced for failing to register. Thus, many births continued to go unregistered between 1837 and 1874.

The period within which registration was required remains the same today at within forty-two days of the birth (six weeks) with rules being set out for late registration; between forty-two days and three months the superintendent registrar had to be present at registration; between three months and a year registration had to be authorised by the Registrar General.

Marriages

Marriages were either conducted by the local registrar at the register office, by an officiating clergyman in the Church of England who himself acted as the local registrar, or at a licensed place under the Marriage Act 1836 subject to the attendance of the local registrar at the ceremony. When a marriage took place in the Church of England, the officiating clergyman would have two identical marriage registers (books) to be completed and signed by the relevant parties. One copy would be retained by the church, the other copy, once the register was full, would be sent direct to the superintendent registrar. In addition, every quarter, clergymen were required to send a copy of their marriage records to the superintendent registrar to update the indexes. This same procedure remains in place today.

For marriages at other locations, the registrar would provide copies to the superintendent registrar in much the same way as for births and deaths.

The GRO indexes are arranged alphabetically. They were prepared quarterly between 1837 and 1984, since when they have been prepared annually. They contain a summary of the registration information held by the GRO and are available online at the GRO website (**www.gro.gov.uk**) and can be searched as various websites such as FreeBMD, (**www.freebmd.org.uk**), Family Search (**www.familysearch.org**), Ancestry (**www.ancestry.co.uk**), and Findmypast (**www.findmypast.co.uk**).

The indexes identify when the event was *registered* not when it took place; this is particularly useful to remember when looking at a birth. For example, a birth at the end of February or in March may be registered in the April/May/June quarter because of the time parents had to register the birth. Foundlings and those who were to be adopted in England were added at the end of the index for the appropriate quarter, although it must also be borne in mind that legal adoption was not introduced until 1927 following the Adoption of Children Act 1926 from when the GRO also holds the Adopted Children's Register. It should be further borne in mind that stillbirths were not registered until 1 July 1927.

The indexes provide the registration district, volume and page number required to order a copy of the actual entry from the GRO. Birth indexes on the GRO website also provide the mother's maiden name.

When searching for a birth, death or marriage entry in the indexes, it is useful to have the name, approximate age and place or registration district of event. It is also important to understand how registration districts have changed since they were first introduced to help determine and differentiate same name entries.

Surrey was originally divided into twenty-two registration districts: Bermondsey, Camberwell, Chertsey, Croydon, Dorking, East Grinstead (partly in Surrey until 1897), Epsom, Farnham, Godstone, Guildford, Hambledon, Kingston, Lambeth, Newington, Reigate, Richmond, Rotherhithe, St George Southwark, St Olave Southwark, St Saviour Southwark, Wandsworth and Windsor.

Each registration district included between one and thirty-nine parishes and was divided into between one and seventeen sub-districts. The website UKBMD (**www.ukbmd.org.uk/reg/sry.html**) has a very useful list of registration districts, parishes within districts and sub-districts existing since 1837.

The first changes to the registration districts within Surrey took place in 1869 when Bermondsey and Rotherhithe were abolished and merged with St Olave Southwark, while Newington and St George Southwark were also abolished and merged with St Saviour Southwark. Following the boundary changes of 1889, Surrey lost the following registration districts to London: Camberwell, Lambeth, St Olave Southwark (Renamed in 1902 as St Olave (Bermondsey)), St Saviour Southwark and Wandsworth.

The next major change in registration districts came in the 1930s. Registration districts did not always follow county boundaries – as in the case of East Grinstead which was partly in Surrey and partly in Sussex – and this continued to be the case following the introduction of the Local Government Act of 1888, which created administrative counties. Thus, in the 1930s boundaries were altered to become fully aligned with local counties and county boroughs.

These changes in Surrey took place in 1934 with the creation of the registration districts of Surrey Mid-Eastern, Surrey North-Eastern, Surrey North-Western, Surrey South-Eastern, and Surrey South-Western in which were merged the following, with some pre-existing districts being split between more than one new district, and Windsor disappearing from Surrey into Berkshire:

Surrey Mid-Eastern	Surrey North-Eastern	Surrey North-Western	Surrey South-Eastern	Surrey South-Western
Dorking	Epsom	Chertsey	Dorking	Chertsey
Epsom	Kingston (also Staines)	Farnham	Epsom	Dorking
Godstone	Richmond	Guildford	Godstone	Farnham
Kingston (also Staines)			Reigate	Guildford
				Hambledon

These new registration districts included the following sub-districts:

Surrey Mid-Eastern	Surrey North-Eastern	Surrey North-Western	Surrey South-Eastern	Surrey South-Western
Coulsdon & Banstead	Merton & Carshalton	Frimley & Egham	Caterham	Farnham
Dorking	Mitcham & Beddington	Runnymede	Dorking	Godalming & Cranleigh
Epsom & Banstead	St Helier	Surrey Heath	Godstone	Godalming & Haslemere
Epsom & Leatherhead	Wimbledon	Walton & Chertsey	Horley	Guildford
Epsom & Ewell		Woking	Reigate	Guildford St Lukes
Epsom Woodcote		Woking & Surrey Heath	Reigate & Banstead	Haslemere
Leatherhead				
Leatherhead & Esher				
Sutton & Cheam				

The next boundary change came in 1965 when the London boroughs of Kingston, Merton, Richmond and Sutton were created and the county borough of Croydon was lost to London. It was also at this time that Staines and Sunbury were transferred to Middlesex. Thus, the registration district of Croydon was transferred to London; the registration district of

Surrey Northern, which was created in 1948 out of Surrey North-Eastern registration district, was divided between Kingston upon Thames, Richmond upon Thames and Surrey Mid-Eastern registration districts with a new Surrey Northern district being created out of Middlesex South and Surrey North-Western registration districts; while the Surrey North-Eastern district was divided between Merton and Sutton registration districts.

Further changes took place in 1996 with the abolition of Surrey Mid-Eastern, Surrey Northern, Surrey North-Western, Surrey South-Eastern, Surrey South-Western and the creation of Mid Surrey, North Surrey, South-East Surrey and West Surrey. Mid Surrey and South-East Surrey merged into East Surrey in 2000 which itself merged into Surrey in 2008. Thus, today the only registration district in Surrey is that of Surrey with district number 759 and no sub-districts. The GRO volume numbers for Surrey are IV between 1837 and 1851; 1d and 2a between 1852 and 1946; 5g between 1947 and 1974; and 17 from 1974 to 1992. From 1993, the format in the indexes changed to register, sub-district, and entry numbers, rather than using a volume and page number.

Copies of birth, death and marriage entries and certificates can be obtained direct from the GRO through its website. These can be obtained as paper copies, PdF or for historic birth (currently from 1837 up to 100 years ago) and death entries (currently from 1837–1957) digital images are now available.

Many parish copies of marriage register entries have been indexed and digitised at websites such as Ancestry and Findmypast. Those indexed and digitised for Surrey can be found on Ancestry in collections 'Surrey, England, Church of England Baptisms, Marriages and Burials, 1538–1812', and 'Surrey, England, Church of England Marriages and Banns, 1754–1937' which includes marriage register entries before the start of civil registration. These can be searched generally by name, date, location or can be browsed by parish. The originals are held at SHC.

There are also specific collections for Sutton, Surrey: 'Sutton, Surrey, England, Church of England Baptisms, Marriages and Burials, 1538–1812' and 'Sutton, Surrey, England, Church of England Marriages and Banns, 1754–1940' which again can be searched generally by name, date, location or can be browsed by parish. The originals of those are held at London Borough of Sutton Archives & Local Studies.

B. Census returns

Census returns provide a record of the population and were first conducted in 1801. They have been conducted every ten years since, except during the Second World War. However, the 1931 census return records were unfortunately destroyed by a fire in 1942. There is 100-year restriction on the release of census returns and therefore with no census returns for 1931 and 1941, the next census returns to be released for public access will be that taken in 1951, which is unlikely to be released until after 2051.

The census returns for 1801, 1811, 1821 and 1831 were, however, only statistical and generally do not contain any useful information for tracing ancestors. That being said, occasionally enumerators' notebooks and other related documents are available which may contain useful information. For Surrey, such records can be found at SHC and include some original records from 1801, some copies and some later transcripts:

- A small notebook relating to the 1801 Census Return for Bletchingley with surnames given and the number of men, women, boys and girls under each name. Held under SHC reference 2727/1/48/84 (dated 1801)
- A parchment-bound book copy of the *Population of Guildford 1801* containing a copy of the census returns of 1801 which was presented to John Nealds, Esq., Mayor, by James Apark, Thomas Piggott and Thomas Mare, vestry clerks. The book is arranged by parishes providing names of owners of houses with number of males and females in their families. Held under SHC reference G93/1 (dated 1801)
- Census returns for Mortlake, taken on 10 March 1801, by Mr Thomas Hill, churchwarden, Mr Thomas Weatherston, overseer, and Mr Woolfe, vestry clerk, giving the names of householder, number of families per house, total males and females, three categories of employment (agriculture; trade, manufacture or craft; other), and includes names of lodgers. Held under SHC reference 2397/6/42 (dated 1801)
- Manuscript volumes for the *Population of Chobham* giving various details including the names of heads of households for 1801, 1811 and 1831. Held under SHC reference P34/17/1-3 (dated 1801, 1811, 1831)
- File of working papers relating to census returns for Chobham which includes transcripts of the census returns for 1801, 1811, 1821, 1831, and 1851 listing properties, landowners and occupiers dating between 1790 and 1850. Held under SHC reference 4515/4 (compiled in the twentieth century)

- File of census working papers in relation to Chobham which includes, among other information, alphabetical lists of families mentioned in the censuses of 1801, 1811, 1821, 1831, 1841 and 1851; along with a comparison of family addresses between censuses a)1851 versus 1841, b) 1841 versus 1831 and c) 1831 versus 1811 and 1801. Held under SHC reference 4515/5 (compiled in the twentieth century)
- Oxted census *c.*1800–1831: Notebooks containing lists and other details of inhabitants relating to the taking of census, Held under SHC reference P3/5/114-123

The census returns which are most useful for family history research begin in 1841 with the most recent available being the census return of 1921 at Findmypast.

Each census return provides slightly different information, as the government adjusted the information it wanted to know about the population. It is also important to understand the records available for 1841 up to and including 1901 are the enumerators returns, i.e. the forms the officials completed rather than those the householders completed. The census was conducted by enumerators providing forms to each household which were then collected and collated in the enumerators' returns. This inevitably results in an increase in errors by mis-transcription.

In some cases where there was no one in the household who was literate, the enumerator may have completed the forms from information they were told, further resulting in incorrect information being recorded due to difficulties with accents and dialects. This also accounts for different spellings of names between census returns. Thus, alternative spellings should be searched.

It is important to bear in mind that if an ancestor cannot be found in the census return there are some parts of the census returns which are missing, having either been lost or destroyed over the years. However, Surrey does have complete census returns, for the most part, save for 1841 when pieces 1074 and 1075 are missing; these covered the parishes of Walton-on-Thames, Hersham, Weybridge, and Malden.

It is also important to remember the census return is a snapshot of where people were living or staying on the specific census night. Only those actually sleeping at a property on census night are supposed to be counted. If an ancestor cannot be found in their known place of abode, a wider search should be undertaken as they may have been staying with relatives, away on business (such as a travelling salesman), recorded in an institution such as a workhouse, gaol, or asylum, or may be missing altogether because they were working through the night. For example, the 1841 census was taken on 6 June, which was harvest season when some agricultural labourers were working and may have slept outside or were away from the family home, particularly those who were seasonal workers.

The 1911 and 1921 census returns should contain fewer of the earlier difficulties because the returns were completed by the householders and should therefore contain an ancestor's own handwriting and signature, although it cannot be said with any certainty who in the household completed the return; this may have depended on which members were literate.

Census returns have always been taken on a Sunday night. They are arranged by civil registration districts, subdivided into enumerators' districts, except in 1841 they were arranged by Hundreds (an administrative subdivision of land). They are further arranged by civil parish or townships, ecclesiastical parish, piece, folio, page and schedule number and are held at TNA under the following reference numbers:

Date	TNA Ref. no.
6 June 1841	HO 107
30 March 1851	HO 107
7 April 1861	RG 9
2 April 1871	RG 10
3 April 1881	RG 11
5 April 1891	RG 12
31 March 1901	RG 13
2 April 1911	RG 14
19 June 1921	RG 15

Census returns have been digitised and indexed and are now widely available at all the main family history research websites; however, in addition to some of the problems and pitfalls with census returns generally discussed above, digitisation and online indexing of these records come with their own significant errors, largely in the transcription of them when indexing the records. Census returns may have been indexed under Christian or first names, having been mistaken as surnames, and vice versa. Names may have been misspelled in indexing due to difficulties reading the handwriting along with ages having been mis-transcribed. It is therefore important to use a variety of spellings, try searching by first name, and/or use a wildcard search. It is also possible to search by county, parish and sub-district and view the digitised images and manually search the census returns.

For Surrey, the WSFHS has produced various indexes, surname indexes and family group indexes for census returns among its CD Collection of publications, available for purchase through the GenFair website, for example:

- CD 3 'The Woking collection' includes indexes for the 1851, 1861 and 1871 Census, plus 1841 for Pyrford and 1901 for part of Woking
- CD 6 '1851 Census Index of Western Surrey' is a searchable index of 92,000 names, 72 parishes with alphabetical listing of family groups, along with an index of birth places and an indexed list of 'addresses' including such places as public houses, mills, etc. The index covers Abinger, Albury, Alfold, Ash, Bisley, Bookham (Great & Little), Bramley, Byfleet, Capel, Chertsey, Chiddingfold, Chobham, Clandon (E & W), Cobham, Compton, Cranleigh, Dockenfield (Hants), Dorking, Dunsfold, Effingham, Egham, Elstead, Esher, Ewhurst, Farnham, Fetcham, Frensham, Frimley, Godalming, Guildford, Hambledon, Hascombe, Haslemere, Horsell, Horsley (E & W), Merrow, Mickleham, Molesey (E & W), Newdigate, Ockham, Ockley, Peperharow, Pirbright, Puttenham, Pyrford, Ripley, Seale, Send, Shalford, Shere, St Martha's, Stoke D'Abernon, Stoke-next-Guildford, Thames Ditton, Thorpe, Thursley, Walton-on-Thames, Wanborough, Weybridge, Windlesham, Wisley, Witley, Woking, Wonersh, Worplesdon and Wotton

The ESFHS has also produced transcriptions and indexes of all the Merstham census returns from 1841–1901 in its 'Merstham Collection', which is also available to purchase through GenFair and Parish Chest websites.

C. Parish registers and Bishop's Transcripts

Parish registers
Parish registers are the mainstay of family history research prior to the start of civil registration and can, in theory, be used to trace our ancestors back to Tudor times. Parish registers of baptism, burial and marriage were first introduced by Thomas Cromwell, Henry VIII's Vicar-General,

in 1536; however, their introduction and use continued to be ignored by many parishes.

In 1558, the Diocese of Canterbury enquired whether the order had to be obeyed and in 1559 the order was reissued. However, it was not until 1597 when the Convocation of Canterbury made a constitution ordering registers to be written on parchment or vellum and further ordering that existing old paper registers were to be transcribed onto parchment or vellum. This was further enforced by Canon 70 of the Book of Canons 1603, requiring baptisms, marriages and burials to be transcribed into parchment books from 1538 where the registers existed or from 1558 when Elizabeth I came to the throne.

Where early registers had been created, they had been written either in paper books or on loose sheets of paper which were perishable and not suitable for maintaining permanent records. By the end of the sixteenth century, many had already deteriorated or disintegrated, thus many registers, where they had existed, were only transcribed back to 1558. Parish registers are, therefore, generally more complete from 1597 than from earlier periods.

Further, the Civil War years resulted in a period of poor keeping of parish registers in many parishes. Ejected ministers were replaced by a 'Register' or parish official; an individual elected every three years by the parishioners of each parish. These appointments may be recorded in the parish registers such as the 'Register' appointed to Horsell parish and noted at the start of the register parish register of baptism in 1653:[1]

> Robert Roake the Elder of Horsell, is elected and chosen Register within the parish of Horsell aforesaid and hath taken his oath for the due execution of his office before us the day and year above written [1 July 1654] according to an Act of Parliament in that case made.
>
> Signed John Hone, Edward Hone, Joseph Hone, Edward Wilson and Arthur Onslow.

The 'Register' was responsible for entering banns of marriages (for a fee of 12d), births and burials (each for a fee of 4d), and baptisms free of charge which was probably to undermine the significance of baptism. Essentially, the register books were taken away from the clergy and surrendered to laymen – much to the resentment of both Episcopal and puritan clergy.

In examining parish registers for Surrey, it does appear most of the registers did continue throughout the period, albeit that in some registers fewer events were recorded, in particular baptisms. It cannot, however, be said with any accuracy whether those were contemporaneously or subsequently recorded. For example, the parish register of baptisms, burials and marriages for Cobham which commences in 1562[2] is, in fact, a transcription from an earlier register for Cobham from 1562 to 1754 (marriages) and 1759 (baptisms and burials), rearranged into chronological order by William James, vicar of Cobham, in 1831, and which in 1644 includes the note:

> Mr KING, vicar of Cobham, did about the beginning of September leave this Parish being afraid lest that he should have been taken by some of the King's party and punished for speaking against his Majesty & justifying the proceedings of the Parliament whose forces were about this time totally defeated in Cromwell. And having left his Vicarage he never returned to it again but was in a short time preferred to the Rectory of Ashtead. And there was no minister settled here until the year 1656 and therefore till then the Register was very imperfectly kept; or rather not kept at all for there is no account of any Burials or Marriages and as for the persons that were baptised their names were not registered presently but when the Rev. Mr Carter was settled in the Parish and parents has had kept an account of their children's baptism got Mr Carter to enter them in the Register; but because they were not brought to him at one time he set them down confused as they came.

The registers do include entries each year between 1644 and 1655. Sadly, the registers for 1656 and 1657 were 'accidentally defaced and unreadable', demonstrating that some registers do not appear to have survived the Civil War and only survive from the 1660s.

The original registers for those parishes within Surrey are generally held at SHC, the exceptions being those parishes which are now in London boroughs whose registers are generally held at TLA rather than SHC. These include the parishes of Ashford (Middlesex before 1965), Battersea, Bermondsey, Camberwell, Clapham, Laleham (Middlesex before 1965), Lambeth, Littleton (Middlesex before 1965), Newington, Putney, Rotherhithe, Shepperton (Middlesex before 1965), Southwark, Staines (Middlesex before 1965), Streatham, Sunbury (Middlesex before 1965), Tooting Graveney, and Wandsworth. Those for Beddington St Mary, Belmont St John, Benhilton All Saints, Carshalton, Cheam St Dunston, Cheam Common, Hackbridge & North Beddington and Sutton are held at Sutton Heritage Central Library.

SHC has a 'Guide to the Parish Registers' it holds, which includes details of those held at TLA and Sutton Heritage Central Library and the periods for which they survive. The records held at SHC have been digitised and indexed and are available to search online on Ancestry and at Findmypast (see further details below).

The content of parish registers varies from parish to parish, incumbent to incumbent and because of legislation. Some registers, particularly early registers, simply record names and dates, while baptisms did include the name of the father.

Prior to 1754, clandestine marriages – that is irregular marriages conducted which ignored the ecclesiastical rules on using banns and licences but were still valid in English law provided the bride and groom had consented – were often conducted by priests in unlicensed buildings. These are sometimes referred to as 'Fleet' marriages and are recorded in the 'Fleet registers' held at TNA under reference RG 7, because many were conducted in the chapels in and surrounding Fleet prison, London.

These became increasingly popular with couples from the south-east, including Surrey. The records have been digitised and indexed on Ancestry and include 27,435 entries where at least one of the parties to the marriage was a resident of Surrey.

On 25 March 1754, Lord Hardwicke's Marriage Act of 1753 came into force to prevent irregular marriages. Until then, many parishes had recorded baptisms, burials and marriages in the same book; others had used separate books. The Act introduced pre-printed registers for marriages. It also introduced the legal requirement that all marriages must now take place following the calling of banns or the purchase of a licence, it being recorded in the marriage register whether the marriage was following the calling of banns or by licence. Separate printed marriage banns books were also introduced to record the calling of banns. These books can sometimes be found, but note the calling of banns is not confirmation the marriage itself took place. Apart from Jews and Quakers, who were exempt, all marriages were required to be solemnised in a parish church.

However, not all incumbents used the printed registers immediately following their introduction, as these entries from Cranleigh in 1781–82 demonstrate – the printed registers not being introduced in Cranleigh until 1789.

It also appears that following Lord Hardwicke's Marriage Act it became increasingly common to find both parents' names in baptism registers, such as these entries from Cranleigh in 1756.

Sample page from Cranleigh marriage register (pre-1774 style), SHC Ref: CRA/1/3.

Marriage by licence had been legal from medieval times, licences being purchased from and issued by archbishops, bishops and clergy appointed as their surrogates. Where a couple were married by licence, additional records may be found in the form of a sworn statement or allegation made by the groom confirming the details of those to be married, their ages and parents' consent. A marriage bond would also be entered into recording the names, occupations, addresses, sum involved as security, and providing an undertaking that both parties were free to marry and would marry lawfully, specifying the church. The allegations

Sample page from Cranleigh marriage register (post-1774 style), SHC Ref: CRA/2/2/1.

and bonds are more likely to survive than the actual licence which would have been presented to the officiating officer at the ceremony, so may be found among other parish records where they survive.

Surrey residents would apply to the Bishop of Winchester because Surrey came under the Diocese of Winchester prior to 1927. While the main records of the Diocese of Winchester are held at Hampshire Record Office at Winchester, records pertaining to the Archdeaconry of Surrey, Archdeaconry Court of Surrey and Commissary Court of Surrey are held at TLA.

Marriage Allegations and Bonds survive from 1673 to 1927 held in Reference DW/MP, the TLA online catalogue providing the names of the parties to the marriage. They have been digitised and indexed on Ancestry in the collection 'All London and Surrey, England, Marriage Bonds and Allegations, 1597–1921'.

Further changes to parish registers occurred in 1813, following Lord Rose's Act of 1812 which introduced printed registers for baptisms and burials and slightly changed the form of marriage registers. Until that point, many parishes had continued to record baptisms and burials in the same book. From 1813, separate books were required for baptisms, burials and marriages. Baptism and burial registers have continued in the same format since; marriage registers changed again following the introduction of civil registration in 1837.

Surrey archives for parish registers
Surrey History Centre, 130 Goldsworth Road, Woking, Surrey GU21 6ND
The London Archive, 40 Northampton Road, London EC1R 0HB
Sutton Heritage Central Library, St Nicholas Way, Sutton SM1 1EA

Research aids for Surrey parish registers
The following are comprehensive lists of the main collections and finding aids available for Surrey parish registers:

Collections available on Ancestry:

- London and Surrey, England, Marriage Bonds and Allegations, 1597–1921
- Surrey, England, Church of England Baptisms, 1813–1921
- Surrey, England, Church of England Burials, 1813–1997
- Surrey, England, Church of England Baptisms, Marriages and Burials, 1538–1812
- Surrey, England, Church of England Marriages and Banns, 1754–1937
- Surrey, England, Selected Church of England Parish Registers, 1599–1812
- Sutton, Surrey, England, Church of England Baptisms, Marriages and Burials, 1538–1812
- Sutton, Surrey, England, Church of England Marriages and Banns, 1754–1940
- Sutton, Surrey, England, Church of England Births and Baptisms, 1813–1915
- Sutton, Surrey, England, Church of England Deaths and Burials, 1813–1985
- The registers of the parish of Wandsworth in the county of Surrey: (1603–1787)
- The registers of Windlesham, Surrey, from 1677 to 1783

Collections available at Findmypast:

- Surrey Baptisms
- Surrey Marriages
- Surrey Burials
- Surrey Parish Registers Browse
- Surrey, Southwark Baptisms
- Surrey Strays Marriage Index

- Surrey, Southwark Burials Birth, Marriage, Death & Parish Records
- Surrey Registers & Records – parish registers by parish
- Surrey, Southwark Marriages

Collections available at Family Search:

- England, Surrey Parish Registers, 1536–1992*
- England, Surrey Marriages Bonds and Licences, 1536–1992*

West Surrey Family History Society (WSFHS)
The Society has several research aids available for purchase through its website, e.g.

- Surrey Parishes with a list of Neighbouring Parishes
- A list of Surrey Parishes – Ancient and Modern

It also has a series of CDs of parish register transcriptions and indexes which can be purchased, such as:

- West Surrey Burials Index to 1865
- The Guildford Collection
- The Surrey Burial Index
- Croydon Parish Registers to 1753 and Croydon Monumental Inscriptions to 1882
- The Elmbridge Collection
- Metropolitan Surrey Burials Index (including some Rural Parishes)
- London and Middlesex Baptisms
- A 2nd Collection of London & Middlesex Baptisms
- An Index of Burials in London and Middlesex
- A 2nd Collection of London & Middlesex Burials
- Parish Register Transcripts and Indexes in the Chertsey District
- Ancient Parishes in the Kingston District
- Ancient Parishes in the Dorking District
- Ancient Parishes in the Hambledon District

---

* The above collections are indexed online with images available at Family Search centres or affiliate libraries.

East Surrey Family History Society (ESFHS)

ESFHS also has a selection of parish register transcriptions and indexes which can be purchased and downloaded via its website (**www.eastsurreyfhs.org.uk**), including (but not limited to):

- Addington, St Mary the Blessed Virgin – Indexes to Baptisms 1813–1851 and Marriages 1813–1837
- Bermondsey, East Lane Chapel (The Most Holy Trinity R.C. Church)–Includes baptisms 1801–1847, marriages 1808–1854 and burials 1839–1854
- Caterham, St Mary & St Lawrence – includes indexes to baptisms 1836–1910, marriages 1837–1920, and burials 1836–1920
- Coulsdon, St John the Evangelist – Transcription and indexes to baptisms 1813–1856, marriages 1813–1915 and burials 1813–1879
- Croydon, St James – Indexes to baptisms 1829–1851 and 1851–1906 (extracts) and burials 1829–1866
- Merstham Collection – includes transcriptions and indexes of parish registers of baptisms, marriages and burials 1538–1855
- Mitcham, St Peter & St Paul – Indexes to baptisms 1779–1812 and burials 1779–1884
- Woodmansterne, St Peter's – Parish Registers 1566–1837 – includes baptisms 1568–1837, marriages 1568–1836 and burials 1566–1837

Bishop's Transcripts (BTs)

These were also introduced by the 1597 Convocation of Canterbury constitution whereby each incumbent was required to copy and send to the bishops, all entries in their parish registers on an annual basis, usually on Lady Day (25 March) (although some incumbents copied them from Michaelmas (29 September) to Trinity term).

They therefore provide a valuable alternative to parish registers, particularly if they still survive in areas and/or for periods where parish registers no longer exist. However, they in themselves were more susceptible to loss and damage because they were produced on an annual basis and were originally written on loose sheets of paper. It is therefore unusual to find a complete run of them.

As they were copies of the original parish registers, they are also susceptible to transcription errors, such as miscopying information (mixing up lines of information), misspelling of names, missing entries, missing information etc.

For Surrey, BTs survive for the majority of ancient parishes (pre-boundary changes). The originals are held at the TLA, among records for the Diocese of Winchester, under reference DW/T. Each parish is listed individually and they vary in survival rate. At TLA they are available to view on microfilm but have been indexed and digitised on Ancestry largely in collection 'London, England, Church of England Baptisms, Marriages and Burials, 1538–1812'. For those parishes not specifically listed in the drop-down menu choose 'Parishes Not in a Borough' and then choose the parish from the further drop-down menu.

It is always worth searching both parish registers and BTs where they survive for a parish as they may contain varying information and one may have records missing from, or unreadable in, the other.

While websites such as Ancestry and Findmypast are more often simply searched by name, dates and locations to produce a list of possible records, it is often worth searching the specific record collections both for specific names/variants as this may produce fewer results to sift through. It can also be worth a manual search of the digitised images for a period as it is not unknown for entries to be missed or mis-transcribed during the indexing process.

D. Monumental Inscriptions

Monumental inscriptions should not be overlooked. Significant family information can often be found on headstones. You may find your ancestors had a family plot in their local parish church.

Where legible, the name, age and date of death of the deceased is given at the least. An occupation, place of origin or information on military service may also be recorded.

Often families were buried together or in adjacent plots, revealing family relationships. They are especially useful in identifying children who died in infancy, of whom the researcher may otherwise be unaware.

Local authorities have often recorded monumental inscriptions and deposited copies with the Registrar General, while retaining the originals. TNA holds transcripts of inscriptions from around 170 burial grounds in series RG 37. For Surrey, these include burial grounds at Western Road, Mitcham (1833–1879); Salem Chapel, Croydon (1081–1843); Horton Hospital Estate Cemetery, Epsom (1910–1945); and Merton Congregational Chapel, Morden Road, Merton (1816–1851).

Indexes and images can also be found at **www.findagrave.com** (which are also indexed on Ancestry) and **www.deceasedonline.com**. These projects are ongoing and the websites are continually updated. There is also a large collection of monumental inscriptions at Findmypast for

St Mary's Church graves.

various counties in England including 'Surrey Monumental Inscriptions' containing 33,644 entries that can be alphabetically searched by surname.

The Society of Genealogists holds three collections of Monumental Inscriptions which have been indexed and can be searched online and viewed by its members. The local family history societies have also produced transcriptions and finding aids for monumental inscriptions which can be purchased through their respective websites. Including but not limited to:

Society of Genealogists

- *Snells Genealogical Collections Vol 2* – Monumental inscriptions recorded by Frederick Simon Snell for the following Surrey churches: Wimbledon (St Mary); Morden (St Lawrence); Merton (St Mary)
- *Surrey monumental inscriptions volume 13* – A collection of monumental inscriptions from the following sixteen Surrey churches: Ashtead, Banstead, Battersea St Mary, Beddington St Mary, Betchworth, Bletchingley, Great Bookham, The Bourne St Thomas, Bramley, Brixton, Burstow, Byfleet, Camberwell St George, Carshalton, Chaldon and Charlwood
- *Ye Olde Mortality Book* miscellaneous book – twenty-six gravestone inscriptions for the parishes of Elstead, Epsom, Ewell, Farnham and Headley recorded by Arthur Weight Matthews

West Surrey Family History Society (WSFHS)

- Croydon Monumental Inscriptions to 1882
- Some Surrey Monumental Inscriptions
- The Monumental Inscriptions of Surrey: A List of Copies
- A List of Middlesex Monumental Inscriptions

East Surrey Family History Society (ESFHS)

- Addington, St Mary the Blessed Virgin (1216–1994)
- Ashtead, St Giles (1272–2003)
- Beddington, St Mary the Virgin (1294–1997)
- Benhilton (Sutton), All Saints (1837–1992)
- Carshalton, All Saints
- Caterham, St Mary
- Chaldon, St Peter & St Paul (1656–1987)
- Cheam Common, St Philip (1881–1983)
- Chelsham, St Leonard (1250–1988)
- Chessington, St Mary the Virgin (1746–1999)
- Chipstead, St Margaret (1303–1989)

- Crowhurst, St George (1675–1987)
- Croydon, St John the Baptist (960–1999)
- East Surrey – includes Bletchingley, St Mary 1559–1942; Charlwood, Provident Chapel 1832–1974; Horne, St Mary 1618–1961; Leigh, St Bartholomew 1646–1983; Lowfield Heath, St Michael 1846–1874; Newdigate, St Peter 1634–1978; Nutfield, St Peter & St Paul 1631–1979; Outwood, St John 1819–1984; Redhill, St John 1807–1981; Reigate, Friends Meeting House 1802–1982
- Epsom, St Martin's (1643–1960) & Congregational Churches (1758–1874) & Bugby Strict Baptist Chapel (1787–1984)
- Farleigh, S. Mary the Virgin (1495–1988)
- Ham Common, St Andrew (1720–1997)
- Headley, St Mary the Virgin (1317–1998)
- Kennington, St Mark – Monumental Inscriptions and Vauxhall Chapel (Independent), Kennington Lane
- Kew, St Anne (1714–1987)
- Kingston, All Saints (1120–1992)
- Kingswood, St Andrew (1814–1987)
- Merstham Collection, St Katharine's (1487–2006)
- Merton Park, St Mary the Virgin (1675–1995)
- Mitcham, St Peter & St Paul (1583–1993)
- Old Malden, St John the Baptist (1613–1979)
- Putney, the Old Burial Ground (1750–1854)
- Reigate, St Mary Magdalene
- Shirley, St John the Evangelist (1803–1996)
- South Croydon, St Peter (1853–1987)
- Surbiton, St Mark
- Tandridge, St Peter (1731–1988)
- Tatsfield, St Mary's (1662–1994)
- Titsey, St James (1579–1988)
- Tooting Graveney, St Nicholas (1670–1989)
- Walton on the Hill, St Peter the Apostle (1775–1991)
- Whyteleafe, St Luke (1867–1997)
- Woldingham, St Agatha (1857–1979)
- Woodmansterne, St Peter's (1771–1991)

E. Wills and Probate

It is often underestimated how many of our ancestors made wills. Conversely, it can be surprising that a wealthier land-holding ancestor did not make one. To understand this, it is necessary to understand a little about the history of the law relating to wills, probate and land.

Historically, there were two probate documents, the 'will' and the 'testament'.

Prior to the Statute of Wills 1540, real property could only be inherited through the rules of intestacy. However, prior to the Statute of Uses 1535, the use of land, i.e. the equitable interest in the land, could be left or *devised* in trust in the document known as a 'will', to the use and benefit of a testator's heirs on his death. That right was abolished by the Statute of Uses 1535 but reinstated by the Statute of Wills 1540.

The document known as a 'testament' dealt with personal property, that is goods and chattels including household belongings, personal belongings, trade tools and equipment, livestock, grain etc., which were *bequeathed by a legacy*.

From 1540, those who held land in fee simple were able to devise all their land (legal and equitable title), while those holding land subject to the performance of military service were able to devise up to two-thirds of their land. Land holding subject to military service was abolished in 1662 from when all land held in fee simple became fully devisable. This change in the law brought together the 'will' and 'testament' into one document, more commonly referred to simply as a 'will' today.

Those who held land in copyhold tenure, that is those who held land from a lord of the manor by copy of the manorial court roll (see Chapter 4) could not devise their holding by will until 1815; however, they were able to surrender their holding to the terms of their will creating a trust in relation to the right to use or equitable interest in the land.

Land held in fee tail or entail, i.e. land which was to pass by operation of law to an heir determined by a settlement deed that specified to whom the property was to descend, was not devisable by will until 1925 when the Law of Property Act 1925 abolished such land holding.

The making of a will was, until the Married Women's Property Act 1882, limited to men over the age of 14 years, widows, spinsters and women over the age of 12 who had their property rights protected in a marriage settlement. With the husband's consent, a married woman could make a will of personal property but this could be revoked by the husband at any time. Further, marriage invalidated a man's will save in the case of a soldier or sailor on active service, when the birth of a child from that marriage, rather than the marriage itself, invalidated a will. The age at which a will could be made was increased to 21 years for both men and women by the Wills Act 1837 which came into force on 1 January 1838.

Consequently, many of our earlier ancestors who were not land holders made a 'testament' rather than a 'will' dealing with the distribution of their personal property. Further, as growing numbers of people held land in one guise or another as laws changed, an increasing number of people sought to determine how their property was distributed on death, often making provisions ensuring widows could remain living in properties or ensuring provisions were made for infant children.

Wills can therefore be full of family details, providing names, relationships, occupations, residence and indications that children were minors when the will was made. They may also name friends and associates. It must be remembered, however, that expressions used for relationship did not necessarily have the same meaning they do today, for instance 'cousin' in middle English (between 1066 and the late fourteenth century) was also used to describe grandchildren, godchildren, nephews or some other relationship, while the term 'in-law' was used extensively, so a stepson might be described as a son-in-law. Similarly, the term 'kinsman' could mean any male relative or may simply have been used to express the importance of a male friend.

Although most wills were written in English, entries in ecclesiastical records will be found in Latin before 1733 and caution must particularly be given to relationship terms if expressed in Latin; for example 'Nepos' is generally thought to be 'nephew' but could also be used to mean grandson or descendant.

Types of will

- **Sworn Will** – this is the more common type of will, which would have been handwritten (typed today) and sworn by the testator (person making the will) and confirmed by two or more witnesses.
- **Nuncupative Will** – this was an oral will, which, up until the commencement of the Wills Act 1837, could be made for personal property (a testament) in the presence of reliable witnesses; their wishes would be written down by the witnesses who swore to its contents in a probate court. They were often made by those who believed they were dying and had not previously made a valid will. Following the Wills Act 1837, nuncupative wills are limited to combatants on active service.
- **Holographic Will** – is a will written entirely by the testator him/herself and not witnessed by others. This kind of will was usually presented to the probate court by witnesses who could swear to its authenticity. Holographic wills can still be valid today provided they are written solely in the testator's handwriting and correctly signed and witnessed.

Where was probate granted?
Until 1858, wills and probate matters were dealt with by the ecclesiastical courts. To search for a will or administration (where no will has been made) pre-1858, it is essential to know which ecclesiastical court(s) had jurisdiction of the relevant parish of the deceased. This was not necessarily the parish in which they lived; the relevant jurisdiction was the one in which the deceased held land or property and the value of that land or property.

The appropriate court was determined by the location and value of property:

Location and value of property	Relevant court
All in one archdeaconry	Archdeacon's court, Deanery or a peculiar court with local jurisdiction
Bona notabilia (i.e. notable property generally being goods valued in excess of £5, or £10 in London) in more than one archdeaconry within the same diocese Appeals from the archdeacon's court	Diocesan Court (Consistory or Commissary court of the bishop)
Bona notabilia in more than one diocese but within the same province Appeals from the Diocesan Court	Prerogative Court of the Archbishop of Canterbury (PCC) or Prerogative Court of Archbishop of York (PCY) depending on location of the diocese
Bona notabilia in more than one province	PCC – Appeals from the PCC were to the Court of Arches or the High Court of Delegates
Persons dying abroad (e.g. soldiers and sailors), holding property abroad or foreigners holding property in England or Wales	PCC

Pre-1858, the only exception to the above rules was during the Interregnum years (1649 to 1660) when the church hierarchy and ecclesiastical courts were suspended and a civil 'Court for Probate of Wills and Granting Administrations' was established from 1653 to 1660 where *all* wills were proved. Following the Restoration in 1660, the church courts were quickly reinstated with the records of the intervening civil court being filed with those of the PCC.

Surrey fell within the province of the PCC, the Diocese of Winchester, and Archdeaconry of Surrey with probate jurisdiction falling under four courts: the PCC; the Consistory Court of the Bishop of Winchester; the

Commissary Court of the Bishop of Winchester; or the Archdeaconry court. The Commissary Court of the Bishop of Winchester essentially replaced the Consistory Court following the Restoration when the bishop no longer held his own court but appointed a Commissary to exercise probate jurisdiction in Surrey on his behalf. Wills in Surrey could, therefore, be proved in any of the four courts subject to the value and location of the estate.

In addition, Surrey had one Peculiar Court, that of the Deanery of Croydon where those who held property in the parishes of Barnes, Burstow, Charlwood, Cheam, Croydon, East Horsley, Merstham, Mortlake, St Mary's and Trinity Church Newington, Putney, Roehampton, St Peter's Walworth and Wimbledon could prove wills, subject to the value of the estate.

Where can I find wills?

SHC does not hold the records of any of the ecclesiastical courts; however, original wills can be found among the records held at SHC. Wills found among ecclesiastical court records are usually the proven registered copies of wills, NOT the originals. Originals were usually returned to the executors, although as will be seen from the collections detailed below, original wills can sometimes be found among ecclesiastical court records.

At SHC, original wills, copy wills, abstracts, extracts, and associated papers relating to the administration of estates can be found within various family, estate, manorial and parish collections, such as the following collections:

- 'Properties of the Sparkes and Eastwood Families in Shalford, Godalming, Witley and elsewhere', which holds nine records relating to wills and probate between 1707 and 1822 (reference G106/17/)
- 'Estates of the Leigh Bennet family in Thorpe, Addington and Stanwell and Staine, Middlesex: deeds and paper', which holds nine records dating between 1692 and 1866 (reference 7624/2/)
- 'Ladbroke family of Randalls, Leatherhead: Deeds and Estate papers' which holds sixteen records dated between 1725 and 1883 (reference 6154/)
- 'Kentwyns Estate in Nutfield and Bletchingley: Deeds and papers' which holds sixty-four records dating between 1526 and the 1920s (reference 3089/7/)
- 'Great Bookham Manor' (reference K34/2/) which holds twenty-one wills dating between 1738 and 1821

These are just a few of those available so it is always worth searching a name or location to see what may be available.

Wills of the Prerogative Court of Canterbury (PCC)

Wills proven in the PCC are held at TNA in series PROB 11 and span the years 1384 to 12 January 1858. They can be downloaded for free from TNA Discovery website and are indexed and digitised on Ancestry in its 'England & Wales, Prerogative Court of Canterbury Wills, 1384–1858' collection.

The Series PROB 10 contains original wills of those proven in the PCC which were not returned to executors, so is also worth searching. The series covers the years 1484 to 1858 and can be searched by name and year. They are not digitised so must be viewed at TNA.

Wills of the Consistory Court

Wills proven in the Consistory Court of the Bishop of Winchester are held at Hampshire Record Office in series 21M65/D2 and survive from c.1540 to 1858. This collection has now been indexed and digitised on Ancestry in collection 'Hampshire, England, Wills and Probates, 1398–1858', and includes the wills of 973 Surrey residents.

Wills of the Commissary and Archdeaconry Court

Wills proven in the Commissary Court of the Bishop of Winchester and the Surrey Archdeaconry Court are held at TLA.

For the Commissary Court, surviving records include:

- Original wills 1663–1856, with gaps (DW/PC/05/1663–1856)
- Registers of wills 1674–1696, 1729–1857 (DW/PC/07/001-008)

For the Archdeaconry Court surviving records include:

- Original wills 1534–1857, with gaps (DW/PA/05/1534–1857)
- Registers of wills 1480–1821, with gaps (DW/PA/07/001-033)

For both courts, those held in the 'Original wills' collections are available on Ancestry in the collection 'London, England, Wills and Probate, 1507–1858' and SHC holds copies on microfilm of some registered wills held at the TLA. Abstracts and summaries of original wills held at TLA can also be searched at Findmypast in the collection 'Surrey & South London Wills & Probate Index, 1470–1856'.

Probate Act Books, which are registers of the grants of probate, are also available, with separate books for each probate court. These record each probate granted and include the name of the deceased, occupation, date of grant of probate, and the executor's name. They can include facts about a deceased that are not given in his will, such as his parish, whether he died married, unmarried, widowed etc., his trade, profession or status or that he belonged to one parish but died in another. They may also provide details of the appointment of executors when an executor died before a testator, or when an executor did not wish to act, and in the event of an executor's death when the court would appoint successive executors. The books often contain unregistered wills (wills not proved in court).

For the PCC, these can be found in series PROB 8 at TNA. There are typed indexes available in seven volumes covering the years 1630 to 1854 which have been digitised and indexed on Ancestry in the collection 'Abstracts of probate acts in the Prerogative Court of Canterbury'. For Surrey, there are also abstracts of wills indexed at Findmypast in the collection 'Surrey, Prerogative Court of Canterbury Will Abstracts, 1736–1794'.

For the Consistory Court of the Bishop of Winchester, the Probate Act books are held at Hampshire Record Office and survive from 1587 to 1694 and are held in series 21M65/D1.

For the Commissary Court of the Bishop of Winchester and the Surrey Archdeaconry Court, Probate Act books are held at TLA as follows in 'Probate and administration act books 1662–1858, with gaps' (DW/PC/01/001-015) for the Commissary Court and 'Probate and administration act books 1674–1858, with gaps to 1725' (DW/PA/01/001-007) for the Archdeaconry Court.

In addition, many wills, probates and administrations were entered in the registers of the Archbishops of Canterbury, many of which date from the medieval period and no longer survive among records of any other court. These registers are held at Lambeth Palace Library.

My ancestor died intestate

Where someone died without leaving a will, Letters of Administration (commonly referred to as Admons) were granted, usually to the next of kin. They provide the deceased's name, address, occupation, date and place of death along with, the name, address, occupation, and the administrator's relationship to the deceased. The value of the estate will also be given. The details of beneficiaries are not provided. They generally contain less genealogically useful information than a will.

Before 1858, these will be found in the records of the relevant ecclesiastical court determined by where the property was held and its value. They can be accessed through Administration (Admon) Act Books. These are registers of the grants of administration covering the period from 1559 to 1858. There are separate Admon Act Books for each probate court.

Admons can sometimes be found with wills attached. This happened when an administrator was appointed because the executor renounced or was unable to act. The will was filed with the administration bond in a separate series and not with the registered wills. It was also entered in the calendar of wills as 'Admon with will annexed'.

When letters of administration were granted, an administration bond was required (with sureties). The bond obliged the administrator to produce an inventory of the deceased's goods and chattels, to pay any debts and to render an account to the court in the same manner as an executor.

Where can I find letters of administration and administration bonds?

Admons in the Prerogative Court of Canterbury

For Admons granted in the PCC, the Admon Act books are held at TNA in series PROB 6 and 7 and date from 1559 to 1858. There are typed indexes available in three volumes covering the years 1581 to 1595 and 1649 to 1660 which have been digitised and indexed on Ancestry in the collection 'Index to administrations in the Prerogative Court of Canterbury'.

Admons in the Consistory Court

Admons granted in the Consistory Court of the Bishop of Winchester are held at Hampshire Record Office in series 21M65/D2 and survive from c.1540 to 1858, while Admon Act books can be found among the Probate Act books in series 21M65/D1. Administrations have been indexed and digitised as part of the collections on Ancestry 'Hampshire, England, Wills and Probates, 1398–1858'.

Admons in the Commissary Court and Archdeaconry Court

Admons granted in the Commissary Court of the Bishop of Winchester and the Surrey Archdeaconry Court are held at TLA.

For the Commissary Court surviving records include:

- Probate and administration act books 1662–1858, with gaps (DW/PC/01/001-015)
- Administration bonds 1674, 1731–1858 (DW/PC/06/1674–1858)

For the Archdeaconry Court surviving records include:

- Probate and administration act books 1674–1858, with gaps to 1725 (DW/PA/01/001-007)

It is worth remembering that among various family, estate, manorial and parish collections held at SHC, associated papers relating to the administration of estates can also be found so it is worth checking the catalogue for names and places.

Inventories

From 1529 to 1782, executors and administrators were usually required to prepare a probate inventory, which was a list of the deceased's personal or moveable goods, assets and chattels, not including real estate or land.

They listed and valued room by room the deceased's movable goods, including cash ('money in his purse') and clothes ('his wearing apparel'), followed by the contents of agricultural buildings, livestock and crops growing in the fields. Anything that was not movable was omitted, so even things like cooking utensils, curtains and household furniture would often be identified by room, thus providing evidence of both rooms and the use of rooms. However, it is impossible to tell whether all the rooms in the house have been listed, unless there are internal inconsistencies (e.g., a 'chamber over the buttery' but no 'buttery'). They provide an excellent insight into an ancestor's life and status.

The objective of the exercise was to ensure that any unpaid debts owing at death could be paid.

Where to find Inventories

Inventories in the Prerogative Court of Canterbury

Inventories filed with wills proved and admons at the Prerogative Court of Canterbury are held at TNA in series PROB 2–5 and those filed between 1660 and 1782 are searchable online via TNA's Discovery catalogue.

Inventories in the Consistory Court

Inventories filed in the in the Consistory Court of the Bishop of Winchester are held at Hampshire Record Office in series 21M65/D3 and survive from 1540 to 1833. Inventories have been indexed and digitised on Ancestry in its wills collection 'Hampshire, England, Wills and Probates, 1398–1858'.

Inventories in the Commissary Court and Archdeaconry Court

There do not appear to be any separate inventory records for the Commissary Court and Archdeaconry Court of Surrey held at the TLA suggesting none have survived; however, Surrey Record Society, Vol XXXIX. *Surrey Probate Inventories 1558–1603* by Marion Herridge (2005) brings together transcripts of surviving inventories from the stated period.

Peculiar Court of the Deanery of Croydon

The records for this court are held at Lambeth Palace Library held in series VH 96/1-2945 and include wills, inventories, court acts, administration, administrators' and executors' bonds and renunciations of administration from 1614 to 1841 listed in alphabetical order.

Finding aids for wills and probate records in Surrey

Probate Jurisdictions: Where to Look for Wills by Jeremy Gibson (published 2002 by the Federation of Family History Societies) provides a countrywide county guide to locating wills and probate records.

Prerogative court of Canterbury

- Index of Surrey Wills proved in the Prerogative Court of Canterbury 1650–1700 (WSFHS)
- Surrey Administrations in the Prerogative Court of Canterbury 1760–1781 (WSFHS)
- Surrey Administrations in the Prerogative Court of Canterbury 1782–1790 (WSFHS)
- An Index to the wills proved in the Prerogative Court of Canterbury 1750 to 1800 (Society of Genealogists, 1976 to 1992, 6 volumes)
- Index to administrations in the Prerogative Court of Canterbury (Ancestry)
- Vol. I. Index of acts of administration in the Prerogative Court of Canterbury. 1649–1654
- Vol. II. Index to acts of administration in the Prerogative Court of Canterbury. 1655–1660
- Vol. III. Index to acts of administration in the Prerogative Court of Canterbury. 1581–1595
- Surrey, Prerogative Court of Canterbury Will Abstracts, 1736–1794 (Findmypast)
- Prerogative Court of Canterbury Wills Index 1750–1800 (Findmypast)

Consistory Court

- *Union index of Surrey probate records which survive from before the year 1650* by Cliff Webb (British Record Society, 1990)
- *Wills, administrations and inventories with the Winchester Diocesan Records* by Arthur J. Willis (self-published 1968 (digitised at Family Search Film 973253 Item 6 continued at Film 973254 Item 1)

Commissary Court

- Index of Surrey Wills proved in the Commissary Court 1660–1751 (WSFHS)
- Index of Surrey Wills and Administrations in the Commissary and Peculiar Courts 1752–1858 (WSFHS)
- Abstract of Wills in the Commissary Court of Surrey 1662–1857 (WSFHS)

Archdeaconry Court

- Index of Surrey Wills proved in the Archdeaconry Court 1660–1751 (WSFHS)
- Abstract of Wills in the Archdeaconry Court of Surrey 1480–1649 (WSFHS)
- Abstract of Wills in the Archdeaconry Court of Surrey 1660–1739 (WSFHS)
- Abstract of Wills in the Archdeaconry Court of Surrey 1740–1858 (WSFHS)
- Abstract of Wills in the Archdeaconry Court of Surrey and Commissary Courts of Surrey 1480–1858 (WSFHS)

Peculiar court

- Index of Surrey Wills and Administrations in the Peculiar Court 1660–1751 (WSFHS)
- Surrey Peculiars Probate Index, 1660–1751 (Findmypast)

Published sources:

- Volume XXXIX. Surrey Probate Inventories 1558 to 1603 transcribed by Marion Herridge (2005) (Surrey Record Society)

- Volume V. Surrey Wills: Spage Register (1922) – probate register of the Archdeaconry Court of Surrey entitled 'Spage', 1484 to 1489 (Surrey Record Society)
- Volume IV. Surrey Wills: Herringman Register (1915 to 1920) – probate register of the Archdeaconry Court of Surrey entitled 'Herringman', 1595 to 1608 (Abstracts) (Surrey Record Society)

Death Duty Wills

Between 1796 and 1903, registers were maintained of those wills and administrations which were subject to stamp or 'death' duty following the Legacy and Residue Act 1795. The registers include an abstract of all wills (from 1812, copies of wills) and administrations which were deposited at the Legacy Duty Department of the Stamp Office. When initially introduced, duty was payable on 'every share or residue of the personal estate of any person dying and leaving such estate of the clear value of £100 or upwards' and before 1805 this included about 25 per cent of estates. However, in the nineteenth century the scope of duty was gradually extended and by 1857 all estates worth £20 or upwards were liable. Estates of those who died while serving their country were exempt.

These wills were still proven in the ecclesiastical courts until 1858, but the death duty registers can be worth searching where no will or administration can be found in the local ecclesiastical courts.

The registers are held at TNA in series IR 26 and can be accessed using the death duty indexes found in series IR 27 to find the appropriate reference in IR 26. The indexes have been digitised and can be searched at Findmypast. The indexes contain 28,169 Surrey resident entries. For years 1796 to 1811, digital copies of the registers for ecclesiastical courts other than the PCC can be searched and downloaded from the TNA website and include 162 entries for Surrey residents. For more information see the research guide 'Country court death duty registers 1796–1811'.

National Probate Calendar

On 12 January 1858, jurisdiction for granting probate and administration was transferred from ecclesiastical courts to the newly created Principal Probate Registry (PRR) with local probate districts being created. From 1858, therefore, basic details of wills and administrations can be found in the National Probate Calendar (NPC). This is a central calendar (or index) compiled annually of all wills and letters of administration since 1858 granted in the PPR and local Probate Registries in England and

Wales. This being a central register, it is no longer necessary to search individual probate courts.

The NPC can be searched online at **www.gov.uk** and can also be found at commercial websites such as Ancestry and Findmypast.

The calendar will provide the name of the deceased, occupation, date of death, place of death, date of probate, the registry in which the probate was granted, the value of the deceased's estate and, until 1967, to whom probate was granted.

It can be searched where a death record cannot be found, although of course not everyone made a will and a grant of administration may not have been required in all cases (such as where the estate was limited to jointly owned property or only had no real property).

Copies of wills and administrations can be obtained from the government probate service website 'Find a Will' (**https://probatesearch.service.gov.uk**) for a small fee (currently £1.50).

Chapter 3

TAKING YOUR ONLINE RESEARCH FURTHER

A. Newspapers

Newspapers can be an invaluable source of information for family history research, including, but not limited to, obituaries, birth and marriage announcements, court proceedings (civil and criminal), coroners' inquests, accidents, bankruptcies and business advertisements. They can provide all sorts of information on individual ancestors and their families. They can also include details of local history which can enhance your family history research such as reports on sporting events, churches, housing, shops and businesses, schools, sport, local shows and local council meetings.

The first local newspaper to be published was the *Worcester Postman* in 1690 and the first national daily newspaper was the *Daily Courant* in 1702. The first local newspaper for Surrey was *The County Chronicle and Weekly Advertiser for Essex, Herts, Kent, Surrey, Middlesex* in 1788. This was followed by the *Sussex & Surrey Chronicle* in 1823, and the *Surrey Herald and County Advertiser* first published in 1826 and 1828, among others.

In the eighteenth century, newspaper circulation was limited, partly due to limited literacy skills but also the high cost of paper with the imposition of stamp duty on newspapers from 1712 further hampering the costs. In this period, paper was still handmade and it was not until the introduction of the Fourdrinier papermaking machine that production costs began to fall.

Through the nineteenth century, with lower production costs, an increasingly literate population, the reduction of stamp duty on newspapers in 1836 and its eventual abolition in 1855, the number of local newspapers began to grow.

The Surrey Comet,

AND GENERAL ADVERTISER,

FOR KINGSTON, GUILDFORD, SURBITON, RICHMOND, CHERTSEY, THAMES DITTON, LONG DITTON, ESHER, EAST AND WEST MOULSEY, HAMPTON, HAMPTON-WICK, HAMPTON-COURT, TEDDINGTON, TWICKENHAM, &c.

No. 14.] SATURDAY, NOVEMBER 11, 1854. [PRICE ONE PENNY.

PHŒNIX LIFE OFFICE.

CAPITAL £100,000.

CHIEF OFFICE,—1, LEADENHALL STREET, LONDON:

Directors:

LT.-COL. ADDISON, (*Managing Director*.)
GENERAL BARTON, H. E. I. C. S.
EDWARD COOKE BOURNE, Esq.
CHARLES GOOLDEN, Esq.

MAURICE EVANS, Esq.
R. H. GOOLDEN, Esq., M. D.
Rev. W. DOUGLAS VIETCH, M. A.
JOHN ALEXANDER WATT, Esq.

Bankers:
MESSRS. MASTERMAN, PETERS, MILDRED & CO.

Resident Manager:
E. DANIELS, Esq. *Chief Office*.

Provincial Superintendent:
J. W. DICKSON, Esq. *Seething Wells, Surbiton*.

Agent in Ditton :—Mr. JOHN HOWICK.

RATES at the Lowest Scale compatible with perfect security. £100 secured to a Life of 20 for £1. 14s. per annum, payable yearly, half yearly, or quarterly.—At 30 years of age, £2. 3s. 7d.—at 40, £2. 17s.—at 50, £4. 1s. 8d.—at 60, £6. 4s. 6d., completed if required in one day. Thus a Life of 20 may assure £100 at death for less than 9s. a quarter. No stamp or entrance fee. Half the premium may remain on credit for five years. Policies once issued are ABSOLUTELY indisputable. A liberal commission allowed to persons bringing business. All Medical men referred to, remunerated.

Veterinary Establishment.

HORSES SHOD on principle of Expansion, by skilful and experienced Workmen, at THOMAS EMM'S Veterinary Establishment, Brick Lane, Kingston-on-Thames. Sick and Lame Horses and all other domestic Animals attended to. Charges moderate.

ARTHUR BROWN,
PHOTOGRAPHIC ARTIST, AND TEACHER OF DRAWING & PAINTING,
KINGSTON-ON-THAMES.

PORTRAITS TAKEN by the VARIOUS PHOTOGRAPHIC PROCESSES, at his residence in LONDON STREET.
Where Specimens can be seen.

Photographic Portraits,
Pure in tone and perfect in definition, taken by
J. BARBROOK,
No. 3, TERRACE, HAMPTON WICK.

THESE PORTRAITS are surpassed by none in brilliance or minuteness of detail, and being taken instantaneously, they combine marvellous truth with singular beauty. A great variety of specimens on view.

ARTHUR DUNN,
PRACTICAL MILLWRIGHT, ENGINEER, SMITH, &c.
Heathen Street, Kingston.

ALL kinds of AGRICULTURAL MACHINES supplied and repaired on the lowest terms. Pumps, Pipes, Cocks, &c., made and repaired. Horticultural Buildings heated by hot water or steam. Castings of all descriptions supplied at London prices. Furnace Bars and Railing Bars 10s. per cwt.
N.B. Ranges, Stoves, &c., supplied.

THE KINGSTON
BOOKBINDING ESTABLISHMENT.
JOHN DIAMOND, BOOKBINDER, AND ACCOUNT BOOK MANUFACTURER,
CHURCH STREET.
Libraries arranged, carefully Packed and Repaired.—Engraving and Copperplate Printing neatly executed.

J. W. A. DICKENSON,
(Late of the White Hart Inn, Hampton,)
WINE AND SPIRIT MERCHANT,
DRUID'S HEAD INN,
MARKET PLACE, KINGSTON.
Well aired Beds and Good Stabling.—Slate Bagatelle and Dry Skittle Ground.

LOWE'S EMPORIUM,
HEATHEN STREET, KINGSTON,

OFFERS TO PURCHASERS OF DRAPERY AND CLOTHING

the advantages of an Extensive Stock,

Bought in the first Markets, for Cash, and consists of every description of useful Goods in

DRAPERY AND CLOTHING, HATS, BOOTS AND SHOES, CARPETS AND DRUGGETS, &c.

GARMENTS OF ALL KINDS MADE TO ORDER BY FIRST RATE WORKMEN.
Agent to the Professional Life Office.

VACHELL'S BREWERY,
AT THE BACK OF THE PLOUGH INN.
SURBITON HILL.

H. W. V. begs to call the attention of the Gentry, Inhabitants of Surbiton, and the Neighbourhood, to his HOME BREWED ALES, strongly recommended for their pure and genuine quality. To be had in large or small casks, at the following prices :—

XXX ALE, 9 Gallons	...	12s.	4½ Gallons	...	6s.
XX ,, ,,	...	9s.	,,	...	4s. 6d.
X ,, ,,	...	7s. 6d.	,,	...	3s. 9d.

Also, Superior **STOUT** and **PORTER** at the above prices.
GUINNESS' STOUT, and ALLSOPP'S and BASS' PALE ALES in bottles.

J. B. ETHERINGTON & SON,
HAIR CUTTERS, DRESSERS, & ORNAMENTAL HAIR WORKERS,
King Street, Twickenham,

PERFUMERY, Combs, Brushes, of every description. Etherington's Hair Wash, strongly recommended for cleaning and beautifying the Hair. Private room for Hair cutting. *Licence dealers in Fancy Snuffs, Tobacco, and Cigars.*

DEALER IN GAME.
JOHN TICKNER,
PORK BUTCHER, TRIPE DRESSER and POULTERER, HEATEN STREET, KINGSTON.
Sausages and Saveloys ; Neats' Feet, New Lard. Home-cured Bacon, Hams, Tongues, & Chaps. New Laid Eggs.

HOUSEKEEPER WANTED.—A respectable person who understands cooking and general superintendence of domestic duties will meet with a comfortable situation. Enquire at the "Comet" Office.

THE BATTLE OF THE ALMA, in a splendidly coloured Plate. Price 2s.—Also, WYLD'S MAP of THE CRIMEA, Price 3s. to be had at T. PHILPOTT'S, *Bookseller and Stationer.*

C. WRIGHTON,
(FROM LONDON),
FRENCH DYER AND CLEANER,
CHURCH STREET, KINGSTON,
Opposite the Mechanics' Literary Institution.
BRITISH AND FOREIGN SHAWLS cleaned. Silk, Satin, Velvet, and Lace, cleaned or dyed, equal to new.—Chintz Furniture, Table Covers, &c.

Extract from Surrey Comet 11 November 1854.

The longest running County newspaper is the *Surrey Comet* first published in 1854 and continuing today under the Newsquest Media Group Limited who purchased it in 1996. The Kingston Heritage Centre holds a complete collection of the Surrey Comet right up to date, with copies available to view on microfilm between 1854 and 1998 (originals are stored off-site) and bound volumes from 1999 available on-site. Copies can also be found at SHC and online at British Newspaper Archives and on Findmypast.

The *Surrey Times* series, first published in 1855 and now part of the Surrey Advertiser Group currently owned by Reach plc., includes three newspapers: the *Guildford Times*; *Godalming Times*; and the *Cranleigh Times*.

The *Surrey Advertiser* is the third longest running county newspaper, first published in 1864 and gradually evolved into the Surrey Advertiser Group of seven more localised versions: Guildford, Cranleigh, Godalming, Woking, Elmbridge, Leatherhead, and Dorking.

The *Surrey Advertiser* group also publishes the *Surrey Herald* which has four localised editions concentrated in the north of the county: Walton and Weybridge, Sunbury and Shepperton, Staines, Ashford & Egham, Chertsey & Addlestone.

The British Library Newsroom holds approximately 60 million issues collected from nearly all newspapers published in the United Kingdom and Ireland, dating back to the early 1600s and continues to receive around 1,500 newspaper titles on a daily or weekly basis, and nearly 100 titles from overseas. Many of these have been digitised and it is this collection that can be found in the 'Newspaper' collection at Findmypast and/or the British Newspaper Archive online, which for Surrey include: (in alphabetical order):

- *Camberley News* (1986–1988)
- *Caterham Mirror* (1950–1999)
- *Chertsey & Addlestone Leader* (1994–1999)
- *Cobham News and Advertiser* (1969–1971)
- *County Chronicle, Surrey Herald and Weekly Advertiser for Kent* (1834–1865)
- *Croydon Chronicle and East Surrey Advertiser* (1855–1912)
- *Croydon Advertiser and East Surrey Reporter* (1872–1999)
- *Croydon Guardian and Surrey County Gazette* (1877–1913)
- *Dorking and Leatherhead Advertiser* (1887–1999)
- *Egham & Staines News* (1897–1906)
- *Epsom Journal* (1871–1902)

- *Esher News and Mail (1938–1999)*
- *Farnham Mail (1986–1990)*
- *Guildford & Godalming Advertiser (1963)*
- *Horley & Gatwick Mirror (1952–1999)*
- *Hants and Berks Gazette and Middlesex and Surrey Journal (1892–1910)*
- *Leatherhead Advertiser (1986–1999)*
- *Middlesex & Surrey Gazette (1877–1878)*
- *Middlesex & Surrey Express (1886–1909)*
- *Staines & Ashford News (1950–1999)*
- *Staines & Egham News (1986–1999)*
- *Staines Informer (1986–1999)*
- *Staines Leader (1994–1999)*
- *Sunbury & Shepperton Herald (1986–1999)*
- *Surrey Advertiser (1864–1973)*
- *Surrey Comet (1854–1910)*
- *Surrey Gazette (1860–1900)*
- *Surrey-Hants Star (1986–1999)*
- *Surrey Herald (1911–1999)*
- *Surrey Herald and County Advertiser (1826–1828)*
- *Surrey Independent and Wimbledon Mercury (1882–1905)*
- *Surrey Mercury (1845–1847)*
- *Surrey & Middlesex Standard (1835–1840)*
- *Surrey Mirror (1879–1999)*
- *Sussex & Surrey Chronicle (1823–1824)*
- *Sutton & Epson Advertiser (1908–1960)*
- *Walton & Weybridge Informer (1986–1999)*
- *Walton & Weybridge Leader (1994–1999)*
- *Wandsworth Borough News (1908–1919)*
- *West Surrey Times (1855–1919)*
- *Woking Informer (1986–1999)*
- *Woking News & Mail (1907–1963)*

Back issues of newspapers held at SHC include:

- *Banstead Herald*
- *Camberley News, Camberley Mail, Camberley News and Mail*
- *Caterham Free Press, Caterham and Purley Weekly Press and County Post*
- *Epsom and Ewell Advertiser*
- *Epsom and Ewell Herald*

- *Esher News and Mail*
- *Farnham Herald*
- *Godalming Times and Advertiser*
- *Guildford Times and Advertiser*
- *Guildford and Godalming Advertiser / Times and Advertiser*
- *Guildford Outlook*
- *Middlesex Chronicle*
- *The Post: Epsom, Ewell and Banstead*
- *Staines and Egham News*
- *Surrey Advertiser*
- *Surrey and Hants News*
- *Surrey Comet*
- *Surrey Herald: Chertsey, Addlestone and Byfleet edition* (also Walton, Weybridge and Hersham edition February 1979 to 1999 at Elmbridge Museum)
- *Surrey Mirror*
- *Surrey Times*
- *Sussex Agricultural Express* (*Incorporating the Surrey Standard*)
- *Windsor and Eton Express*
- *Woking Herald, Woking News and Mail, Woking Review*

SHC also holds several useful volumes of the *Illustrated London News* covering the years 1843 and 1890. The *Illustrated London News* was the world's first illustrated weekly news magazine, first published in 1842 and published weekly until 1971 when it moved to monthly publication until 1989. It was then published quarterly in 1994 after which it was published twice yearly until ceasing publication in 2003.

SHC holds the *Gentleman's Magazine* from 1731 to 1842. This was a monthly magazine which was perhaps the most influential of its period. First published in 1731, it ran uninterrupted until 1922, and was created to provide news and commentary on a wide range of topics its target audience, 'the educated public', may have been interested in.

Kingston Heritage Centre holds the following (in addition to the *Surrey Comet*), either in hard copy or on microfilm, all of which are localised newspaper to Kingston and the surrounding area:

- *Kingston and Malden Borough News* (1963–1980)
- *Kingston and Surbiton News* (1882–1899)
- *Kingston, Surbiton and New Malden Times* (1994–1999)
- *Kingston Express* (1886–1893)
- *Local Illustrated News* (1922–1924)

- *Malden and Coombe Times* (1937)
- *Surbiton News* (1959–1961)
- *Surrey Daily Post* (1913)
- *Wimbledon Borough News* (1949–1953)

Sutton Local History and Archive Centre has a Newspaper Index as part of the online catalogue which including articles from the following newspapers from November 1998 onwards:

- *Croydon Advertiser*
- *Surrey Comet*
- *Sutton Guardian*
- *Sutton Herald*
- *Sutton Independent*
- *Sutton Post*

B. Directories

Trade, county, town and street directories were the forerunners of telephone directories. Trade directories were first published covering London in the mid-seventeenth century, providing lists of named merchants and their locations, in alphabetical order. They gradually spread across the major towns and cities and by the mid- to late nineteenth century, directories could be found for almost every county, produced annually by either the Post Office, Kelly and White (Kelly's Directories), Pigot's and some other smaller publishers.

They include lists of traders, businessmen and principal inhabitants of each town, and can include information which may not be easily found elsewhere. Between 1841 and 1921 they can help bridge the gaps between the decennial census returns. They also include advertisements providing a good source of illustrative material.

Tradesmen and anyone else wishing to appear in the directory had to pay for their entries but they offered a valuable form of advertising before the invention of the other forms of media such as radio, television and, of course, the internet of today. However, it must be remembered that information printed in a directory could be up to a year out of date by the time it was published.

Guildhall Library, London holds the largest collection of trade directories including those which cover Surrey or parts of ancient Surrey:

- Pigot's London Directory 1826–28, 1832–33
- Robson's London Directory 1838

- Pigot's London Directory 1839
- Robson's General Directory 1839
- Essex directories 1845, 1847, 1851–52, 1855 (vol.2), 1859
- Surrey directories 1862, 1866
- Essex directories 1867
- South London Blue Book 1869
- Surrey directories 1870, 1874
- Surrey directories 1876 ('West Surrey' edition)
- Surrey directories 1878, 1882
- County Companion 1884
- Surrey directories 1887, 1890–91, 1895, 1899
- Surrey directories 1903 ('Kelly' edition)
- Surrey directories 1905, 1907, 1909, 1911
- Surrey directories 1913 (2 editions: 'Kelly' & 'West Surrey')
- Surrey directories 1915, 1918, 1922, 1924, 1927, 1930, 1934
- Surrey directories 1936 ('North-West Surrey' edition)
- Surrey directories 1938 (2 editions: 'Kelly' & 'North-West Surrey')
- Surrey directories 1949

South-Eastern Counties directories 1960–61 The following directories have been digitised and can be searched on Ancestry:

- 1839 Pigot's Directory, Surrey
- 1851 Post Office Directory, Surrey
- 1867 Post Office Directory, Surrey
- 1878 Post Office Directory, Surrey
- 1891 Kelly´s Directory of Kent, Surrey & Sussex (Pt 3: Surrey)
- 1911 Kelly´s Directory, Surrey
- 1913 Kelly´s Directory, Surrey
- 1918 Kelly´s Directory, Surrey

Findmypast has the following directories digitised and searchable:

- 1851 Gray's Directory, Croydon, Surrey
- 1855 Kelly's Directory for Essex, Hertfordshire, Kent, Middlesex, Surrey, Sussex
- 1867 Kelly's Directory, Surrey
- 1881 Kelly's Directory, Surrey
- 1913 Kelly's Directory, Surrey
- 1924 Kelly's Directory, Surrey

The Genealogist website also has the following directories digitised and searchable:

- 1839 Pigot's Directory
- 1938 Kelly's Directory Kent, Surrey, Sussex

SHC also holds a good collection of both original and microfiche copies of local, county and national directories going back to the late eighteenth century.

The first telephone directory was introduced in England on 15 January 1880; it contained 248 personal and business names in London but no telephone numbers! Callers could simply ring the telephone exchange and ask to be connected to someone else listed in the directory.

Historic telephone directories covering each year from the first publication are held at the British Telecommunications Archive where the original directories can be viewed on microfilm to the year 2000. Years 1880 to 1984 have also been digitised and are available to search on Ancestry. The coverage for Surrey is unclear and varies across the county.

The first Yellow Pages directory was published in 1966 and historic copies are available at The Royal Berkshire Archives, 9 Coley Avenue, Reading, Berkshire RG1 6AF.

C. Poll books and electoral registers.

The right to vote in parliamentary elections was first introduced in 1429 when men aged 21 or over who held freehold land or property with an annual net value of 40 shillings or more could vote. The right to vote in local borough elections, however, depended on local custom, with some boroughs allowing all male heads of households the right to vote, while others allowed only freemen, or some other designated group of men in so-called 'rotten' or 'pocket' boroughs.

Following the Land Tax Act 1780, the payment of Land Tax (see next section) confirmed a man's right to vote in parliamentary elections with duplicate Land Tax assessments being deposited with the Clerk of the Peace for the purpose of electoral registration. This helped to reduce the number of disputes over who qualified to vote. Those who held copyhold land only were specifically excluded by an Act of Parliament in 1758.

The right to vote in local elections continued to be based on local customs until the qualification to vote was standardised by the Great Reform Act 1832 when electoral registers were introduced.

Poll books recorded those who voted at a given election and can include details of their parish of residence, their occupation and the candidate who they voted for (this being public knowledge as secret ballots were not introduced until the Ballot Act 1872).

In Surrey, parliamentary boroughs returning members of parliament from the fourteenth and fifteenth centuries were: Bletchingley, Farnham, Guildford, Kingston, Reigate and Southwark. Gatton became a parliamentary borough in 1450 and Haslemere in 1584.

The right to vote in these Surrey boroughs differed across the county. For example, in the boroughs of Bletchingley, Haslemere and Reigate, the right to vote was conferred on owners of specific plots of land in those boroughs; in Gatton, any freeholders of the borough who occupied their own freeholds and were not receiving alms were able to vote; and in Southwark and Guildford those freemen and freeholders who paid 'scot and lot' (a local tax) could vote in local elections.

Poll Books for Surrey held at SHC include:

- Guildford Poll Books 1796–1841 (reference BR/PAR/2/) with selected earlier volumes available under reference 1251/1-6)
- Bletchingley Poll records 1660–1769 (among papers of the Clayton Family; reference K60/9/)
- Polls for Reigate Borough from 1698 to 1722 compiled by William Bryant, attorney, (among papers of William Bryant; Reference 445/1) (Copies of polls are also held at Hertfordshire Archives and Local Studies under reference D/ECd E156-72)

Poll books for Surrey have also been digitised and are searchable on Ancestry from 1705. Further details of what poll books are available and from which archives can be found in Gibson and Rogers' 'Poll Books c.1696–1872'.

The Land Tax returns for Surrey between 1780 and 1832, which were used as evidence as a man's right to vote, are held at SHC under reference QS6/7/ and have been digitised and can be searched on Ancestry (see next section).

Great Reform Act 1832
Following the Great Reform Act ('the Act'), electoral registers were introduced and have been produced annually since, except during the war years 1916–1917 and 1940–1944.

The Act widened the criteria for those able to vote in parliamentary elections to include not only those who held freehold land or property with an annual net value of 40 shillings or more but also:

- Those with an estate for life or lives of any tenure worth £10 per annum
- Copyholders of property with an annual value of £10 or more
- Leaseholders of property let for sixty years or more with an annual value of £10 or more
- Leaseholders of property let for twenty years or more and with an annual value of £50 or more which included sub-lessees where the sub-lease was for that period, provided they occupied the premises

It also set down criteria for those able to vote in local elections to include anyone who previously had a right to vote plus any male householder who had property worth £10 or more a year, whether owners or tenants.

The criteria were extended in 1867 to include, in parliamentary elections:

- All male freeholders or leaseholders of property with an annual value of £5 or more
- Tenants who paid annual rent of £12 or more

And in local elections:

- Owners of houses who had been resident for a year
- Most occupiers who paid annual rent of £10 or more

In 1884, the criteria were further extended to enable those with local voting rights from 1867 to vote in parliamentary elections. These criteria remained in place until the universal right to vote was introduced in 1918 for men aged 21 years and over and women aged 30 years and over. The age for women was reduced to 21 in 1928 with the qualifying age being reduced to 18 for all in 1969.

SHC holds electoral registers for the county of Surrey from 1832 to present, including to 1889 and 1962 respectively for those parishes lost to London boroughs. The TLA holds electoral registers for the parishes lost to London boroughs from the respective dates.

Surrey electoral registers have also been digitised and can be searched on Ancestry between 1832–1962 including in collections:

- Surrey, England, Electoral Registers, 1832–1962
- Sutton, Surrey, England, Electoral Registers, 1931–1970
- Electoral Rolls from Carshalton, Beddington, Wallington, Sutton and Cheam for the years 1931 to 1970

D. Land Tax records

Land Tax was the longest running tax, introduced in 1693 and continued until 1963, although the largest surviving collections cover the period 1780 to 1832 when they doubled as evidence of the right to vote. It was a tax on both real and personal property, certain public pensions, and salaries of anyone holding land worth an annual value of 20 shillings or more, with Catholics being charged double. The records consist of assessments and returns listing landowners, with additional information added over time:

- From 1772 they include details of occupiers of property
- From 1799 they include an additional column for sums assessed but exonerated (redeemed by payment of a lump sum)
- From about 1826 they include a column for a description of the type of property

Land Tax records are held locally; those for Surrey are held at SHC (reference QS6/7/) for the ancient county of Surrey between 1780 to 1832. The records are available both on microfilm at SHC and as digitised copies searchable on Ancestry in its series 'Surrey, England, Land Tax Records, 1780–1832'. SHC also holds a surname index in its search room.

The survival rate of Land Tax assessments before 1780 and after 1832 varies across the county. There is no comprehensive list of earlier or later assessments; however, various assessments and associated records can be found among manorial, family and estate papers, parish records, and 'Hundred' records by searching 'Land Tax Assessments' in the SHC catalogue. For example:

- Land Tax papers in the Hundred of Godalming and for Linchmere, Sussex among the papers of Heath Hall estate for 1723–1740 (reference 1225/93, 1225/94 and 1225/95)
- Land Tax assessments for Old Malden 1751–1830 (reference 2473/6)
- Land Tax assessments, parish of Ashtead in the Hundred of Copthorne, later Copthorne and Effingham Division, 1796–1804, 1807, 1873–1874, 1898–1899, 1903–1904, 1910–1911 and 1934–1946 (reference 648 (six boxes))
- Wallington Hundred and Division: Land Tax Assessments 1798 to 1949 (reference 657)
- Division of Kingston and Elmbridge: Land Tax Assessments 1854–1940 includes assessment for Claygate, Cobham, East

Proprietors	Occupiers	£	s	d	Proprietors	Occupiers	£	s	d
Jn.º Blanch	Himself		8	0	Wm.ᵐ Bayly	Rich.ᵈ Manwell	1	0	0
D.ᵒ	Ja.ˢ Pilan		1	0	John Brewer	Himself	1	0	0
Jn.º Sayers	Himself		14	0	Tho.ˢ Stilthorpe	Mary Weaver	1	16	0
The heirs of Jn.º Prease	Jn.º Sayers		16	0	Jn.º Downer	Himself	1	0	0
The heirs of Tho.ˢ Puttock	Ric.ᵈ Clapton		12	0	Rev.ᵈ Wood	Himself		12	0
Ric.ᵈ Clapton	Nathan Harris		4	0	Sam. Denyy	Rev.ᵈ Wood	1	0	0
Jas Champion	Himself		8	0	John Hamsher	Himself	1	12	0
W.ᵐ Frost	Jas Harris		12	0	Rich.ᵈ Stedman	Himself	2	16	0
Rich.ᵈ Falkner	Himself		4	0	W.ᵐ Martindeno	Himself		6	0
Mrs Tickner	Himself	2	16	0	D.ᵒ	W.ᵐ Penor	1	10	0
David Whitehorn	Himself		4	0	Jas Chearman	Himself		2	0
D.ᵒ	W.ᵐ Pilard		3	0	W.ᵐ Wooner	James Shaw		1	0
W.ᵐ Lee	Himself		8	0	Rob.ᵗ Holt	Himself		10	0
D.ᵒ	Rob.ᵗ W.ᵐ Smith		4	0	D.ᵒ	Henry	1	10	0
W.ᵐ Puzzett	Jn.º Puttock		4	0	Geo Hill	Geo L.ˢ R.		10	0
Baldwin	Hen. Farmer		4	0	James Turner	Tho.ˢ Sherif / James Boate	1	4	0

Extract of Land Tax extract for Cranleigh 1787 (SHC Ref: QS6/7/59).

Molesey, Ember and Weston, Esher, Ham, Hook, Kew, Kingston upon Thames, Long Ditton, Malden, Malden Rushett, Coombe and New Malden, Petersham, Richmond, Stoke d'Abernon, Surbiton, Walton-on-Thames, and Weybridge (reference 635/1)
- Godley Hundred Land Tax assessments 1803–1951 (reference 6200)

From 1798, those liable for Land Tax could commute their future Land Tax liability to a one-off payment equivalent to fifteen years of tax, hence there being an additional column in the Land Tax assessments until 1832 indicating a person had commuted their liability to ensure they remained eligible to vote.

Registers were compiled in 1798 by the Land Tax commissioners, listing all those who were liable to pay tax that year. These are held by TNA in series IR 23 and form an almost complete set of Land Tax assessments for all counties in England and Wales arranged by parish. These records list owners, occupiers, the amount of tax assessed and date of redemption (where applicable) but no details of properties are included.

When Land Tax was commuted, Land Tax Redemption certificates were issued. Registers of Redemption Certificates are held at TNA in series IR 24 covering the years 1799–1963. SHC, however, also holds a selection of redemption certificates, again found largely among manorial, estate and family papers. For example:

- Certificates of land tax redemption held among estate records of the Tollemache family covering the years 1897–1949 (reference 58/13/)
- Certificates of land tax redemption held among estate records of the Somers Cock family for the year 1847 (reference 371/9/65a-f)
- Certificates of land tax redemption held among estate records of the Ewell Castle Estate papers covering the years 1812–1892 (reference 940/44/1-10)
- Certificates of the contracts for redemption of land tax, with annexed plans held among estate records of the Hatfield estate in 1869–1909, Morden, Mitcham, Merton, Malden, Carshalton, Cheam, Sutton and elsewhere (reference K85/5/)

Commutation of Land Tax was made compulsory in 1949 with Land Tax finally being abolished in 1963.

E. Tithe records.

Tithes were a local payment of one-tenth of an individual's annual produce or earnings, taken as a tax to support of the parish church and local clergy.

The Tithe Commutation Act 1836 allowed tithes to be converted into cash payments. These payments were known as Tithe Awards (the records being known as apportionments or schedules) and were based on land values and the price of corn. The Tithe Commutation Act converted tithes into a tithe rent charge, which were finally abolished in 1936.

The records also include altered apportionments which may have been conducted when land or property changed ownership, although this did not always happen, as there may have been an informal agreement made between the tithe-owner and landowner. Altered appointments can usually be found attached to the original apportionment. There were also various Acts before 1918 which allowed the tithe rent charge to be redeemed by payment of a lump sum.

In most cases, three copies of the award were made: one for the parish; one for the diocese; and one for the Tithe Commission. The award provided details of landowners and occupiers, a brief description of the property or land, and the amount measured in acres, roods and perches. They were arranged by tithe districts usually based on parish boundaries. The tithe award had a reference number to an accompanying large-scale tithe survey map of the parish showing what land was occupied as well as features such as houses, parish boundaries and field names.

Tithe Commission copies of the records can be found at TNA in series IR 18 (Tithe Files), IR 29 (Tithe Apportionments) and IR 30 (Tithe Maps). Copies made for the parish and diocese can be found at the local or diocesan record office. Tithe records have, however, been digitised at The Genealogist website in its 'Landowner & Occupier' collection. They include the collection for Surrey.

Original parish copies of tithe maps and apportionments for the ancient county of Surrey, including those parts which are now London boroughs are held at SHC. For those parishes in Surrey which were formerly in Middlesex (Ashford, Laleham, Littleton, Shepperton, Staines and Stanwell) records are held at TLA although copies and a transcript of the apportionments are available at SHC. The tithe map and apportionment for Dockenfield are held at Hampshire Record Office.

Digital images and transcripts of the apportionments for 103 tithe districts are also available to purchase on CDs and DVDs (one for each tithe district) from SHC and via its website. Tithe record name indexes can also be downloaded as PdF documents free of charge from the SHC website.

F. Inland Revenue valuation records – Lloyd George Domesday Survey

This was a survey conducted between 1910 and 1915 following the Finance Act 1910 under the authority of the Valuation Office of the Board of Inland Revenue. The project was part of a plan to tax increases in land values measured from the initial purchase to the sale or transfer. Business premises are also included in the survey, as were properties which fell below the tax threshold.

Freehold owners were recorded and some leaseholders. The records might include common and waste land.

The main records include Valuation Office plans, Valuation books and Field books. Each property was identified on a large-scale plan by the assessment or hereditament number and the information collected was then entered initially into Domesday or Valuation books and finally into Field books.

Valuation Office plans

These are based on 1908 Ordnance Survey maps with each property or parcel of land being allocated an assessment number. Two sets of plans were created, the official copy, where it survives, being held at TNA in series IR. Sadly, few such maps for Surrey appear to have survived in the TNA collection, but can be searched in series IR 121/1, IR 124/1 to IR 135/9.

However, the original working copies can often be found at local archives and SHC holds a large collection of such maps in series reference 4639/1/ containing 130 maps. It should be noted, however, these do NOT cover the whole of Surrey.

Valuation (or Domesday) books

These were the first records created by the Valuation Office at the beginning of the survey and include the assessment number for the property, thus where the plans have not survived, they can be used to identify the property in the Field books. These books contain a brief description of the property including an estimate of the extend of any land, address, names of the occupiers and the name and address of the owner, if different.

For the administrative county of Surrey prior to 1965, surviving Inland Revenue Valuation Survey books are found in series reference 2415/ covering:

- Reigate – parishes of Abinger, Ashtead, Betchworth, Leigh, Bletchingley, Great Bookham, Little Bookham and Effingham, Burstow, Capel, Caterham, Caterham, Chaldon and Merstham, Charlwood, Chelsham and Farleigh, Fetcham, Chessington, Leatherhead, Fetcham, Chessington, Leatherhead, Gatton, Godstone, Horley, Horley, Horne, Ifield (Sussex), Limpsfield and Titsey, Lingfield and Crowhurst, Newdigate, Nutfield, Ockley, Oxted, Reigate and Buckland, Tandridge, Tatsfield, Woldingham, and Wotton
- Sutton – parishes of Banstead, Beddington, Carshalton, Chipstead and Kingswood, Cuddington and Ewell, Epsom, Sutton, Wallington, Walton on the Hill and Woodmansterne
- Richmond – parishes of Barnes, Hampton, Mortlake, Richmond, Teddington, and Twickenham
- Guildford – parishes of Albury, Alfold, Ash, Bookham, Bramley, Chiddingfold, Clandon (East and West), Compton, Cranleigh and Ewhurst, Elstead, Frimley, Godalming, Guildford, Hambledon, Hascombe, Haslemere and Thursley, Horsell, Horsley (East and West), Merrow, Ockham, Pyrford, Shere, Wanborough, and Woking
- North Surrey – parishes of Esher, Molesey (East and West), Walton-on-Thames
- Kingston – parishes of Chessington, Ham, Kingston, Malden, Surbiton, Thames Ditton, and Tolworth
- Croydon – parishes of Addington, Coulsdon, Croydon (North, South and West), and Sanderstead

Field books
The Field books are the final records produced and include the information from landowners and surveyors written up in small printed bound volumes with each Field book containing space to record 100 plots. They can be found at TNA in series IR 58, Field Books.

Field books contain the name and address of the property/landowner and any occupiers/tenants, a description and situation of the property and how the property was being used, often with detailed inspection notes which could include the date a property was built, number of rooms or structure of property and sometimes a sketch. The nature of ownership and the property's rateable and market value along with details of former sales may also be found.

The Genealogist is undertaking a project to digitise and index the Field books and the series for Surrey has now been completed and is therefore available to search online by name and parish without the need to consult the maps or valuation books and includes more than 225,000 heads of households and property owners. They can be found within the 'Landowner and Occupier records sets'.

G. Useful indexes available from the Surrey History Centre website

- Index of names at the manorial court of Pyrford, 1654 to 1675
- Military records indexes
- Criminal court and prisoner indexes
- Surrey mental hospital records
- Annual Reports of Reed's School, Cobham
- Surrey Poor Law Union minute books
- Surrey Poor Law Union Boarding Out Committee minute books.
- Surrey Poor Law Union vaccination registers 1872 to 1909
- Dorking Poor Law Union application and report books
- Richmond Poor Law Union application and report books
- Chertsey Poor Law Union admission and discharge books *
- Deaths in Surrey County gaol 1798 to 1878 *
- Dennis Specialist Vehicles drawings and photographs *
- Godstone Poor Law Union application and report books *
- Guildford Workhouse births 1866 to 1910, deaths 1887 to 1914 and infirmary deaths 1933 to 1939
- Mayford Industrial School admissions 1895 to 1907 *
- Patients in the St Peter's Memorial Home in Woking *
- Princess Mary Village Homes pupils 1870 to 1890 *
- The Royal Philanthropic School at Redhill registers of admission*
- Chertsey School of Handicrafts pupils 1887 to 1920

---

* These indexes can also be searched together using the advanced search on the Exploring Surrey's Past website (**www.exploringsurreyspast.org.uk**).

Chapter 4

RESEARCHING IN LOCAL ARCHIVES

So, with all the records that have been digitised and are available online, why would you need to visit the local archives? Because only a small percentage (10 to 15 per cent) of records available to use for family history research have been digitised and made available online, highlighting the importance of taking research into the local archives where the records to be found can be vast, varied and offer much more insight into the lives of our ancestors.

The main archive for Surrey is the Surrey History Centre (SHC) at Woking, having 6 miles of shelving holding thousands of records dating back to the twelfth century. However, due to the boundary changes which took place in Surrey in 1889 and 1965, records for those parts of the ancient county that are now London boroughs can also be found at the The London Archive (TLA) at Clerkenwell. Records may also be found at The National Archives (TNA) and there are several local heritage/history centres and societies offering smaller collections and/or finding aids/research guides.

A. Parish chest records – beyond the registers

Parish chest records are not limited to parish registers. Before the introduction of local governments (by the Local Government Act 1888) and parish councils (by the Local Government 1894), the parish and its officers were responsible for the governance and administration of the local people, generating a wide range of records, the survival of which varies from parish to parish.

The parish was responsible for not only matters pertaining to the church but also the management and care of the poor, local highways and bridges, levying and controlling of the church rate, parish rate and poor rate; it dealt with every aspect of parish life, the community, and anything which may have touched upon the church, the parish and its parishioners. The importance of the parish increased significantly from the sixteenth century, following the decline of the manorial courts.

Generally, where they survive for Surrey parishes, these records are held at SHC except as listed below:

Archives	Parishes
TLA	Battersea, Camberwell, Clapham, Deptford, Lambeth, Newington (some), Putney (some), Rotherhithe (some), Southwark Christ Church (some), South St George (some), Southwark St Olave (some), Southwark St Thomas, Staines, Totting Graveney (some), Wandsworth (some)
Wandsworth Heritage Centre	Battersea St Mary, Clapham (some), Putney, Streatham, Tooting Graveney, Wandsworth
Sutton Archive and Local Studies	Beddington, Cheam, Sutton, Carshalton, Sutton
Southwark Local History Library and Archive	Bermondsey, Camberwell, Newington, Rotherhithe, Southwark Christ Church, South St George, Southwark St Olave, Southwark St Saviour, Southwark St Thomas (some)
Lambeth Archives	Clapham (limited), Lambeth, Streatham (some)
Royal Berkshire Archives	Old Windsor

The Vestry

The Vestry was the governing body of the parish, akin in some ways to the parish council of today, made up of the incumbent, parish officers and any parishioner who paid rates, although over time select vestries did start to emerge in some parishes which were usually made up of an agreed number (between twelve and twenty-four) of rate payers, usually wealthier parishioners.

Meetings would be held regularly; depending on the business to be conducted, this could be weekly, bi-weekly or monthly, with an annual meeting to appoint parish officials, approve accounts and set the amounts and criteria for the various rates. Parish officials would include (depending on local arrangements) churchwardens, overseers of the poor, constables, parish clerk, sextons, and waywardens. The main officials producing records useful for family history research are the churchwardens, overseers of the poor, and constables.

Vestry minutes record the details of vestry meetings. while the greater content of the minutes can provide a picture of the day-to-day life of the parish, including information from which relationships between parishioners may be deduced; the minutes can also contain the names of:

- Those appointed as parish officials
- Those assessed as eligible to pay the poor rate and the amount they had to pay
- Those who would be excluded from paying the rate

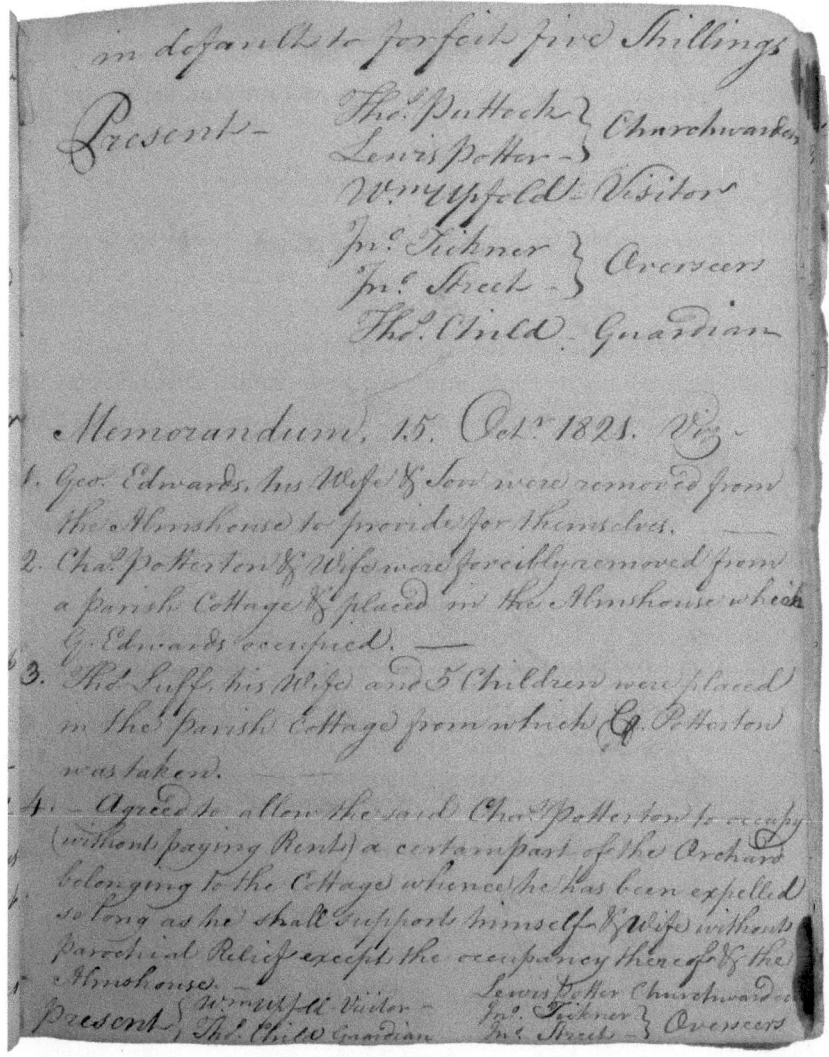

Extract from Cranleigh Parish Vestry Minutes dated 15 October 1821 (SHC Ref: P58/1/1).

- Those who had failed to pay the poor rate
- Those who were to be paid poor relief, provided with clothing, medical expense etc.
- Migrants and any provision made for their passage through the parish
- Apprenticed children

Vestry minutes survive for approximately a third of parishes in Surrey of which just under half of those survive from the seventeenth and eighteenth century onwards with the rest surviving for the nineteenth century only. Few dated in the twentieth century have been deposited. It should be noted that vestries still exist, but since 1894 their role has been restricted to church and wider ecclesiastical matters and are most likely to be retained by church offices.

Churchwardens

Churchwardens can be traced back to the fourteenth century or earlier although few records of their accounts exist from that time, with none surviving for the parishes of Surrey before the 1500s. At least two churchwardens (larger parishes could appoint more than two) would be appointed annually, one appointed by the incumbent the other by the parishioners, who were required to act together to ensure their actions could be legally enforced.

Churchwardens were responsible for, among other things:

- The upkeep and maintenance of the church building and everything in it
- Provisioning the church for worship (utensils, wine, bread etc.)
- Bringing offenders before the archdeacon's court at his parish visitation, such as those who had failed to attend church, anyone committing adultery or who had entered into a clandestine marriage along with any incumbent who was failing in his duty to the parish
- The administration of the church rate and funds

They were required to account annually to the parishioners and thus proper accounts were kept and these are the main records of the churchwarden, although in larger parishes there may be separate church rate and parish rate records.

The accounts can be quite detailed, naming parishioners who worked for and were paid by the parish, such as tradesmen who carried out

Jn° Farmer

1840					
	Paid Geo Steer for Work done for Bell frame &c	18	18	10
June 27	D° D°	1	4	3
"	D° Sarah Holden for 4 Bottles of Wine O A Dusey	1	2	—
"	D° Edw Stedman for shoveling Snow in Church Yard	—	1	—
"	D° H & Rowland's Bill O A		1	6½
Mar 25	D° William King for Dinners for Electing Parish Officers	3	12	—
"	D° for Ringers	1	14	—
1841	D° for Tradesfolks Work at Church		8	5
April 13	D° Geo Peto on acct of Stone Window Frame	9	—	—
27	D° Edw Charman in Part of Bill	10	—	—
"	D° Jn° Snatt for Bell ropes & Clock line	3	7	—
"	D° Tho° Elliott (Clerk) for Salary	6	—	—
"	D° D° 2 years Register Bread for Sacrament	—	13	—
"	D° Mat Taylor's Salary	2	—	—
"	D° for Washing Surplice & Communion Linen	—	6	6
"	D° Cleaning Church Yard & Lighting Fires	—	8	—
"	D° Leathering Bells	—	6	—
1841	D° Geo Holden on acct	22	14	6½
June 17	D° Tho° Elliott 2½ Days in Churchyard	—	5	—
"	D° Jas Reeves for repairing Church Clock	1	—	—
"	D° Rich Crawson for Glazing	2	18	5
"	D° C Herrington Bill for this Book & Parchment	—	11	—
"	D° Visitation Expenses	3	10	0½
"	D° For Cleaning Church	1	0	—
		90	2	6¾
	Bale Brought down	68	15	10½
	Out Pocket £	21	6	8¼

Extract from Cranleigh Churchwardens Accounts dated 1840/1841 (SHC Ref: CRA/7/3).

maintenance and repair of the church: masons, carpenters, glaziers, bakers who provided bread, and shopkeepers who provided wine and candles. Some, however, may simply be lists of names and amounts of who provided goods and services or those who paid the church and/or parish rate. Churchwarden accounts per se may therefore be of little value in tracing ancestors but can provide an overview of family/local life.

Further, names may appear in the accounts if they contributed to the 'church rate' or 'parish rate' and their inclusion or disappearance may be an indication of the family's wealth, their movements in and out of the parish or even a death, but it is unlikely those entries would provide sufficient information to determine family members and relationships. Church rate and parish rate records may be found in separate books to the churchwarden accounts.

Churchwarden accounts (including where there are separate church rate and parish rate books) survive for approximately a third of parishes in Surrey of which about a third again date from the seventeenth century (although not necessarily complete runs from the period). Of the remainder, about a quarter survive from the eighteenth century and the rest from the nineteenth century. Some of the early records solely comprise lists of churchwardens and other parish officers.

Overseers of the poor (Overseers)

Following the Poor Law Act 1572, the parish had responsibility for the poor. The office of Overseer of the Poor was created by the Relief of the Poor Act 1598 and they were responsible, as the name suggests, for managing or overseeing the poor.

Following the Great Poor Law Act 1601, their responsibility included collecting the 'poor rate' and paying poor relief (whether that was in money, clothes, food, other items, or putting them to work). Following the further Act of Settlement and Removal 1662, they were also responsible, along with churchwardens, for issuing settlement certificates and removing those who did not have settlement in the parish if/when they become a burden on the parish.

Their records include overseers' accounts which can provide a great deal of information valuable for family history research, particularly those from poor backgrounds. Agricultural labourers and their families were among those most often appearing in the overseers' accounts because they were among the lowest paid workers. In years when crops failed or prices crashed, it would be those workers who suffered the most and may have relied on poor relief to survive until the following year.

Poor rate assessment

Under the Poor Law Act 1572, contributions to the assist the poor were voluntary. The Great Poor Law Act of 1601 introduced a tax on 'every inhabitant, parson, vicar and other and every occupier of lands, houses, tithe impropriate and proprietors of tithes, coalmines or saleable underwood' – the poor rate – which remained in force until the Poor Law Amendment Act 1834.

The vestry and its officers were responsible for setting the rate, usually based on the value of a parishioner's land or property irrespective of whether they owned it or just occupied it. The overseers were responsible for conducting the annual poor rate assessment, recording it either in their own accounts (in smaller parishes) or in separate Poor Rate books (in larger parishes). The assessments usually include the names of those assessed and the amount paid so these could provide an indication of an ancestor's wealth. Further, because the rate was collected annually, an ancestor's appearance or disappearance from these records may indicate their death, movement between parishes or change in their financial circumstances.

Parishioners failing to pay their assessed rate could be sent to gaol and details of those ancestors may be found in the constables' accounts (see below).

Poor relief

Poor relief was available to the sick, the unemployed or the elderly. Anyone who was simply unwilling to work would not receive poor relief. There was no set rate; anyone seeking poor relief would have their need assessed by the overseer and/or the vestry and appropriate provision would be made. Relief could be provided in various forms and for specific purposes, for example money to pay rent, buy clothes, pay for coffins/funeral expenses and medical treatment.

From the eighteenth century, this would include housing those in need in workhouses or poorhouses. Those who were able to work would be put to work – women would often be provided money, food, clothing etc. in return for caring for the sick or undertaking laundry work; men would be set to work repairing parish roads and bridges in exchange for relief.

Poor relief records will include a recipient's name and may provide details of family members they needed to support. They will also include the amount or type of relief given and the purpose of the payment.

The survival rate of overseers' accounts, poor rate and poor relief records again varies from parish to parish with such records surviving

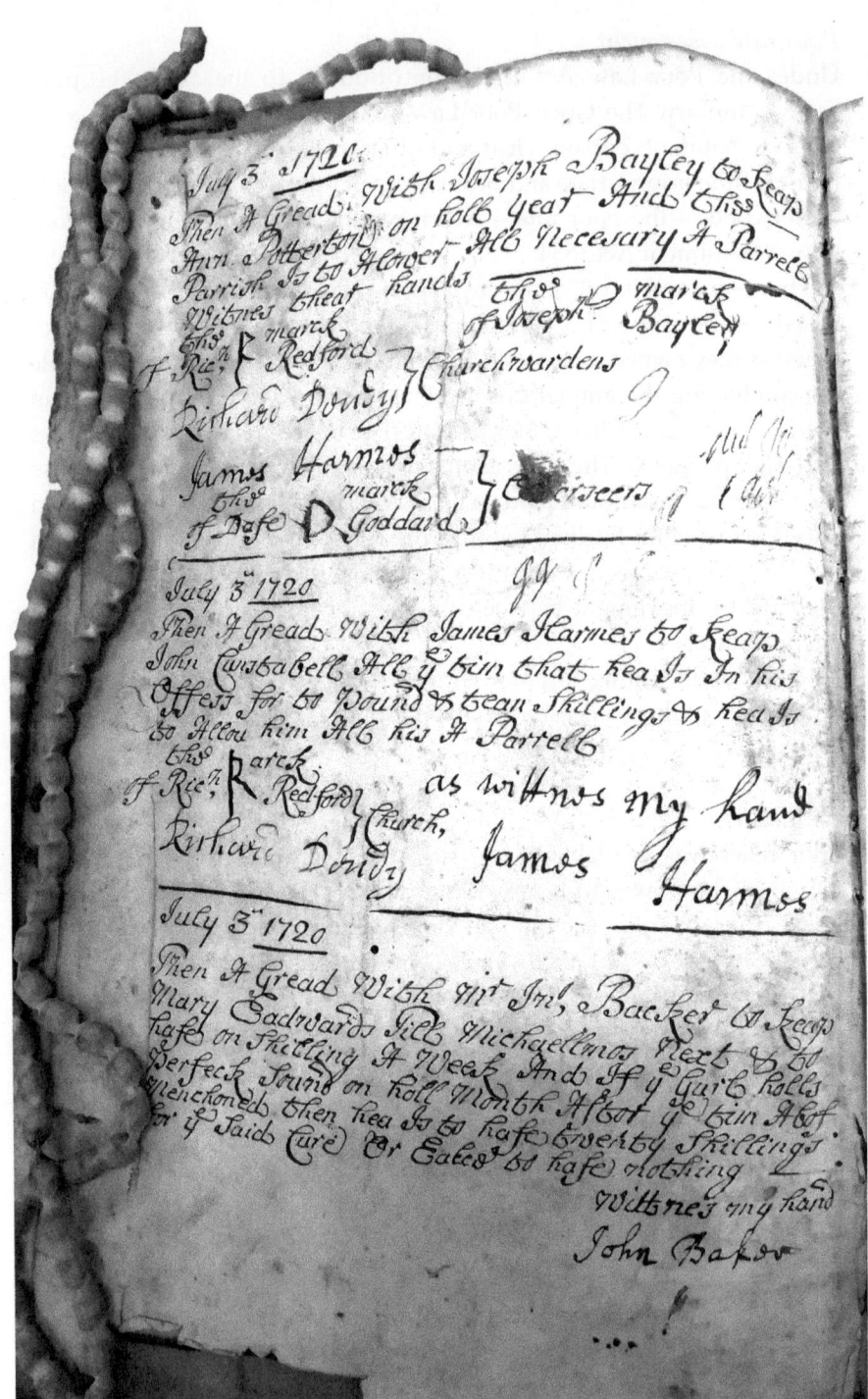

Extract from Cranleigh Overseers of the Poor rate book 1820 detailing the payment of poor relief for specific reasons (SHC Ref: P58/4/1).

At the 5th monthly meeting of the Churchwardens and overseers of the poore and other Inhabitants of the parish of Cranlye one Sunday the Seventh day of September in theare parish Church in the afternoon after devine Service touching the Releife of the poor of the Said parrish it is ordered as followeth by us whose names are hereunder Subscribed

It is ordered that Assessment be made within the said parish for the Sum of 114:16 Shillings for and towards the necessary Releife of the poore of the Saide parish and for the provideing a Convenient Stock therein for Seting of poor people to work and for placeing forth the poore Children which assessment is made for one half year due at michillmas next Ensueing it is allsoe ordered that the severall poor people of the Said parish whose names are here under Subscribed be Alowed weekly pay the Respective Sums hereunder mentioned towards their Releife

widow woodhatch 01·09	John Tickner 2·3	wid Baucheom 1·3
widow Clark 01·09	wid: Semens 1·0	wid: Poterten 4·0
Tho: Beety 01·00	Rich: Kitchill 1·3	wid: march 2·3
Goody nicholl 01·06	Elonar plaw 1·9	wid Tickner 1·6
Edward Gloar 02·00	widow Heorly 0·6	wid: Kite 1·6
James Smith 2·3	Robert Sherlock 2·0	Goody hampsher 1·3
Kenny glem Sherlock Child	Jenny gon Ses Child	mary morver 3
	wid Sherlock 1·3	

Extract from Cranleigh Overseers of the Poor rate book 1820 listing the names of those to receive, along with the amounts, poor relief (SHC Ref: P58/4/1).

for approximately a third of parishes in Surrey of which over half date from the eighteenth century onwards.

Settlement and Removal
To further 'control' the payment of poor relief, following the Act of Settlement and Removal 1662 poor relief could only be claimed in the parish in which a person was legally settled. Settlement could be obtained in several ways:

- Renting property in the parish to the annual value of £10 or more
- Working in the parish for a year (if unmarried)
- Being a woman marrying a man of the parish
- Being a legitimate child under 7 years of age whose father lived in the parish
- Before 1743, being an illegitimate child born in the parish (after 1743 an illegitimate child took the settlement of the mother)
- Being a child or person apprenticed to a master in the parish for more than forty days
- Being a person who has moved to the parish and lived there for forty days after giving the parish authorities written notice of his intention to do so
- From 1691, holding public/parish office

These new restrictions made it increasingly difficult for the poor to move around to find work, resulting in the introduction of settlement certificates in 1697. Settlement certificates were provided by the overseer and churchwarden of the parish in which a person had legal settlement and confirmed the parish would accept them back should they require poor relief. This enabled people to move between parishes to obtain work. A copy of the certificate would be retained by the originating parish with a further copy being provided to the overseer and churchwarden of the parish to which the person had moved, thus it is worth checking both parishes for surviving records.

Settlement certificates can provide valuable genealogical details such as:

- Names of all family members
- Ages of family members
- Details of their parish of settlement
- Names of the churchwardens and overseers of the parish issuing the certificate

Copy Settlement Certificate from the parish of Ewhurst dated 15 September 1703 (SHC Ref: P38/3/199).

SURREY. To the Constable or Tythingman of the Parish of *Albury*
in the said County, And to the Churchwardens and
Overseers of the Poor of the Parish of *Ewhurst*
in the same County.

WHEREAS *Samuel Palmer*
Rogue and Vagabond *was* apprehended in the
said Parish of *Albury* on *Wednesday* the
9th Day of *April instant*

And by the Examination on Oath of the said *Samuel Palmer*
it appears to me that the said Parish of *Ewhurst*
is the Parish where *he was* last
legally settled. And whereas, I have ordered the said *Samuel*
Palmer to be *punished in the House*
of Correction
for such *his* Offence.

NOW I do hereby require you, the said Constable
or Tythingman, of the said Parish of *Albury*
to convey the said *Samuel Palmer*

to the said Parish of *Ewhurst*
and *him* to deliver to the Churchwardens and Overseers of the Poor there, or to some, or one of them,
together with this Pass, and the Duplicate of the Examination of the said *Samuel Palmer*
which I have caused to be ~~annexed hereto.~~ *hereunder written* And you
the said Churchwardens and Overseers of the Poor of
the said Parish of *Ewhurst*
are hereby required to receive the said *Samuel*
Palmer
and Employ or Place *him* according to Law.

Given under my Hand and Seal this *10th* Day
of *April* 1777.

William Godschall

The Examination on Oath of Samuel Palmer Hair Brown, Eyes 5 feet 9 Inches high 28 Years of Age Razor grinder and Broommaker taken the 9th instant in Heath Bason in Albury and brought before me one of his Majestys Justices of the peace in and for the said County. Saith that his last legal Settlement is in the Parish of Ewhurst and that he belongs to Captain Waterhouses Company in the Surrey Militia

Taken and Sworn
before Me
William Godschall

The Mark of
X
Samuel Palmer

Copy Settlement Examination from the parish of Ewhurst dated 10 April 1777 (SHC Ref: P38/3/254).

Where someone's legal settlement was in doubt and they had become a burden on the parish, the overseers and churchwardens would seek to establish where their legal settlement was. They would bring the individual before the Justice of the Peace (JP) at the quarter sessions (QS) court to be examined on oath as to their legal settlement. The resulting records were settlement examinations and settlement and removal orders (as was appropriate and assessed by the JP).

Surviving examination records can be found among both parish records and QS records, in particular among session papers (see QS records). They can include what essentially amounts to a short biography of the person's life and provide valuable information for family history and clues to what and where other records for the person and their family may be found, such as:

- Place of birth
- Age
- Parentage
- Employment history
- Apprenticeships
- Places in which they have previously lived
- Marriage
- Children's names and ages

The justices would issue an order confirming the persons legal place of settlement and if different from the parish in which they were residing, they would also issue a removal order, ordering removal of the person and any dependent family to their place of legal settlement.

As with settlement examinations, removal orders can be found among both parish records (both for the parish from which the person is being removed and the parish they are being removed to) and QS records.

For Surrey, the survival rates of settlement and removal records among parish records is limited to about a quarter of all parishes. However, further records can be found among QS rolls and bundles (see QS records).

It should also be noted there may be reference to people and families being removed in parish records such as vestry minutes and constables' accounts. Constables were required to escort those being removed to the parish boundary and where a person or family had to pass through a number of parishes to get to their parish of legal settlement, the constables in each parish would escort them through – thus there may be reference in the constables' accounts of each parish they had to pass

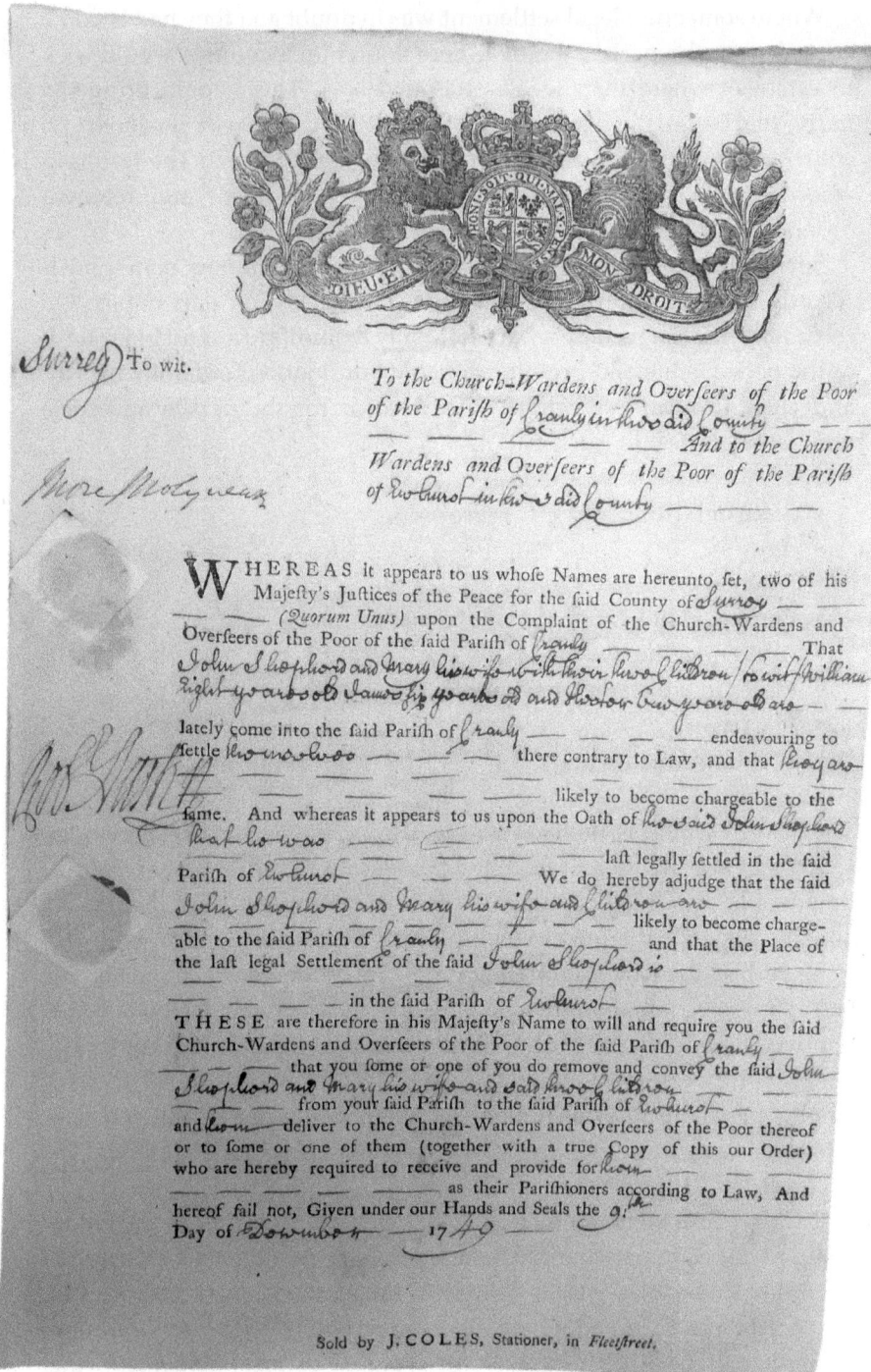

Copy Removal Order from the parish of Ewhurst dated 9 December 1749 (SHC Ref: P38/3/147).

through. These references would be by way of the constables' expenses in connection with the removal, which could include the names and details of those being escorted. Constables' accounts may also be found among parish records.

Workhouse Records

While almshouses have existed in England since about the tenth century to provide charitable housing and aid to the poor, sick, elderly and others in need, there was no legal requirement to provide such places until the Great Poor Law Act 1601, which stated that those who were unwilling but able to work, i.e. the 'idle' and/or 'disorderly', were to be sent to 'houses of correction' or prison where, as a form of punishment, they would be set to work. The Act also provided for the building or provision of housing (almshouses) for the poor who were unable to work.

By the Workhouse Act 1722, 'houses of correction' became 'houses of industry' or workhouses. Records for these institutions will be found among vestry minutes and overseers' records.

The office of the overseer continued until the Poor Law Amendment Act 1834, which introduced Poor Law Unions and Poor Law union workhouses, with overseers being replaced by Guardians of the Poor.

Records for Poor Law Unions can include (but are not limited to) minutes recording the day-to-day running of the union; admission and discharge registers; application and report registers recording those who were applying for poor relief without entering the workhouse ('out-relief' or 'out-payments'); creed registers recording the religion of 'in-mates'; and birth, baptism and death registers. Poor Law Union workhouses, their 'in-mates' and staff should also be found in the census returns recording those staying in the workhouse on census night.

The Poor Law Unions of ancient Surrey (prior to the boundary changes of 1889) including where the records are held were:

- Bermondsey (inc. Bermondsey, Rotherhithe and St Olave) (TLA)
- Camberwell (TLA)
- Chertsey (SHC)
- Croydon (Museum of Croydon)
- Dorking (SHC)
- East Grinstead (part of) (WSRO)
- Epsom (SHC)
- Godstone (SHC)
- Guildford (SHC)
- Hambledon (SHC)

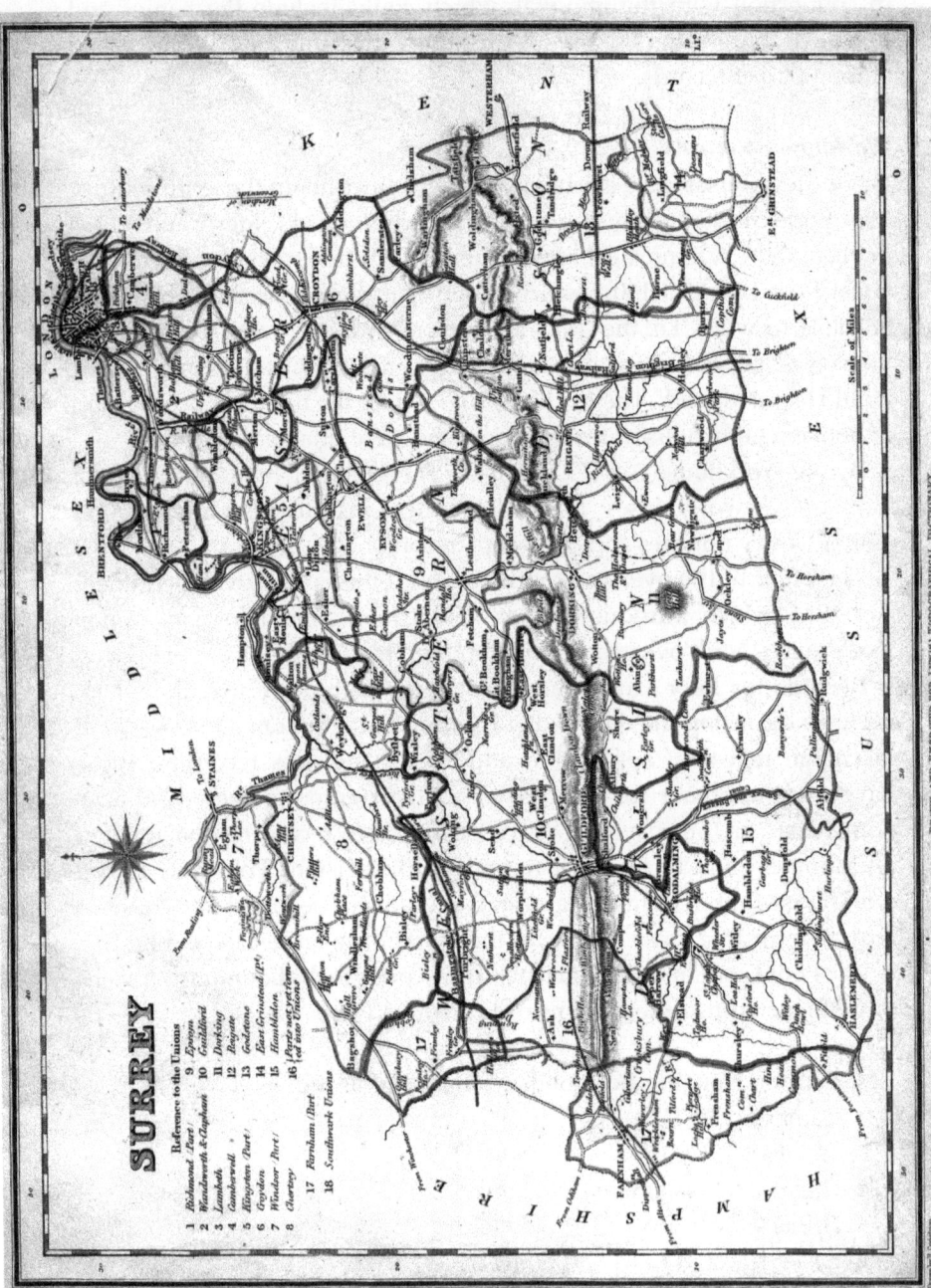

Poor Law Unions map (undated) reproduced under licence CC By-SA 4.0.

- Kingston (SHC)
- Lambeth (TLA)
- Reigate (SHC)
- Richmond (SHC & Richmond local studies library)
- Southwark (inc. St George Southwark, Newington, St Saviour, Wandsworth) (TLA)
- Windsor (part of) (RBA)

For some of the Poor Law Union records available at SHC, there are searchable indexes available at its website:

- Chertsey Poor Law Union admission and discharge books
- Dorking Poor Law Union application and report books
- Godstone Poor Law Union application and report books
- Guildford Workhouse births 1866–1910, deaths 1887–1914 and infirmary deaths 1933–1939
- Richmond Poor Law Union application and report books
- Surrey Poor Law Union Boarding Out Committee minute books.
- Surrey Poor Law Union minute books
- Surrey Poor Law Union vaccination registers 1872–1909

Some Board of Guardian records held at the TLA, including for those for Poor Law Unions previously part of ancient county of Surrey, have been digitised and can be searched on Ancestry.

The Workhouse website (**www.workhouses.org.uk**) provides a wealth of information on the history and workings of workhouses generally and individual workhouses around the United Kingdom.

Bastardy Bonds
The birth of illegitimate or bastard children (as it was commonly referred to) was an unusual occurrence in the sixteenth and early seventeenth century. However, during the later seventeenth century and the eighteenth century the birth rate of illegitimate children increased, increasing the burden on the parish with many illegitimate children and their mothers requiring poor relief. Several Acts of Parliament were therefore passed to control these growing rates and the burden was placed on the parish to maintain illegitimate children and their mothers, including:

- A mother of an illegitimate child being imprisoned for up to one year (Act of 1609/10)

- A mother having a second illegitimate child being sent to prison unless she could provide security for 'good behaviour' which lead to an increase in abortions and infanticide (Act of 1609/10)
- The killing of an illegitimate child was an offence of murder (Act of 1623/4).
- Overseers, on the order of two Justices of the Peace, being able to seize goods of parents who abandoned their bastard children (Act of 1662)
- A woman pregnant with an illegitimate child was to declare such to the overseer and to name the father (Act of 1732–1734)
- An illegitimate child was to take the settlement of the mother who could be punished by public whipping (Act of 1743/4)

While most illegitimate births produced few records other than being recorded in parish baptism registers, for mothers brought before the quarter sessions, bastardy examinations were held to establish who the father was. Once identified, the father would either agree, by way of a bastardy indemnity bond, or be ordered to pay for the child's upkeep. Illegitimate children who were a burden on the parish were also frequently apprenticed from the age of 7 (see apprenticeships).

Parents were sometimes persuaded (perhaps by way of bribes or financial incentives) to marry, thereby ensuring the child would take the father's legal settlement, particularly if that was of a different parish and meant they could then be removed. Such events may have been recorded in vestry minutes.

Bastardy examinations, bonds and orders survive among parish records for only about one-tenth of all parishes; however, further records may be found among QS records session rolls and bundles. They may also be found in specific record series such as those for the period 1750 to 1836; 'Examination Books' can be found among Poor Law Administration records for the Borough of Guildford held in series BR/QS/4 at SHC.

Miscellaneous records

Parish records discussed above represent those which are most frequently found and can provide the most use for family history research. However, other records may be available, including, but not limited to: constable accounts; tithe records; militia relief records; and charity records. Records can be quite varied between parishes such as this example from Cranleigh parish records – Midwifery book of John Ellery (doctor) recording names and dates of patients between 1812 and 1841 held at SCH under reference CRA/17/1.

Copy extract from 'Midwifery book of John Ellery' amongst Cranleigh Parish records (SHC Ref: CRA/17/1).

'A Guide to Surrey Parish Documents' Research Aid' has been produced by WSFHS (RA 42) detailing what parish records survive, the periods covered and where they are held and is include in their CD series within CD 7 'A Collection of Surrey Research Aids'. Both can be purchased from WSFHS direct or through the GenFair website.

B. Quarter Sessions, Petty Sessions and associated records.

Following the Norman Conquest in 1066, sheriffs and their courts were introduced in each county of England to administer local justice. The Sheriff of Nottingham in the story of Robin Hood might be brought to mind! While the story of Robin Hood may be based on legend and folklore it is the case that over time the sheriffs acquired a reputation for dishonest practices and embezzlement. In 1195, Richard I, who believed his sheriffs were guilty of abusing their authority while he had been away on the Third Crusade, commissioned knights from every shire to assist in keeping the peace and ensure the law was upheld. These knights were known as 'Keepers of the Peace' until 1327, when Edward III first referred to them as 'Justices of the Peace' (JPs) by which time they had taken over many of the cases previously heard by the sheriffs.

Following a statute passed by Richard II, from 1388, commissions of the peace were held in every quarter of the year, on or within a month of each quarter day (Michaelmas, 29 September (Michaelmas session); Christmas 25 December (Epiphany session); Lady Day 25 March (Easter session); and Midsummer, 24 June (Trinity session) and they became known as Quarter Sessions (QS).

Over the next two centuries, their jurisdiction increased to the demise of the sheriffs. In 1388, there were six justices in every county and by the reign of Elizabeth I there were between thirty and forty in each county. There were also several non-county boroughs entitled to hold their own QS, most of which were ancient boroughs that had been established by charters granted by the Crown at various times.

Each QS was presided over by at least three justices, one of whom was the Custos Rotulorum, the Keeper of the Rolls, later known as the Clerk of the Peace. Other officials in attendance would be the sheriff, the high constable, constables, and the coroner. The jury would be made up of local freeholders, while others in attendance included plaintiffs, defendant, witnesses, those held on criminal charges, the county gaoler and keepers of the houses of correction.

Quarter sessions dealt not just with criminal cases, gaols and houses of correction but also a variety of other civil and local matters, matters similar to the business of a modern-day local council.

Civil jurisdiction

The QS were responsible for the regulation and registration of various activities required by legislation, such as traders' weights and measures, victuallers and alehouse licensing, slaughterhouse licensing (from 1786), gamekeepers licensing (from 1710), Nonconformist meeting house licensing, along with the regulation and licensing of printing presses, friendly societies, private lunatic asylums (from 1774–1860s), agreements of Acts of Enclosure, canals, railways, turnpike companies and other public bodies.

Other records can include oaths of allegiance of military and civil officers, papists, dissenting ministers and dissenting teachers; records of freeholders from whom jury members could be selected; land tax and other taxes collected locally. Further, records such as those concerning the enclosure of common land and plans of public infrastructure, services and utilities such as the development of canal, railways, gas, electric etc. were ordered to be deposited at QS. Civil matters may also have been dealt with or referred to the assizes, most commonly where the assize court was to be convened sooner than the next QS.

It should be noted that most, if not all, of the civil/administrative functions of QS were transferred to local governments which were established following the Local Government Act 1888.

Criminal jurisdiction

By the fifteenth century, this included cases such as murder, riot, assault and poaching. By the later sixteenth century, however, QS generally referred more serious offences to the assizes (see Chapter 5) with local justices concentrating on lesser non-capital offences, although in practice there remained some overlap between the type of criminal cases the two courts dealt with.

Typical offences dealt with by the QS included (but were not limited to):

- Assault, affray, theft, larceny
- Offences against byelaws and licensing laws
- Drunkenness
- Non-payment of tithes, taxes and fines
- Debtors
- Anything not attracting death penalty.
- Anything attracting a transportation order for seven years

Petty Sessions

These emerged in the sixteenth century from committees of justices who would meet between QS to conduct much of the court's administrative business, and by an Act of 1541 justices were required to meet six weeks prior to QS to make enquiries about vagabonds. This requirement was extended by an Order of Council 1605 compelling justices to meet at least once between each QS to inquire as to labourers, alehouses, the assize of bread, rogues and vagabonds and more.

There was a gradual extension to the work the petty sessions undertook and by the mid-nineteenth century most minor crimes were tried by petty sessions (also known as magistrates' courts by this time). These would include minor theft and larceny, assault, drunkenness, bastardy examinations, and arbitration. They would also decide whether to refer a case to the QS or assizes with many justices most likely adopting a common-sense approach and sending offenders for trial to whichever came first, QS or assizes, thus minor offences may have found their way to the assizes if they were to be held sooner than the next QS.

The records
The records for QS and petty sessions are held at local or county archives, again with a variable survival rate; generally, there are no surviving records in any county before the sixteenth century.

The main records of the QS and petty sessions which are the most valuable for family history research are:

- **Minute, Process or Session books** which provide details of those who should have attended each court session (and those who did) along with a summary of the matters dealt with including civil/administrative matters.
- **Order books** which were the formal records of the proceedings, recording civil/administrative decisions of the justices, along with a summary of cases, including criminal trials presented and the verdicts and sentences of the justices.
- **Sessions rolls/files/papers** which contain the documents used during the sessions including: lists of justices, county officers, and jurors; petitions; reports and records to civil/administrative matters such as reports on roads, bridges etc.; witness depositions; indictments (formal criminal charges) and presentments (accusations made by a jury or its own volition) of criminals; recognizances (financial bonds) to appear at court or for good behaviour; removal orders and other papers relating to Poor Law cases; and calendars of prisoners. Some of these records may be stored under individual record sets.

Surrey
Surrey county QS were held at key towns of the county on a rotary basis, including Guildford, Kingston upon Thames, Newington, and Reigate.

Guildford, Kingston and Southwark had their own borough QS, the towns having been granted ancient borough status – Guildford by the first known charter of Henry III in 1257 although there is reference to 'burgi de Geldford' in 1130 both by the sheriff and in a writ;[1] Kingston upon Thames by charter of Edward IV in 1484; and Southwark by charter of Edward I in 1295. Croydon was also granted county borough status and its own court of QS in 1889.

County QS records

These are held at SHC in series 'QS'. They contain a vast collection of a wide variety of records. The earliest records in the collection date from 1659 and continue to 1971. It may be that earlier records were lost or destroyed during or shortly after the turmoil created by the civil wars and Commonwealth period of the 1640s and 1650s. At the QS held at Michaelmas 1660 the former clerk of the peace, John Launder, was ordered:

> to deliver into the handes and possession of Henry Byne, gentleman, the present Clerke of the Peace ... all such rolles, records, proces[s] books and other writings as he hath in his custody concerninge the Sessions of the peace.

If this order was complied with it is not known what happened to the records.

Some earlier records (late sixteenth and early seventeenth century) can be found among estate and family papers which have been deposited at SHC, such as those of the Carew family of Beddington (under SCH Ref: 643) and the More family of Loseley (SHC Ref: LM).

In respect of the main records (SHC Ref: QS) the following survive:

- Order books 1659 to 1971 (QS2/1/)
- Sessions rolls 1661–1799; 1889–1915 (QS2/5/)
- Session bundles 1630, 1637, 1701–1888 (QS2/6/)
- Minute books 1694–1971 (QS2/2/)
- Process books 1671–1968 (QS3/5/)

Early order books have been filmed and are available on microfilm, such as those in reference QS2/1/1 (covering period 12 July 1659 to 12 January 1664) as have some selected later order books such as QS2/1/18 (covering period 9 January 1750–13 February 1755).

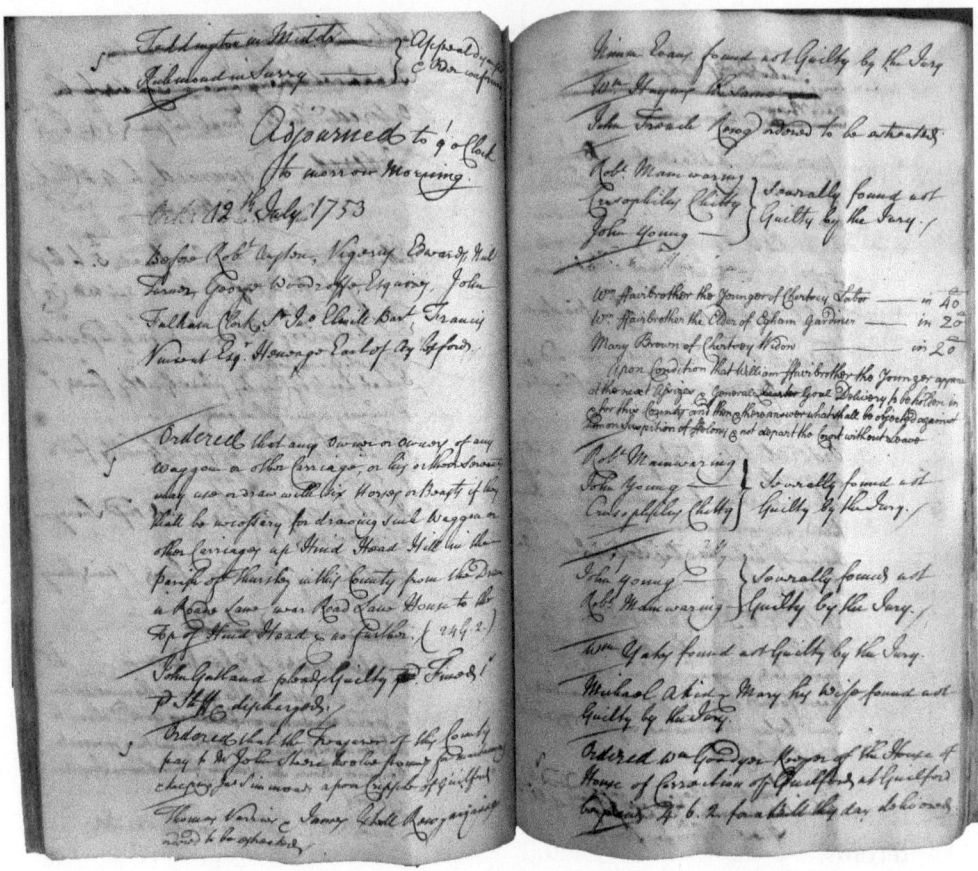

Extract from Minute Book for session dated 12 June 1753 (SHC Ref: QS2/2/1).

The early Order Book and Sessions Rolls covering the years 1659 to 1668 were also transcribed and published by the Surrey Record Society in 1934, in four volumes, which are now out of print but may be found at online and second-hand book shops with copies available at SHC and selected reference libraries.

In addition to main records detailed above, other records within the QS civil jurisdiction include, among many others:

- Land Tax Assessment books 1780–1982 (QS6/7/)*
- Freeholders' books 1696–1824 (QS3/10A/)*
- Registers of licensed victuallers 1785–1935 (QS5/10/)*
- Electoral registers 1832–1889 (QS6/7A/)*
- Public entertainment licensing 1882–1889 (QS5/11/)
- Slaughterhouse licensing 1802–1844 (QS5/11A/)
- Weights and measures 1800–1887 (QS5/13/)

Session roll for Easter 1661 QS session (SHC Ref: QS2/5/1661 Easter).

- In/Enclosure awards 1779–1906 (QS6/4/)
- Freemasons returns 1799–1915 (QS6/5/)
- Public Asylums 1774–1933 (QS5/5/)
- County Asylums 1838–1889 (QS5/6/)
- Institutions for Mental Defectives 1914–1960 (QS5/6A/)
- Removal Orders: Notices of abandonment following appeal 1849–1881 (QS2/9/)
- Vagrant passes 1816–1821 (QS2/10/)
- Records of Charities 1812–1888 (QS6/1/)

Those marked* are also available to view and search on Ancestry in collections:

- Surrey, England, Land Tax Records, 1780–1832
- Surrey Jury-Qualified Freeholders and Copyholders Lists 1696–1824
- Surrey Licensed Victuallers Registers 1785–1903
- Surrey, England, Electoral Registers, 1832–1962

---

* Calendars of prisoners between 1848 and 1902 have been digitised and are available to search and view on Ancestry in collections.

With regard to criminal records, in addition to the main records detailed above, records available include:

- Indictments 1759–1971 (QS2/7/)
- Appeal papers 1846–1888 (QS2/8/) for which there is a PdF document which can be downloaded from the SHC website detailing the contents of the collection
- Estreat book 1689–1967 (QS3/1/) recording fines and recognizances
- Debtors' appearance books 1691–1798 (QS3/2/1-13)
- Debtors' prisoner books 1760–1811 (QS3/2/15-67)
- Calendars of prisoners: Surrey Quarter Sessions & Assizes 1848–1971 (QS3/4/) earlier calendars of prisoners can be found in QS2/6/ among the session bundles*
- Calendars of prisoners: Central Criminal Court 1857–1894 (QS3/3/)
- Conviction registers 1911–1971 (QS3/5a/)
- Case files: trials 1694–1971 (QS3/5c/)
- Case files: appeals and committals for sentencing 1964–1971 (QS3/5d/)
- Calendars of prisoners whose cases were heard at Surrey quarter sessions and assizes 1848–1902
- Index to returns of prisoners whose cases were heard at Surrey quarter sessions and assizes 1912–1918

For the period 1780 to 1820, there is a searchable name index and hearing transcriptions available on CD from SHC (published by Surrey History Trust) and online at Findmypast (Surrey Quarter Sessions 1780–1820). These are compiled from process books (in series QS3/5/) and session bundles (in series QS2/6/). The names index includes 54,208 defendants (and aliases), accusers, victims and witnesses. The hearing transcriptions include 47,543 records which, as well as names, include details of the date of the hearing, occupations, parish of abode, offence type and description, prison, outcome of the case (plea/verdict, sentence), committing magistrate, and any other information available given in the original records. The entries also provide the archive reference for the original record(s). The original records are not digitised and would need to be viewed at SHC. The records at Findmypast can be searched by accuser, defendant, victim and witness.

Borough of Guildford QS and petty sessions records
The records for these QS are also held at SHC, the main series being under reference BR/QS (covering period 1698–1971) with further records

held in other series such as: '1736' ('Guildford Borough Council' series covering period 1608–1978) and '1557' ('Indictments' for the year 1752) among others.

Borough of Kingston upon Thames QS and petty sessions records
These are held at Kingston Heritage Centre. QS records are held in series KE2 dating from the mid-seventeenth century to early/mid-nineteenth century and include:

- Session files 1668–1748
- Session file of presentment and recognizances 1676–1772
- Miscellaneous documents relating to sessions 1663–1829
- Minute books 1705–1779
- Licensing
- Enforcement of Conventicle Act (forbidden religious gatherings) 1660–1679
- Arrests and convictions
- Accounts of fines and warrants

Miscellaneous records from 1665 to the early nineteenth century Petty Sessions are held in series KT1 and include:

- Court registers 1913–1944 (provide name of defendant, offence, plea and sentence)
- Minute books 1882–1938 (some missing years)

An earlier minute book survives in series KS2/1/1 for the years 1723–1751 and later records, which are largely marked as closed (although criminal court proceedings are only usually closed for thirty years), are held in series KT165 covering 1920s to 1979 including registers, minutes, licensing records and minutes of justices' meetings. NOTE that series KT165 is stored at SHC but is not available to view there. Request for access to those records should be made to Kingston Heritage Centre.

Borough of Southwark QS and petty sessions records
The records for both the QS and petty sessions for Southwark are held at TLA. QS records are in series CLA/046/. The surviving records are limited to:

- Session/minute books 1666 to 1768; 1785 to 1929 (CLA/046/01/)
- Session files 1667 to 1870 (CLA/046/02/)

- Session papers 1654; 1667–1784; 1814–1846 (incomplete) (CLA/046/03/)
- Other records (CLA/046/04/) which includes recognizances, victuallers recognizance and associated records

Petty sessions in Southwark were held at the Newington Petty Sessions which were described as the 'Petty Sessions for the East Half Hundred of Brixton and the Town and Borough of Southwark'. However, its jurisdiction largely concerned the licensing of public houses. The records are held in series PS/NEW and include:

- Court minutes 1794–1966
- Calendars and registers of licences 1775–1953

Borough of Croydon QS records
The records for the Borough of Croydon QS established following the granting of borough status to Croydon in 1889, are held at London Borough of Croydon Archives between 1889 and 1964 when South-East London Commission Area was established under the Administration of Justice Act 1964. These records are held in its series QS for the years 1889 to 1965 and include:

- Calendars of prisoners (after trial)
- Indictments
- Depositions and certificates
- Deposition and Appeal Papers
- Highway Diversion Orders
- Accounts of Fines
- Returns of Members of Freemasons Lodges
- Agenda and Forms Book
- List of Barristers and Solicitors Willing to Act for Poor Prisoners

Register of Barristers, Solicitors and Cases South-East London Quarter Sessions covered:

- The London boroughs of Bexley, Bromley and Croydon and superseded Bromley and Penge Petty Sessional Divisions and part of Dartford Petty Sessional Division both originally part of the county of Kent
- Croydon County Borough and part of Wallington Petty Sessional Division both originally part of the county of Surrey

The records for the South-East London QS for the period 1925 to 1978 are held at SHC in series 2877 and include:

- Indictments
- Register of Criminal Cases
- Registers of Appeals
- Register of Leave to Appeal
- Minute Books

Other sources:

- A number of QS order books and session rolls have been transcribed and published covering the period 1659 to 1668 which can be found at the TNA reference library and SHC
- Surrey quarter sessions records: the Order book for 1661–1663 and the Sessions rolls for Michaelmas, 1661, to Epiphany, 1663 / edited by Hilary Jenkinson and Dorothy L. Powell (1938) (Surrey Record Society)
- Volume XXX. The Deposition Book of Richard Wyatt, JP, 1767 to 1776 edited by E. Silverthorne (1978) (Surrey Record Society)
- Volume XLI. Surrey Gaol and Session House, 1791 to 1824 edited by Christopher Chalklin (2009) (Surrey Record Society)

Houses of Correction and prisons

The first prison in England was at the Tower of London which housed enemies of the king from around AD 1100. During the twelfth century, when royal charters were granted to towns, they included an obligation to establish and maintain a gaol to keep the peace which would be the responsibility of the towns' corporations (or governing bodies).

Early prisons were used purely for those who owed money to the Crown (until 1352 when imprisonment for debt was extended to those who owed money to individuals) or prisoners awaiting trial. Imprisonment was not used as a form of sentence/punishment until the early nineteenth century. Sentencing before this usually involved fine, torture, capital punishment or transportation.

Houses of correction or 'Bridewells' were established from 1556 to manage social problems associated with poverty, the first being Bridewell Hospital in London which became a 'house of correction' for petty criminals, beggars, vagabonds, and even unmarried mothers. By the early 1600s, there were approximately 170 houses of correction across England and Wales.

A View of the South Front of the North Side of the Marshalsea Prison (Yale Centre for British Art, reproduced under license CC0 1.0 Universal).

The earliest prisons found in the county of Surrey were the King's Bench prison and Marshalsea, both in Southwark and dating back to the fourteenth century. These were prisons for specific uses: King's Bench prison was for the incarceration of prisoners of the court of King's Bench who were largely debtors; while the Marshalsea held a variety of prisoners such as men accused of crimes at sea and political figures charged with sedition, but in particular, like the King's Bench prison, it became known for its incarceration of debtors and thus later became known as a debtors' prison.

The main records for these prisons are held at TNA in series PRIS 10; however, SHC holds the following debtors' prison records (QS3/2/) for the King's Bench prison and Marshalsea:

- Debtor appearance books 1691–1798 which include details of those appearing in court to be discharged from debt and the outcome which can include conditions of discharge such as joining regiments or ships.
- Debtor prisoners' books 1760–1811 include lists provided to the quarter sessions by keepers of King's Bench prison, Marshalsea prison and Surrey County gaol, where debtors were held in custody. They include not only those incarcerated for debt but those who had been discharged, died, or removed to another prison.

There is no evidence that a county gaol existed in Surrey before 1513 when a commission of gaol delivery was issued for 'Surrey Gaol, Southwark', and from 1580 the county gaol was kept in a house called the 'White Lion' near St George the Martyr church on Borough High Street, Southwark. The prison expanded over time and was finally abandoned in 1798, there having been a new county gaol built in 1791 at Horsemonger Lane, Newington. This prison remained in use until 1878 when Wandsworth prison, built in 1851, became the county gaol and remains in use today.

The main prison records are held at TNA in various sets, although for researching incarcerated ancestors, the starting point should be series PCOM 2 (1770–1951) which contains prison minute books, visitors' books, journals, records relating to Gibraltar prison and some ship prisons and includes records for Wandsworth prison.

Records for Wandsworth prison are also held at TLA in series ACC/3444/PR between 1879 and 1984, including but not limited to:

- Nominal registers of admissions
- Indexes to prisoners' names
- Registers of executions
- Files on condemned prisoners
- Record of daily discharges
- Reception and discharge sheets
- Wing occurrence books
- Landing books
- Petitions of prisoners
- Files
- Medical records
- Photographs

Other local prisons which served Surrey, most of which held debtors or those awaiting trial or transportation rather than those serving a sentence included:

- Kingston upon Thames Town Gaol established by 1264.
- Guildford had a house of correction at Castle Hill between 1822 and 1852.
- Croydon Town Gaol and Lock-up house between c.1820 and c.1848.
- Brixton House of Correction between 1820 and 1852 and from 1853 to 1869 was a female convict prison. It reopened for male

prisoners in February 1870, was a military prison between 1882 until 1898 since when it remained a male prison until 2012 when is changed from a local prison to a Category C training establishment in 2012.
- Southwark Borough Compter between 1717 and 1852 and which from 1840 was used exclusively for female prisoners.
- Woking male prison between 1859 and 1889 primarily for invalided male convicts.
- Woking female prison between 1869 and 1895 which was the first purpose-built female convict prison from which those in Brixton were transferred.

Sadly, no records of prisoners for any of the above listed local prisons appears to have survived although some management records relating to the running of prisons do and can be found at SHC in series QS5/4/ in relation to the gaols at Horsemonger Lane, Southwark, Brixton, Guildford and Wandsworth.

Records for Woking prisons (male and female) are held at TNA and include:

- Registers of Prisoners 1846–1889 in series PCOM 2/141-146
- Quarterly returns of prisoners in Hulks and Convict Prisons 1859–1876 in series HO 8/140-207

It is also worth noting that SHC also holds probation service and after care records for Surrey between 1937 and 1989 in series ref. 3290 and 4504.

C. Land ownership and occupation

Deeds

Deeds are an important source for family history research. They provide a description of the property often described by their location in relation to neighbouring properties including the names of the holder and often previous holders; the size of the plot; the names of the parties to the deed including names and occupations; details of previous holders which may include several generations of a family and their relationships. They will also include the names and often the occupations of occupiers of anyone renting the property.

For example, this deed in respect of a property in Cranleigh provides details of three generations of a family.

Deed for Oliver house Lease and release dated 1 and 2 June 1714, between Arthur Foster of Bramley And James Harmes of Rudgwick (SHC Ref: G96/4/11).

This Indenture made the Second Day of June in the [...] year of the Reigne of our Soveraigne Lady Anne by the grace of God of Great Britain France and Ireland Queene Defender of the Faith &c and in the yeare of our Lord God one thousand Seven hundred and fourteene **Between** Arthur Foster of Bramley in the County of Surrey yeoman Son and heire of Arthur Foster late of Alfold in the said County yeoman Deced who was the Son and heire of Jane Foster the wife of [...] Foster late of Alfold aforesaid Deced who before she was Married was called Jane Smallpeece the Daughter of John Smallpeece Sometime of Cranley in the County of Surrey Taylor long since Deced of the one part and James Harmes of Kyworke in the County of Sussex yeoman of the other part Whereas the said James Harmes either in his own right or the right of his wife hath good right and title to the Lands & tenemts herein after mentioned and hath bin long in possession thereof without interruption and the writings that should evidence such right are either lost or mislaid and the said Arthur Foster is Consenting to confirme establish and assure the sd premisses unto James Harmes and his heires **Now Thereupon** This Indenture Witnesseth That for the establishing confirming and assuring the said premisses to the said James Harmes and his heires, and in consideration of two pounds & three shillings of lawfull money of Great Britain to him the said Arthur Foster before the Sealing hereof in hand paid by the said James Harmes the receipt whereof the said Arthur Foster doth hereby Acknowledge and thereof doth clearly acquit release and Discharge the said James Harmes his Exors & Admrs for ever by these presents Hee the said Arthur Foster Hath granted bargained Sold aliened remised released confirmed and for ever quitclaimed and by these presents doth grant bargaine sell aliene remise release confirme and for ever quit claime unto the said James Harmes (now being in the actuall possession of the One Messuage or tenement and premisses herein after mentioned by vertue of a bargain Sale and Demise thereof for a yeare to him made by the said Arthur Foster by Indenture bearing date the day next before the day of the date of these presents and by force and vertue of the Statute made for transferring uses into possession) and to his heires and assignes for ever All those messuages or Tenemts with the Appurtenances and the reversion and reversions rents and rents thereof and all the estate and interest of the said Arthur Foster therein scituate and being in Cranley in the said County of Surrey abutting on the Lands of John [...] on the East part the lands of Dodstone on the west part [...] the Highway leading from Horsham to Guilford on the South and now in the severall tenure or Occupation of [...] Wassell [...] his assignes which said premisses were sometime the estate of the said John Smallpeece but one of the children [...] of the sd John Smallpeece of Cranley [...] And all houses outhouses buildings yardes orchards gardens [...] yards backsides wayes waters [...] and appurtences to the said messuages or tenemts and premisses belonging or in anywise [...] during the redemn and reversn [...] and rents thereof And all Charters deeds writings and evidences touching or concerning the premisses and the Estate right title interest property possession action claime and demand of the said Arthur Foster and his heires or assignes of in or to the said premisses or any part thereof **To have and to hold** the said messuages or tenemts and premisses before mentioned to be hereby bargained Sold and released or hereby meant or intended to be bargained Sold and released with the appurtenances and the rednn revns and rent thereof unto the said James Harmes his heires and assignes for ever And the said Arthur Foster doth covenant promise and agree for himselfe his heires Exors and Admrs to and with the said James Harmes his heires and assignes by these presents in manner and forme following (that is to say) that he the said James Harmes his heires and assignes shall or lawfully may from time to time and at all times for ever hereafter well and in peace have hold use and enjoy the said messuages or tenemts and premisses with their appurtenances and the rents issues and profits thereof receive perceive and take up to and for his and their own use without any lett trouble interruption contradiction or denial of or by the said Arthur Foster his heires or assignes and without any lawfull lett or interruption of or by any other person or persons claiming or to claime any estate or interest in the premisses in by from or under the said Arthur Foster his heires or assignes **Freed and Discharged** and from time to time well and sufficiently Saved and kept harmlesse of and from all former and other gifts grants bargaines Sales wills estates joyntures dowers judgmts executions charges titles troubles burdens and incumbrances whatsoever had made committed done or willingly suffered to be done or to be had made committed done or willingly Suffered by the said Arthur Foster his heires or assigns **In Witness** whereof the parties first above Named to these present Indentures interchangeably have sett their hands and Seales the day and yeare first above written Arthur Foster Sealed and Delivered in the presence of Lee Child Mattrese [?] Shotter the day and yeare first within written Recd by me the within named Arthur Foster of and from the within named James Harmes the full Sume of two pounds and three Shillings being the consideration money within mentioned to be paid me witness my hand Arthur Foster Witnesses Lee Child Mattrese & Shotter

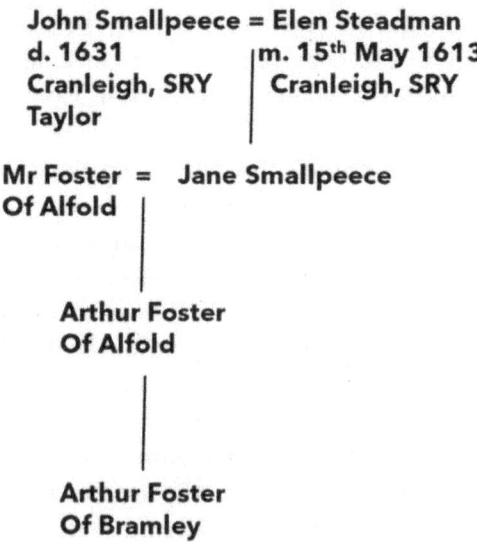

Smallpiece Family tree.

What deeds might be found?

Title deeds are some of the oldest documents to survive in any quantity dating as far back as the late twelfth century, when the keeping of written records first became widespread. Although prior to the Statute of Frauds Act 1677 deeds were not necessary to transfer land, written deeds had been in use for centuries before this and had increased in use.

But what is a deed? A deed is any legal document that is signed and delivered for whatever purpose but most commonly transferring the ownership of property or legal rights.

The earliest surviving deeds dating from the Anglo-Saxon period were almost exclusively grants by Letters Patent, for example royal charters which granted borough status to important towns and cities. From the twelfth century, private charters or 'deeds of gift' used by the nobility can be found granting property or rights to significant beneficiaries such as monasteries.

More widely, however, physical possession of land was evidence of title with property being transferred by an act known as feoffment and the taking of possession of the property by 'Livery of Seisin', in which the feoffer (transferor) physically gave the feoffee (transferee) a clump of the ground, blade of grass, twig from a tree etc., as a symbol of the transfer and/or made an oral declaration of the transfer. Such transactions may have later been witnessed by a deed, but that was largely unnecessary; populations were much smaller, communities tighter knit, so everyone knew whose property it was, its value and location.

Where deeds or legal documents concerning the transfer of property may have come into existence in this period include where property was transferred by Final Concords (or Fines), Common Recoveries, Quitclaims and Leases.

Before the sixteenth century, there also developed the practice of feoffments to uses, enabling land to be devised by way of conveying land to a trust granting the use and beneficial interest to a third party who would then be able to pass on such use and interest by will. These were evidenced in writing, resulting in numerous forms of deeds and conveyance being created. They were, however, disliked by the king and lords as property 'transferred' in this way was not subject to fines and escheats, thus depriving the king and lords of income.

The Statute of Uses 1535/6 was therefore introduced as a result of which the 'user' or life tenant became the legal owner of the property, not the trustees. The statute automatically transferred the legal interest (incorporeal hereditament) in property, and the beneficial interest (corporeal hereditament) could now be conveyed without the physical act of livery of seisin but by way of 'bargain and sale'. Technically, this required no legal document until the Statute of Enrolments was passed in 1535/6 requiring such transfers to be made by deed – which had to be enrolled within six months at the courts of Westminster, most commonly in the Court of Common Pleas (found within Close Rolls held at TNA) or with the Clerk of the Peace (found at local record offices). A separate deed of feoffment was also often prepared in lieu of livery of seisin to confirm the same, as the courts judged the 'bargain and sale' deed did not enfeoff the land.

Letters Patent continued to be an important means of conveying property during the period following the dissolution of the monasteries, under which grants of land were made to individuals 'recovered' by the Crown from the monasteries. They were also used to grant permission to sell property where a manor was held by the Crown in Chief. Letters Patent were enrolled and can found in the Patent Rolls at TNA.

By the sixteenth century, the manorial system was in decline (see Manors and Manorial Records) which resulted in manorial land being sold and many private transactions being recorded by deed as evidence of transfer of title. In the seventeenth century, the Statute of Frauds was introduced (16 April 1677/8) requiring:

- All leases, estates, interest in freehold or term of years assigned granted or surrendered to be by deed or note in writing signed

- All conveyances in trusts of land must be in writing signed by the maker or by will
- All grants and assignments of trusts in land must be in writing signed by the grantor or by will

It also included provisions changing the effect of some existing property holdings:

- All leases, estates, interest in freehold or term of years created by livery of seisin which were not in writing and signed by the maker would now have the effect as an estate of lease at will save for all leases which did not exceed three years in term where the rent was equal to two-thirds of the value of the improved land
- Trusts that arise or result by implication of construction of law, i.e. resulting trusts and constructive trusts

Methods of 'livery of seisin' and 'bargain and sale' became unpopular with many who did not like the public nature of either method, being unable to keep their land transactions 'secret' which they may have wished to for many reasons. While Final Concords, Common Recoveries (which were finally abolished by the Fines and Recoveries Act 1833), Quitclaims and Leases continued to be used by seventeenth-century lawyers, they also began to devise new ways of conveying land, which circumvented legal restrictions on the transfer of property. The methods employed and relating deeds include, Lease and Release (whereby a lease was granted for a year providing an equitable interesting in the property, with a release being entered into the very next day releasing the legal title to the lessee at the end of the term of the lease), Trusts and Settlements, Mortgages, and Deeds of Enfranchisement.

The deeds and methods of conveyance considered above largely concerned property freehold land and leasehold land. From 1852, under the Copyhold Act, manorial tenants of copyhold land could demand enfranchisement, the conversion of their property from copyhold to freehold. Copyhold was eventually abolished and converted to freehold by the Law of Property Act of 1922, which came into force on 1 January 1926 (see Manors and Manorial Records).

Deeds were important records in proving a person's entitlement to property prior to 1925, thus large bundles of documents were retained and required for any conveyance to take place. Conveyancing could, therefore, be quite complex and expensive. The Law of Property Act 1925 sought to help by providing that a vendor was only required to prove their title to property over a period of the previous thirty years (later amendments to the Act have reduced this to fifteen years).

Many old deeds have been destroyed (seen as no longer necessary), although records of them may exist in abstracts of title which are summaries of title deeds and documents that prove an owner's right to property, together with any encumbrances (mortgages, rights of others etc.) that relate to it. In more recent years, these became known as an epitome of title which should have copies of the documents attached.

It was not until the Land Registration Act 2002 that land registration became compulsory (for most property transactions) although it had been voluntary since the Land Registration Act 1925 for some transactions. Thus today, it is much less common on the conveyance of property that a bundle of deeds will be available.

Types of Deed:

- Letters Patent
- Final Concords
- Common Recoveries
- Quitclaims
- Leases
- Bargain and sale.
- Trusts and Settlements, including marriage settlements
- Conditional Release/Mortgages
- Deeds of Enfranchisement

Letters Patent can be found in the Patent Roll held at TNA in series C 66, while those which were not enrolled can be found at TNA in series C81–83. Final Concords, Common Recoveries and Quitclaims (which were all forms of fictitious court claims to record the transfer of property) can be found among the relevant court records held at TNA (see Chapter 5).

Enrolled bargain and sales can be found in the Chancery Close Rolls, again held at TNA in series C 54 from the thirteenth century to c.1930, while ancient deeds may also be found among other collections held at TNA.

WSFHS has produced, in its Record Series (RS), 'A handlist of some Surrey Deeds in the Public Record Office [TNA] c.1100–1800' which have been abstracted and indexed by Cliff Webb. This index lists deeds in chronological order by parish with names of parties and various other details, including the TNA reference. Many of these are held among the records of the Exchequer (series E), Chancery Court (series C), Court of Common Pleas (series CP), records of the Duchy of Lancaster (series DL), Land revenue records (series LR), King's Bench (series KB) and other collections.

The index includes 1,654 deeds, of which the vast majority are pre-eighteenth century. Before about the year 1500, these deeds were written in Latin; from about 1500 they start to be written in English.

There is also an index of names.

Copies of earlier deeds held at TNA can sometimes be found at local record offices along with later deeds such as Leases, Bargain and Sale, Lease and Release, Trusts and Settlements, Mortgages, and Deeds of Enfranchisement. These can often be found among manorial/estate/family papers and other collections. It should, however, be borne in mind they may not be at the archives local to the property; where families moved around, papers may be deposited at the local archives where the family later settled.

SHC holds a vast number of deeds for properties in Surrey, which can be searched at its online catalogue in numerous ways, such as by 'deeds' and the location, or the type of deed such as 'Lease and Release/Bargain and Sale' etc. and the location, or by family name and the location etc. Many records can be found among collections of manorial/estate/family papers rather than as individual documents. They may also be found among records deposited by solicitors, institutions, and other organisations.

It should be remembered that not all surviving deeds may be held by the archives, some may still be held in private hands. I have located some more recent (nineteenth-century) deeds held by my local history society and recent owners of properties, so it is always worth contacting local societies and living descendants of manors/estates/prominent families to see if they retain any records.

Abstracts of title can be searched in the SHC online catalogue in much the same way, simply by 'abstract of title', location, name, etc.

There are some published records for Surrey which act as a finding aid for those deeds recorded in the Feet of Fines:

- *Vol XIX. Surrey Fines, 1509 to 1558* edited by C.A.F. Meekings (paperback reprint 1968) (Surrey Record Society
- *A List of Surrey Feet of Fines 1558–1706* (five volumes; Research Series (RS 20, 22, 24, 26 and 28) (WSFHS)

Window Tax

Window Tax was an annual tax imposed 'only upon the Inhabitants or Occupiers for the time being of such Dwelling House his Executors or

Administrators and not on the Landlord who let or demised the same his Heirs Executors Administrators or Assigns' introduced in 1696 by 'An Act for granting to His Majesty several Rates or Duties upon Houses for making good the Deficiency of the clipped Money'. The tax in fact comprised two taxes:

- House tax charged at a flat rate depending on the number of occupiers in a property and from 1778 included a further charge based on the rateable value of the property
- Window tax charged on a graduated scale of bands based on the number of windows of more than ten, initially, in the property

So, those with fewer windows, initially ten, were subject to a 2-shilling house tax but exempt from the window tax; houses with more than ten windows were liable for both taxes which increased in line with the number of windows:

- Between 1696 to 1766, window tax was paid on houses with more than ten windows
- Between 1766 and 1825 on those with seven windows or more
- Between 1825 and 1851 on those with eight windows or more

In respect of both taxes, those who were exempt from paying the church and poor rates were exempt from the paying the taxes.

The house tax element was abolished in 1834, while the window tax element continued until its abolition in 1851.

Window Tax is often the reason why old buildings today have blocked-up windows. Those liable often sought to reduce or negate their tax liability by blocking up windows either permanently or temporarily until the inspector had been.

From 1784, various other taxes were also included in the same assessment forms as the window tax, such as taxes on servants, shops, horses, carriages, carts, waggons and even a tax on hair powder!

Survival rates of window tax assessments vary from county to county but are held in local record offices. For Surrey, only a handful survive and are held at SHC:

- Battersea – includes a house assessment recording bachelors, windows, shops, servants, horses, carriages, wagons and carts 1786 (SHC Ref: QS6/7/10–11)

- Old Malden – rate assessments for houses, windows and lights 1756, 1759, 1770–1773, 1778 (SHC Ref: 2473/6/)
- Mortlake – windows and lights tax 1779, 1781–1782; inhabited houses duty 1779–1780; house and window and lights tax assessment 1782–1785 (SHC Ref: 2397/5/)
- Thursley – land tax and window tax 1785 (SHC Ref: QS6/7/281)
- Effingham – assessed taxes 1804–1812 (SHC Ref: EFF/19/)
- Newdigate – 'William Wonham his Book of Parish Officers', containing names of parish officers, 1740–1749; vestry minutes, 1879–1880; copies of land tax, poor tax and window tax assessments, 1735–1736 (SHC Ref: NE/4/1)
- Shere – assessment for window tax 1718 (SHC Ref: G85/20/5)

Enclosure awards and maps (or Inclosure awards)

Enclosure awards enclosed larger areas of land either by enclosing areas of common land for the exclusive use of the landholder, enclosing areas of arable land for pasture, or by groups of tenants who perhaps held several strips of land over a wider area, consolidating their landholdings into larger units to make farming more efficient. The process began in the twelfth century but became widespread from 1750.

In early times, this may have been done simply by agreement between landholders and may have been recorded in deeds or evidence in manorial and estate records.

From the mid-sixteenth century, enclosures may be found enrolled in the courts of equity, in particular the Court of Chancery (series C 78) and the Court of Exchequer (series E 159, E368, E 123–E 131). Early enclosures may have caused some controversy and resulted in court proceedings, often in the Court of Requests (held at TNA in series REQ) or the Court of Star Chambers (held at TNA in series STAC).

Also, from the sixteenth century private Acts of Parliament can be found. While the earliest cases largely concern drainage and enclosure of marshes, over time, and particularly from 1750, the granting of enclosure of waste land, common land and open fields by private Acts of Parliament became more frequent until the general Enclosure Acts of between 1801 and 1845, which significantly reduced the costs and time of Enclosure by the appointment of permanent Enclosure commissioners who were authorised to issue Enclosure awards without submitting them to parliament for approval.

The Acts of Parliament listed the landowner who had brought the case and the name of the appointed Enclosure commissioner. The enrolled award detailed how the land was to be divided up, with the survey providing a written physical description of the land and its boundaries including the names of the pre-enclosure fields, footpaths, roads and other features. The award lists the wealthy landowners and then the farmers and cottagers allotted land in lieu of their former common rights. Names of tenants might appear in the schedules, but the awards do not list landless people, so many parishioners are not recorded because they did not have a legal claim to waste and common land.

Enclosure awards were usually accompanied by large-scale Enclosure maps of the consolidated land; these can show boundaries, public roads and footways, land allotted for public purposes, stopped-up roads, old enclosures and land drainage.

Many Enclosure awards and maps for the ancient county of Surrey granted under private Acts of Parliament and under the Enclosure Acts, are held at SHC, where a list, arranged by parish, is available along with a guide showing the boundaries of the Enclosure maps available.

The main series of Enclosure awards and maps are held in series QS6/4/1–74 relating to the enclosure and allotment of open fields and meadows or commons, heaths and greens. They date between 1779 (Cobham) and 1906 (Beacons Heath, Merrow Downs). Further records of and relating to Enclosure awards can be found in various references at SHC for several parishes, including (but not limited to):

- Ewell (1803) (also available on CD) (enrolled in the Common Pleas Recovery Rolls)
- Cheam (1806–1810)
- Byfleet and Weybridge (1811)
- Windlesham (1814–1904)
- Lingfield (1816)
- West Horsley (1817)
- Great Bookham (1822)
- Burstow (1855)
- Thorpe, 1811 and Chertsey, 1814
- Cobham, 1789–1904
- Walton-on-Thames, 1804
- Bletchingley and Horne, 1810
- Shottermill, 1853
- Chertsey, 1814

They can also be found among manorial/family/estate papers such as the Loseley family (series LM); the Tilford family (series 1487); and the

Wyatt family (Survey of Egham parish giving details of old enclosures and lands allotted (with later additions) series 185/16/2 (c.1815)).

The TLA holds Enclosure awards and maps for Spelthorne (formerly in Middlesex), Sunbury, Laleham and a copy of the award for Ashford.

Urban and rural district council records
These are records generally covering the nineteenth and twentieth century relating to the various urban and rural district councils of Surrey. Survival of records varies greatly in the type and age of records. For family history purposes, these can include valuation lists and rate books for the nineteenth and twentieth centuries.

In the SHC series LA, many records relate to highways and sanitary provisions but may provide insight into what life was like in the area for the given period; they also include, in some cases, parish records such as poor rate assessment books and valuation lists. The urban/rural districts found in the series are:

- Barnes borough incl. the parishes of Barnes and Mortlake (LA1) (1765–1938)
- Caterham and Warlingham incl. the parish of Chaldon (LA2) (1730–1933)
- Godstone incl. the parishes of Farleigh, Limpsfield and Warlingham (LA3) (1836–1918)
- Dorking and Horley incl. the parishes of Abinger, Betchworth, Buckland, Capel, Charlwood, Effingham, Headley, Leigh, Merstham, Mickleham, Newdigate, Ockley, and Wotton and the Rural District Council of Reigate (LA4) (1703–1958)
- Mitcham
- Hambledon incl. the parishes of Alfold, Bramley, Chiddingfold, Cranleigh, Dockenfield, Dunsfold, Elstead, Ewhurst, Frensham, Hascombe, Peper Harrow, St Martha, Shalford, Thursley, Witley, and Wonersh (LA6) (1842–1969)

Among these records can be found rate and valuation books, which, where a good run survives, can provide evidence of an ancestor's home and business. For example, for Cranleigh, rate books (described in the catalogue as 'poor rate books') survive for the period 1860 to 1926.

Urban and rural district council records are not confined to the above series. A wider search of the SHC online catalogue for urban/rural district council records and the location will reveal all relevant results for a district. Such records may not provide details of individual families

Extract from Cranleigh Supplemental Valuation Lists and Rate Books (SHC Ref: LA6/13/2).

or ancestors but can help provide an understanding of the area for the particular time period and how our ancestors may have lived.

Maps
SHC holds a large selection of Ordnance Survey (OS) maps. They can be found in the map drawers in the reading room and copies of many, dating between 1860 and 1947, can also be purchased on a set of five CDs from SHC. Individual digital maps can also be purchased which do not only include OS maps but manorial and other maps such as the Cobham Manor Map of 1807 or the Crowhurst Manor map of 1679.

SHC also holds a large selection of manorial, estate, parish and utility maps which can be found in its online catalogue among manorial/estate records. A selection of these have been made available on CD which can be purchased from SHC and include:

- Horsell Map by Edward Ryde 1851, SHC Ref: 6198/11/188 (map, transcript of key; and for further research an Excel spreadsheet containing reference book data, digital images of the reference book and a comparison with the 1851 census)

- Cobham Manor Map 1807, SHC Ref: 2610/1/38/21 (just the map which includes names and acreages; this map does not have a separate key)
- Crowhurst Manor Map 1679, SHC Ref: 6960/1 (map, transcript of key; and for further research an Excel spreadsheet containing the transcript of the key in reference number order)
- Ewell Enclosure Map 1802 and Award 1803, SHC refs 6054/1 and 8887/1 (map, transcript of the Award and Award Schedule and images of the original Award; and for further research an Excel spreadsheet containing the Award Schedule data in plan number order)
- Molesey East and West Enclosure Map 1821, SHC Ref: QS6/4/30/1 (map which includes names and acreages; this map does not have a separate key)
- Molesey Matham and Molesey Prior Manors Map 1781, SHC Ref: K81/3/1 (map and transcript of the key; and for further research an Excel spreadsheet containing the transcript of the key in parcel number order)
- Thorpe Manor Map 1809, SHC Ref: 2675/81/11–12 (map, transcript of the key and images of the original key; and for

further research an Excel spreadsheet containing the transcript of the key in plan number order)
- Woking Manor Map 1719, SHC Ref: G97/5/63 (map, transcript of key to the map and images of the original key; and for further research an Excel spreadsheet of the key)

D. Manors and manorial records

Manorial records, where they survive, can be one of the most voluminous record sets held by an archive beyond parish registers and can provide substantial genealogical information, substantiating family history research, fillings gaps in other record sets, and distinguishing between family members with the same name.

The manorial system dates from the Anglo-Saxon system of the local Hundred courts, Anglo-Saxon agricultural estates and the feudal system when the village chief known as the Thegn held land directly from the king in return for military service.

Following their conquest of England, the Normans developed the system further when William the Conqueror granted land dispossessed from Anglo-Saxon nobility to his supporters. The evolved system is more commonly referred to today as the manorial system, a system which actually continued until it was finally abolished by the Law of Property Act 1925, albeit its importance and role changed and gradually fell into demise.

Originally, the lord of the manor was granted land – usually in return for military service. He would be obliged to provide an agreed number of trained armed men to fight in the Crown's army. From the thirteenth century, however, the need for such military might was greatly reduced and the need to provide military men was replaced with a payment known as Scutage. There were also ecclesiastical lords who provided ecclesiastical services to the Crown rather than military men.

In its simplest form, the manorial system was a system of administration of land under a lord of the manor who held land directly from the Crown as 'tenant-in-chief' or 'demesne' lord. Lords of the manor could grant their knights land in return for their service; these would be 'mesne' lords, i.e. not holding directly from the Crown.

The lord could also grant land within his manor to tenants, most commonly as customary or copyhold tenants, i.e. by copy of the manorial court roll. Such grants of land were made in return for services to the lord, such as working manorial land and fealty (sworn loyalty) to the lord although over time the feudal system of people owing services to their 'superiors' died out and by the mid- to late seventeenth century had been replaced by monetary payments. Copyhold tenants represented the larger part of the population.

Copyhold land could be inherited (by custom of the manor or from the mid-sixteenth century by enrolling a copy of the tenants will in the court records), bought and sold, sub-let and mortgaged, all subject to the agreement of the lord of the manor. Copyhold land continued until it was abolished in England and Wales by the Law of Real Property Act in 1922, which required copyhold tenure to be converted into freehold on the payment of compensation to the lord of the manor (enfranchisement). However, the lord of the manor continued to retain some rights over land converted to freehold until such rights were finally abolished by the Law of Property Act 1925.

Manors varied greatly in size and often spanned parish and county boundaries and may be spread over different locations. The manorial courts were the central administration for the manor. They consisted of two main courts:

- **The Court Leet** which was responsible for minor criminal offences which occurred within the lord's manor, such as breach of the peace. It was responsible for the effective working of the system of Frankpledge in which each area was divided into groups of ten or twelve households, known as tithings, whose members were responsible for the good behaviour of each other. This system began to decline from the fourteenth century with the emergence of the Justices of the Peace following the Justice of the Peace Act 1361 and the developing criminal justice system with the introduction of quarter sessions. Usually held every six months.
- **The Court Baron** was responsible for regulating and administering the affairs of the manor. It was this court which enforced local customs, dealt with minor civil disputes such as boundary disputes and debts, and the transfer of land and property rights, most commonly customary or copyhold land. Freehold and leasehold land was less likely to be recorded in the court records because these did not require the permission of the lord of the manor to be conveyed. Lists of freeholders and leaseholders, however, may be found in court records particularly when the lord of the manor changed. The Court Baron was originally held every three weeks, although its sittings became increasingly infrequent during the fourteenth century, and by the fifteenth century it was often convened only twice a year.

What types of records might you find?

- **Manorial Court Rolls/books** Include names, occupation and locations of copyhold tenants through surrenders of and admissions to copyhold land, conditional surrenders (akin to a mortgage), surrenders to will (creating a trust), permissions, death and inheritance, proclamations which took place on the death of a copyhold tenant. Proclamations were requests made by the lord of the manor for those with an interest in the land (heirs/prospective tenants) to attend court and claim their interest. They would take place on consecutive courts (usually three but could be more) until someone came forward, and if no one came forward the property fell back to the lord of the manor. In the case of a death, the lord of the manor would then be free to admit anyone who so wished to be admitted.
- **Surveys:**
- These include:
    - **Extents** (an extended valuation listing every building, piece of land on the demesne, every labour service and rent, placing a value on each);
    - **Rentals** (beginning in the fourteenth century, list the amounts of rent in cash or produce due from each tenant);
    - **Terriers** (gave a topographically arranged description of the land);
    - **Custumals** (common in the twelfth and thirteenth centuries, recorded the tenants and their holdings but also set out the theoretical customary obligations of the tenants, enshrined in 'the custom of the manor' that can be corroborated by the manorial account).
- **Estreat rolls**: These include offences tenants committed, heriots and reliefs imposed on deaths, fines paid on the admission of new tenants with names and description of property/land. They can provide some insight into life on the manor.
- **Accounts/Compoti**: These can include all sorts of information relating to the lord of the manor and the running the of the manor, which can provide fascinating insights into the social economy of the community. They may also record fines imposed at the Court Leet and fines, heriots (frequently not money but animal) and reliefs paid in the Court Baron, which can provide a snapshot of change of tenants each year.

- **Stewards' records/papers**: These can include individual surrenders of property/land (absolute and conditional), transfers, powers of attorney, and draft court records written in English (particularly useful for those records pre-1733 when the court rolls are written in Latin).
- **Legal Papers**: These can pertain to cases over grazing rights, documents relating to chancery cases where inheritance has been challenged, boundary disputes etc.
- **Correspondence**: Often relating to a wide range of matters concerning the management of the manor, tenants, property etc.
- **Deeds of Enfranchisement**
- Maps

Manorial records can be challenging both to locate, search and use. They are rarely indexed, although manorial court books can be indexed with the names of the main landholder who had dealings with copyhold

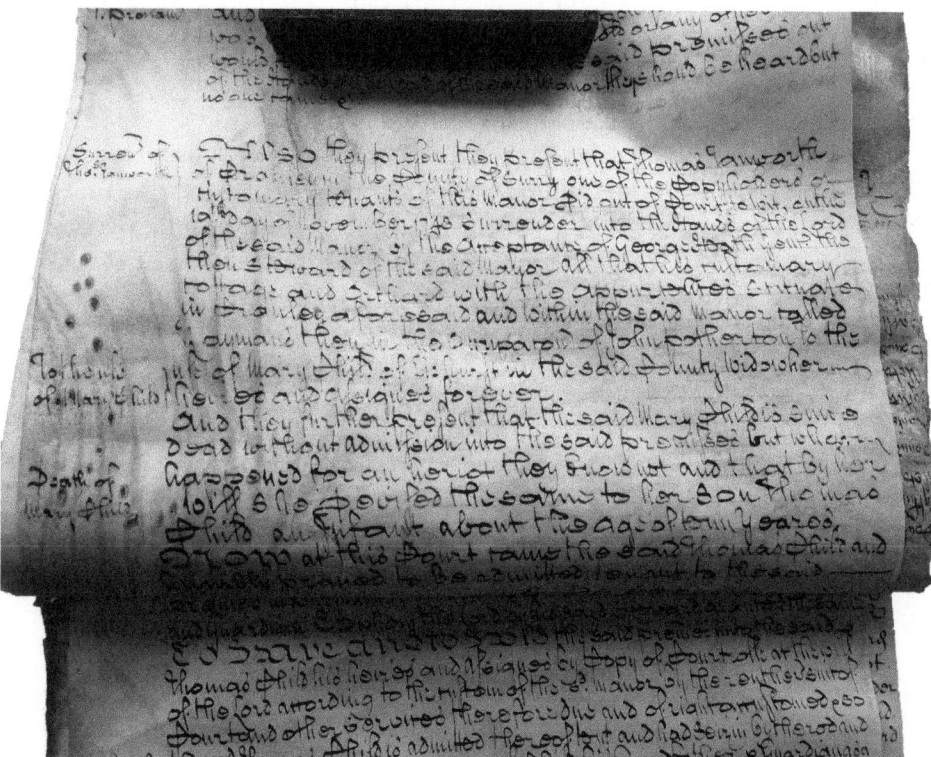

Extract from Manorial court roll for Shere Vachery and Cranleigh dated 19 November 1743 (SHC Ref: G85/10/14). By kind permission of the Bray family and Surrey History Centre.

land. It must also be remembered that before 1733 the records are most likely to be written in Latin which can be heavily abbreviated. Manorial records have rarely been digitised although records for some manors (not in Surrey) have been digitised at various websites and this is steadily growing.

Survival rates of manorial records vary greatly; some manors have no known surviving records while others have a vast collection. Where they do survive, they may not be held at the local archive in the county or area in which the manor existed; there are several reasons for this. Firstly, manors could change hands frequently and a lord of the manor may have taken his records with them when he moved. Secondly, there were many wealthy landowners, both private families and institutions such as monasteries and university colleges, who frequently acquired manors in several counties. Further, many manors were at one time or another held directly by the Crown. For these reasons, manorial records may not be held where expected.

Lords and their records may have been resident elsewhere with their records therefore being held by the local archive in which they were at some time or last settled. It must also be remembered that manorial boundaries could span both parish and county boundaries – also resulting in records being held across several record offices.

Locating surviving manorial records has, however, been made relatively easy with the creation of the Manorial Documents Register (MDR) found at TNA's discovery website (**https://discovery.nationalarchives.gov.uk/manor-search**), described as 'the official index to English and Welsh manorial records. It provides brief descriptions of documents and their locations in public and private hands. The documents recorded in the MDR include and are defined as 'court rolls, surveys, maps, terriers, documents and books of every description relating to the boundaries, franchises, wastes, customs or courts of a manor'. They do not include title deeds. It should be noted that even though records have been deposited at archives, they largely remain private property and are simply deposited at archives for safe keeping and access can be restricted.

Another good source for finding out what manors existed in a parish is the website British History Online (**www.british-history.ac.uk**) (BHO) and its digitised version of the Victoria County History (VCH) series published in the early 1900s. This can be searched by county and parish and provides details of the history of the parish, the manors within the parish and details of the parish church and advowson.

According to the MDR, in searching for manors in the historic county of Surrey there were 454 manors although not all have surviving records or known surviving records. For those manors where records do survive, and are known, the largest collections can be found at either SHC, TLA or TNA. It is clear from the MDR that some records are scattered further afield. Some records can also be found among collections at the British Library and other national collections including the National Trust; others can be found in local archives further afield such as those for the Manor of Merstham.

The majority of records for Merstham Manor are split between Canterbury Cathedral Archives (generally pre-sixteenth century) and Somerset Heritage Centre (generally sixteenth century onwards) with the odd record being held at TNA and SHC. This is most probably because prior to the dissolution of the monasteries, the manor was held by Chertsey Abbey but was ultimately in the possession of the Abbey of Christchurch, Canterbury. Post the dissolution, the manor was granted to Sir Robert Southwell from whom the manor descended through various inheritances and the sale to the family of William Jolliffe whose grandson became the first Baron Hylton and in turn whose descendant, William George Hervey Jolliffe, 4th Baron Hylton (2 December 1898–14 November 1967), served as Lord Lieutenant of Somerset.

WSFHS in 1993 (and revised in 2005) produced a research guide (RA35) of Surrey manors and their surviving records. The guide is no longer available in printed form but is included as a digital copy in its CD series (CD7).

As the MDR is now complete and can be accessed free of charge, the easiest way to locate manors and surviving records for Surrey is through the MDR's search facility, which can be searched by name of the manor (if known), parish and historic county (the ancient county of Surrey pre-boundary changes).

In comparing the MDR and WSFHS research guide, it was noted there are at least two manors, listed in the WSFHS guide but not listed in the MDR: the Browns Manor is listed in the MDR under Kent not Surrey because the manor straddled the border of the two counties; while the manor of Dockenfield in Frensham, Surrey, is listed under Hampshire as it was historically part of Hampshire. There were therefore actually 456 manors in Surrey.

Not all were mentioned in the Domesday Book. At the time of the Domesday Book there were listed only thirty-six land holders, including the king, the Archbishop of Canterbury, the Bishop of Winchester, Bishop Osbern, the Bishop of Bayeux, six abbotts, an abbess, the Canon of St

Paul's (London), the Church of Lambeth, two counts, a countess and an earl. The remainder were largely supporters of William the Conqueror, many of whom were of Norman origin. In the following centuries, land was sold, bought, exchanged, seized and redistributed by the Crown and divided by inheritance, for example the manor of Pollingfold in Ewhurst which in the later fifteenth century was divided between the daughters of William Sydney (son of William Sydney of Loseley) on his death, into two moieties, creating two manors – East and West Pollingfold.

Prior to the dissolution of the monasteries, the larger landholders appear to have been the Crown and religious institutions, with some of the other main land-holding families through the centuries including the Warren family (de Warrene; William de Warenne was the Earl of Surrey at the time of the Domesday Book), the Clare family (de Clare founded by Richard Fitz Gilbert), the More and More Molyneux family, the Bray family, the Evelyn family and the Onslow family, to name a few.

Many of the manors named by WSFHS but not listed in the MDR, are listed as having no known surviving records; however, this can be somewhat confusing for the researcher. On further delving into the history of these manors, in particular with reference to BHO and its digitised version of *A History of the County of Surrey* (the four Surrey volumes of the Victoria County History series published between 1902 and 1912), it appears most of those not appearing in the MDR were smaller estates, farms or tenements which were either:

- Originally conveyed as a manor but with no further reference to them as manors
- Were sub-manors and later descended as part of the larger manor
- Were later sold and amalgamated with a larger manor
- Have simply been given slightly different names in the MDR, e.g., West Purley Manor as named in the MDR is simply named as Purley Manor in the WSFHS research guide

For example, the manor of Henfold in Capel listed in the WSFHS research guide, was designated a manor by the time of the reign of Henry VIII but quickly declined to generally being referred to as a farm within the manor of West Betchworth.

Another example is that of Ottershaw manor in Chertsey, which was possibly once held of Chertsey Abbey but was later referred to as simply woods and land known as Ottershaw – although by the fourteenth century it was described as a messuage and 40 acres of land, which by the seventeenth century may have been held by Owen Bray and by the eighteenth century of the Roake family of Horsell.

Yet another example is the manor of Woodbridge in Stoke-next-Guildford listed in the WSFHS research guide but not in the MDR. According to BHO, in 1324 this was a messuage and 5acres of land held by the Doyle family of Guildford and Tongham. By the end of the sixteenth century, it was in the hands of the Stoughton family who held Stoke and Stoughton manor. While the WSFHS guide states no records survive for Woodbridge and both the MDR and WSFHS guide state no records survive for the manor of Stoughton, records do survive for Stoke-next-Guildford manor from the mid- to late seventeenth century (under SHC Ref. 1320) that include deeds relating to the manor of Stoughton between 1329–1624. While there is no mention of manorial court records, the later Stoke-next-Guildford manorial records most likely include land and property that was once part of the manors of Woodbridge and Stoughton.

One last example of a manor listed under a different name in the MDR is that of Papworth, aka Papercourt, at Ripley and Send which, according to BHO, descended as part of West Clandon manor until the seventeenth century, when it descended as part of Ockham manor until the nineteenth century, from when it descended as part of Wisley manor.

There are also manors which appear in the MDR, are not listed in the WSFHS research guide, but are detailed in BHO, many of which are described as 'reputed' manors due to lack of records of their existence and/or where records survive the property/land not being referred to as a 'manor' but simply as lands/property/tenement etc.

Out of the 456 manors named, 107 have no known surviving records, while many others only have limited surviving collections such as Burstow Lodge Manor for which there is only a plan of the manor surveyed in 1703 showing the boundaries between the Manor of Burstow Lodge and the Manor of Burstow which were added in 1743 (SHC Ref. 3611/1).

Another example of where few records survive is that of the manor of Tullesworth in Chaldon for which only a court roll covering the period 1540–1547 is known to survive and is part of a court roll with other manors (which would have been held by the same lord). This record is held at TNA (Ref. SC2/204/49).

One last example of where few records remain is that of the manor of Suffolk Place aka Mint Liberty in Southwark for which only two records survive: a rental from the year 1549 held at TNA (Ref. E 36/169 ff.159–161) and three rentals covering the years 1811–1813 held at SHC (Ref. K26/10/2–6).

Names of manors also changed over time and/or were known by various aliases, for example, Godstone Manor as named in the MDR, was also known as Walkhampstead and/or Lagham at different times according to BHO; Graveney Manor as named in the MDR was also known as Hall Place manor as named in the WSFHS research guide, Hall Place manor having been originally granted to the Graveney family, according to BHO.

Another example is that of Molesey Matham Manor which was most likely also known as East Molesey, Molesey and possibly Esher Matham manor when considering the history as set out in BHO.

It is noteworthy that the earliest surviving records for several manorial court rolls are from the thirteenth century with a varying degree of continuity from that period. These include, but are not limited to, court rolls for the manors of Addington, Brockham, Friern, Frensham, and Farleigh. Although a thorough analysis has not been conducted, it is reasonable to state that for the greater number of manors, records are more likely to survive from the sixteenth century onwards.

Sadly, it is not possible to plot the boundaries and changing boundaries of the manors of Surrey. While there are many manors for which either maps or surveys survive, providing either a visual or descriptive record of the boundary, there are many more which do not. It can often, therefore, be unclear in which manor an ancestor lived and/or held property if there were several manors in a parish, unless other records, such as a will, specifically name a manor. In those circumstances, where rentals survive, it may be easier to examine those first as they will list all the tenants of the manor at a given time and thus, hopefully, be able to identify (without the need of scouring court rolls for several manors), which manor an ancestor lived/held property.

Other finding aids available for Surrey manors are limited, with only one manor, that of Pyrford (comprising land in Pyrford, Horsell and Chertsey (Woodham)) having an index of names recording tenants and freeholders who appear in the court records (held in SHC Ref: G97/4/2) between 1654 to 1675, which is available to download for free as a PdF from the SHC website.

Publications by Surrey Record Society include:

- Volume XV. *Surrey Manorial Accounts* edited by H.M. Briggs (paperback reprint 1968) Surrey Record Society – includes manors belonging to Merton College, Oxford: four account rolls for the manors of Malden, 1270 to 1271 and 1300 to 1301, Farley, 1277 to 1278, and Thorncroft in Leatherhead, 1282 to 1283
- Volume XLVI. *The Accounts for the Manor of Esher in the Winchester Pipe Rolls, 1235 to 1376* edited by David Stone (2017)

- Volume II. *Court Rolls of the Manor of Carshalton* edited by Dorothy L. Powell (1916)
- Volume XXI. *Chertsey Abbey Court Rolls Abstract* (covering 1273–1793) edited by Elsie Toms (1937 to 1954)
- Volume XXIV. *Guildford Borough Records, 1514 to 1546* edited by Enid M. Dance (1958)
- Volume XXVI. *Fitznells Cartulary* edited by C.A.F. Meekings & Philip Shearman (1968) (the manor of Fitznells in Ewell, Cuddington, Epsom and Cheam)
- Volume XLVI. *The Accounts for the Manor of Esher in the Winchester Pipe Rolls, 1235 to 1376* edited by David Stone (2017)

One last source of information worth a mention is that of *The History and Antiquities of the County of Surrey* by Rev. Owen Manning and William Bray, published in 1804 in two volumes, from which much of the VCH and BHO information is also comprised.

E. Surrey schools

In 1851, a census of educational facilities was conducted across England and Wales. The returns revealed that most children, by that time, did have access some schooling. It was not, however, until W.E. Forster's Elementary Education Act 1870 (Forster's Education Act) that statutory provisions for education for all children aged between 5 and 13 were introduced. The act empowered local education boards to make by-laws regarding the attendance of children at school up to the age of 13. Each local education board could decide whether those children should attend school. Such schools were initially funded by a mix of school fees, local rates and government subsidies. The school fees were unpopular and provisions were introduced in 1891 which provided government funding to cover school fees for the first time. However, schools could still charge fees under certain conditions until they were finally abolished altogether in 1918.

The 1880 Education Act introduced minimum requirements for children to attend school to the age of 10 years, increasing to 11 in 1893 and 12 in 1899. The upper level was increased to the age of 14 by the Education Act 1918, to 15 after the Second World War in 1947 and to 16 in 1972. More recently the age has increased to 17 in 2013 and 18 in 2015, subject to 16-year-olds being able to leave full-time education to take up apprenticeships or traineeships or part-time education or training alongside employment, self-employment or volunteering for twenty hours or more a week.

Before Forster's Education Act, children were frequently employed from very young ages in agriculture and industry, particularly in the emerging factories of the Industrial Revolution. Church schools, however, have existed for many centuries, with their roots in the monasteries educating young monks; the oldest school in England is believed to be King's School, Canterbury founded as a cathedral school in 597.

Grammar schools were introduced in the fifteenth century, funded by charities, university colleges, companies, and guilds. Oxford and Cambridge universities were established many centuries prior to this, with evidence of teaching at Oxford from 1096; it expanded rapidly from 1167 when English students were banned from attending the University of Paris, by Henry II. Cambridge University was established in 1209 by scholars leaving Oxford following a dispute with the local residents there.

Charity schools were first established in the late seventeenth century in poorer urban areas to provide education free of charge for the 'deserving poor' and Sunday Schools were introduced in Gloucester in the eighteenth century by Reverend Thomas Stock and nationally in 1780 by Robert Raikes.

Following the General Workhouse Act 1723, workhouse schools were also established to prepare pupils for apprenticeships with the aim they would no longer be a burden on the parish. Church schools known as National Schools were established in large numbers from the early nineteenth century by the National Society for Promoting Religious Education, providing elementary education centred around the doctrines of the Church of England.

Orphanages frequently had their own schools, such as the Royal Female Orphanage, Beddington, Surrey, which was established in 1762 by Sir John Fielding to house and school orphaned girls to set them up for apprenticeships in domestic service (from the age of 14) and married life, teaching them to read, sew, knit, clean, cook, run a kitchen etc.

Among other schools established were: The Royal Masonic Institution for Girls in 1788, followed by a similar institution for boys in 1798; ragged schools providing education for poor children, free of charge; dame schools set up locally by women to educate young children; private boarding schools; Quaker schools; and military schools.

One only need look in local census returns to find details of local schools such as this extract from the 1841 census for Cranleigh:

Reference	Address	Household members	Occupation
Class: HO 107 Piece: 1045 Book: 9 Folio: 27 Page: 21	Cranley Street, Cranley School Cranley	Thomas Child Snr, 70 Sarah Child, 70 Thomas Child Jnr, 35 Sarah Child, 30 Thomas Child, 3 Sarah Puttock, 8 Frederick Briant, 15 Henry Ansell, 13 George Cooke, 13 John Browne, 14 William Head, 13 Frederick Rothwell, 13 John Honer, 14 Thomas Mayne, 12 James Elwin, 12 George Enticknap, 13 William Holden 11 William Enticknap, 11 John Davis, 12 Henry Boyes, 14 James Martin, 12 Jane Bonsey, 15 Martha Botting, 13	Yeoman Schoolmaster Boarder Pupil Boarder Pupil Boarder Pupil Boarder Pupil Boarder Pupil Boarder Pupil Boarder Pupil Boarder Pupil Boarder Pupil Boarder Pupil Boarder Pupil Boarder Pupil Boarder Pupil Boarder Pupil Boarder Pupil Female Servant Female Servant

By the time the National School (to which parents had to pay a contribution for children to attend) opened in Cranleigh in 1847, it is known there were at least five dame schools in the village, at least one of which continued to operate in the 1881 census return:

Reference	Address	Householders	Occupation
RG 11/793	The village, Cranleigh (previously known as Cranley)	Mary Warner, Head, 76, Unmarried Sarah Warner, sister, 69, Unmarried Mary Jane Warner, Niece, 20, Unmarried Albert Warner, Nephew, 14, Unmarried Edith Butcher, Boarder, 13 Grace Elizabeth Herington, Boarder, 6 Mary Jane Charman, Servant, 15	Proprietress of school Annuitant Teacher Scholar Scholar Scholar General Servant

The oldest schools in Surrey include the Royal Grammar School, Guildford (originally 'The Free School'), which owes its founding to

Robert Beckingham who left provision in his will to 'make a free scole at the Towne of Guldford' with a governing body being set up to form the school in 1512, and Kingston Grammar School founded by royal charter in 1561. Charterhouse School in Godalming is also thought to be one of the oldest schools; however, it was originally founded on the site of an old Carthusian Monastery in Smithfield, London in 1611 by Thomas Sutton, moving to Godalming in 1872.

There were, however, many schools, too numerous to mention, established in the nineteenth century and, with an ever-increasing population, the number of schools has continued to grow in the twentieth and twenty-first centuries.

For many schools, records may only survive from the nineteenth century onward because there was no requirement for records to be maintained prior to this. School logbooks were in quite common use from around 1840 although not required until 1863 in government-financed schools. These can include details of attendance, accidents and illnesses (of both students and staff) and inspectors' reports. They can provide a picture of everyday life such as the weather, the success of the crops, epidemics, celebrations such as coronations, the end of the two world wars; essentially details of anything which may affect school

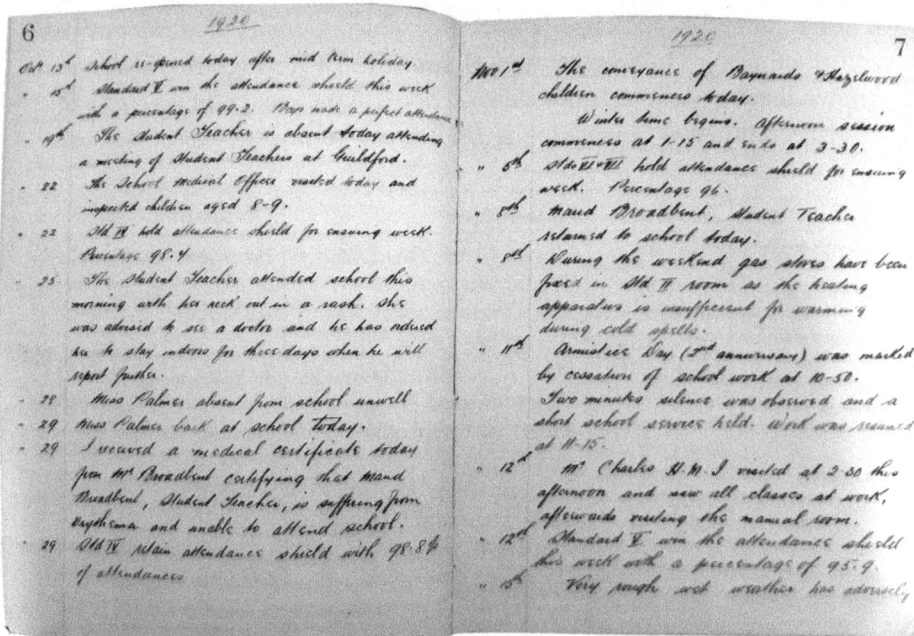

Extract from the school log book in 1920 for Cranleigh Church of England school by kind permission of the Headmistress, Mrs Kate Pelazza.

attendance. These were documented because attendance could affect their local grant.

Following the introduction of education boards in 1870, minute books of their meetings may survive which can provide further information on the pupils, teaching staff and board members. They can include correspondence, inventories, building plans/drawings, photographs and anything which may have affected a schools' funding.

School registers of admission were not mandatory until the Elementary School Code 1903 but may be found prior to this and usually give dates of entry and withdrawal, together with the pupil's age, residence and father's name and occupation. There may be notes as to whether a pupil was baptised. Secondary school admission registers can include educational achievements and may also give details of a pupil's later career either in secondary education or employment. The Elementary School Code of 1903 required such records to be retained for a minimum of ten years following the last entry.

The records for local schools are generally held at local county record offices. Records for schools in Surrey are largely held at SHC with Croydon Local Studies Library holding records for many schools within the Borough of Croydon. Schools in old Surrey parishes now within London boroughs (Battersea, Bermondsey, Camberwell, Clapham, Deptford, Lambeth, Newington, Penge, Putney, Rotherhithe, Southwark, Streatham, Tooting Graveney, and Wandsworth) are held at TLA. Smaller collections can also be found at locally at local study libraries.

Cliff Webb produced a fairly extensive research guide to 'Surrey Schools and their records' published by WSFHS (Research Aid 57), setting out the schools by town/village with details of surviving records and their locations excluding those in towns/villages now within London boroughs; his guide 'Index to London Schools and their Records', published by the Society of Genealogists, includes details of surviving records for schools within towns/villages which were once in Surrey but are now within London boroughs.

More recent records may still be held by individual schools and can include photographs not just of pupils but those which document school life, so it is always worth contacting them. Newspapers are also a good source of information for schools and pupils with school events often being reported in local newspapers.

There are a limited number of records also available online, such as the register of girls admitted to the Royal Female Orphanage, Beddington, which have been indexed and digitised on Ancestry between 1890 and

1913. The registers for Charterhouse between 1872 and 1910 are also digitised and indexed on Ancestry.

Findmypast hosts, among other record sets, 'National School Admissions Registers & Logbooks 1870 to 1914' which includes approximately 567,000 indexed and digitised records for National schools in Surrey such as St Giles' Church of England School, Ashtead; Grayshott Church of England School; St Paul's Church of England School, Hook; Winterbourne Boys' School, Croydon and Haydon's Road Church of England School, Wimbledon (Girls').

University records should not be overlooked. Many have been published extensively such as the *Alumni Oxonienses* edited by Joseph Foster and the *Alumni Cantabrigienses* (Cambridge). But many other universities and colleges have also published their alumni records – the main source for researching an ancestor's university education and qualifications. For more details, 'Registers of the Universities, Colleges and Schools of Great Britain and Ireland' compiled by Phyllis Jacobs and published in 1964 provides a comprehensive listing.

F. Apprenticeship indentures and associated records

Private apprenticeships

Apprenticeships may, arguably, be one of the oldest methods of learning a trade or occupation which still continues today. It is believed the first historical mention was in texts associated with guilds in 1156. Guilds have, since the Middle Ages, been associations of craftsmen focusing on a specific trade, with each guild having well-defined positions of apprentice, journeyman, and master. The first national apprenticeship system of training was set up by the Livery companies of London in 1563, such as the Worshipful Company of Goldsmiths (created by royal charter in 1327).

Indentures were bipartite written contracts binding an apprentice to his or her master and were more often than not, private arrangements between the master and the parent or guardian of the child. Indeed, the master was frequently a friend, relation, or someone found through personal recommendation. Some trades kept apprenticeships very much in the family, and their expertise became the monopoly of a small handful of connected families.

While apprenticeship indentures are not generally digitised and found online, from 1710 to 1811 masters were required to pay stamp duty on apprenticeship indentures, which was recorded in apprenticeship books. These are held at TNA in series IR 1 and have been digitised on Ancestry, with 'Indexes to Apprenticeship Books (1710–1774)' being available at Findmypast (compiled by the Society of Genealogists).

The apprenticeship books are divided into Town Registers (London) and Country Registers (elsewhere), depending on where the stamp duty was paid. For those apprenticed in Surrey (and other home counties and Middlesex) the duty may have been paid in London and the details entered in the Town Registers.

The payment could be made at the start of the apprenticeship or any time up to one year after the expiry of the indenture, the date given in the register representing the date of payment not the date of the start of the apprenticeship.

Some of the terms of apprenticeships were far different to those of today, for example an apprentice could not marry until the expiration of the term of their apprenticeship. There were often rules regarding visiting taverns and the like and becoming intoxicated. Breaching the terms of an apprenticeship indenture would see the breaching party (master or apprentice) being brought before the quarter sessions.

Apprenticeships also lasted much longer; private apprenticeships were mostly for seven years or more, today they range on average between one and three years.

The actual apprenticeships indentures, where they survive, are most likely to be held at the local record offices with SHC holding private apprenticeship indentures for those apprenticed in the ancient county of Surrey. The earliest indenture found at SHC is an 'Apprenticeship indenture of George Bracewell, son of the late Christopher Bracewell of Doncaster, Yorkshire, yeoman, apprenticed to John Swerder, citizen and goldsmith of London, for nine years' dated 10 August 1488 (SHC Ref: LM/1659/17). Some collections held at SHC include records into the twentieth century such as the 'Apprenticeship indenture of Jack Baker of "Albury", Maybury Hill, Woking. Apprenticed for seven years to Billing & Sons Ltd of the London Printing Works, Guildford, letterpress and offset printers and electrotypers etc' dated 1 July 1927 (SHC Ref: 4640/1/2).

They can be searched using the SHC online catalogue by name, date, place and using terms such as 'apprentice', 'apprenticeship', and 'apprenticeship indenture'.

In addition, the following are also available online:

- Surrey and City of London Livery Company Association Oath Rolls, 1695–96 (Findmypast, complied by Cliff Webb, WSFHS)
- Surrey, Southwark, Newington Apprentice Register 1891 (Findmypast, transcripts created by Peter Shilham)

Apprenticeship indenture of George Bracewell, son of the late Christopher Bracewell of Doncaster, Yorkshire, yeoman, apprenticed to John Saverder, citizen and goldsmith of London, for nine years dated 10 August 1488 (SHC Ref: LM/1659/17). By kind permission of the More-Molyneux family and Surrey History Centre.

- Guildford Freemen's Books 1655–1933 (Family Search website Film no. 007941880 images 619–657 Edited by Hector Carter, pub. Guildford Corporation 1963; original record at SCH in BR/BUR/2 or BR/BUR/3 (Burgess rights – private apprenticeships))
- Surrey Apprenticeships 1711–1793 (Family Search website Film no. 007717899 pages 427–578, Surrey Record Society, printed by Butler & Tanner Ltd, 1929)

The following publications are available from Surrey Record Society:

- Volume XXVIII. *Kingston upon Thames Register of Apprentices 1563 to 1703* edited by A. Daly (1974): reproducing the register of apprentices maintained by the Borough of Kingston upon Thames, following the passing of the Statute of Artificers in 1562
- Volume X. *Surrey Apprenticeships, 1711 to 1731* edited by Hilary Jenkinson (1929): Includes Surrey entries, 1711 to 1713, extracted from registers of apprenticeships at TNA, following the introduction of a duty on apprenticeships

East Surrey Family History Society has produced indexes (purchased via Parish chest or GenFair, records available at SHC):

- Wimbledon Apprenticeship Indentures & Poor Law Record: Indexes to Apprenticeship Indentures 1690–1895 and Poor Law Records 1698–1842
- Mortlake Apprenticeship, Poor Law & Militia Records: Indexes to Apprenticeship Records 1614–1915, Poor Law Records 1631–1834 & Militia Records 1801–1809
- Mitcham Poor Law, Apprenticeships and Militia Records: Indexes to Settlement Certificates 1700–1806, Bastardy Examinations 1715–1819, Apprenticeship Indentures 1700–1844, Apprentices' Registers 1802–1844 & Militia Records 1709–1811
- Reigate Poor Law Records: Contains an index to Poor Law Records 1669–1794 and index to Apprenticeships Records 1672–1796

West Surrey Family History Society has also compiled finding aids:

- MS 12. Calendar of Surrey Apprenticeships 1711–1749 Downloads following the introduction of a duty on apprenticeships

- Surrey Apprenticeships III – An Index of Apprentices of Surrey Interest in some London Livery Company Records 1563–1928 Research Series (RS) 33, Edited by Cliff Webb. This series includes those who were sent up to London to be apprenticed.

With Surrey's close proximity to London, it is not surprising that many Surrey residents were apprenticed in London, along with other surrounding counties. For those who became Freemen of the City of London, the records between 1681 and 2004 are held at TLA.

Parish Apprenticeships
Under the Poor Law Act 1601, children of those who found themselves reliant on poor relief, including orphans and foundlings, could be apprenticed by the parish from the age of 7. Parish apprenticeships could be entered to learn a trade but also less-skilled occupations such as agriculture, domestic service etc.

Such apprenticeships were often entered into without the agreement of the parent(s). The indentures should have been executed before a Justice of the Peace by the child, his/her parents, their master and the parish officers and enforced by the execution of a bond. Two copies were made: one for the master and one for the parish, with the master having a legal obligation to feed, clothe and teach his/her trade/occupation for the duration of the contract. By the seventeenth century, children of the middle classes and even gentry who found themselves under economic pressure may be found among parish apprenticeships. Typically, children of fallen gentry would be bound to manufacturers, merchants and the professions.

Parish apprenticeships also lasted much longer. Bearing in mind children from the age of 7 could be apprenticed by the parish, they would normally continue until the age of 24 for boys and 21 for girls (apart from in London parishes where the age limit was reduced to 21 for both boys and girls, or a maximum of a seven-year term following Hanway's Act 1767).

Parishes were also required to maintain apprenticeship registers following an Act of Parliament in 1801, although many do not survive. Where they do survive, they should provide the date of Agreement, the name of the child being apprenticed, the name of the Master, the names of the Churchwarden(s), Overseer(s) and Justices of the Peace endorsing the apprenticeship, the trade in which the child is to be apprenticed and the term of the apprenticeship. Later registers will also include the sex and age of the child, the name of his/her parents (especially the father), and the residence of the parents. Compulsory parish apprenticeships continued until 1844.

Where parish apprenticeship indentures do not survive, details of apprenticed children may be found among overseers' accounts and vestry minutes. Parish apprenticeships were not subject to stamp duty and will not, therefore, be found among the stamp duty collections at TNA or online.

Parish apprenticeship indentures and any associated records (such as bonds) are generally held among parish records, particularly among overseers' records. The collections held at SHC generally range from the seventeenth to the nineteenth century. Details of parishes for which apprenticeship records survive can be found in the WSFHS 'Guide to Surrey Parish Documents' in its Research Aid 42 available from its website.

According to that guide, sadly, apprenticeship indentures appear to survive for only about one-eighth of the ancient parishes of Surrey, and often in limited numbers, such as the parish of Morden for which only one record survives: 'Notice of application by parish of St Pancras, Middlesex, for permission to apprentice poor child to Robert Williams of Morden' dated 1831 (SHC Ref: 2065/4/236).

However, if no such records are listed for the parish you are interested in, it is always worth searching the SHC catalogue. For example, the WSFHS guide does not list any apprenticeship records for the parish of Farnham; however, there are 166 indentures (folio nos. 82–248) in a box (SHC Ref: 1505/Box32) among overseers' records, which also holds bastardy bonds and other parish bonds, and date between the seventeenth and nineteenth centuries.

Later nineteenth-century records may be held under Poor Law Union records rather than parish records. For example, there are no apprenticeship records listed for the parishes of Dorking in the WSFHS guide; however, there are two later indentures listed in the SHC catalogue under Dorking Poor Law Union (SHC Ref: BG2/18/1–2). These inconsistencies may have arisen simply because records have either been deposited or identified since the WSFHS guide was created in 1999. So, again it is always worth searching the SHC catalogue and/or asking the staff at SHC.

G. Locally held military, militia and defence records

Military records

There are generally held at TNA with a growing number of records being available at various commercial websites and/or downloadable (often free of charge) from the TNA Discovery website. However, the following records are also held locally at SHC:

- Military records of the Queen's Royal Surrey Regiment and its predecessors (SHC Refs: QRWS, ESR and QRS)
- Queen's Royal (West Surrey) and East Surrey Regiments Recruitment District registers, 1908 to 1933 (SHC Ref: 2496)
- Nominal rolls for officers of the Queen's Royal (West Surrey) and East Surrey Regiments, 1914 to 1919 (SCH Ref: 8227)
- Registers of enlistments, discharges and transfers for the Queen's Royal (West Surrey) and East Surrey Regiments, 1920 to 1958 (SHC Ref: 7791)

These do not include service records for soldiers who served in the regiments; they do, however, provide information about the regiments themselves with some named individuals, along with a large collection of photographs in which many individuals are named.

The following registers, indexes and rolls for Surrey regiments can also be searched:

On Ancestry:

- Queen's Royal West Surrey Regiment enlistment registers 1920 to 1946
- Queen's Royal West Surrey Regiment transfers in registers 1939 to 1947
- Queen's Royal West Surrey Regiment World War II Honours Indexes [1939] to 1946
- Queen's Royal West Surrey Regiment nominal rolls of officers 1914 to 1918
- East Surrey Regiment enlistment registers 1920 to 1946
- East Surrey Regiment transfers in registers 1924 to 1946
- East Surrey Regiment World War II Honours Indexes [1939] to 1946
- East Surrey Regiment nominal rolls of officers 1914 to 1919

- 21st to 24th Battalions the London Regiment nominal rolls of officers 1914 to 1918
- Surrey World War II Home Guard Records 1940 to 1945

At Findmypast:

- British Army, Queen's (Royal West Surrey Regiment) 1901–1918
- Surrey Recruitment Registers 1908–1933
- British Army, East Surrey Regiment 1899–1919
- British Army, London Regiment, Surrey Battalions 1914–1940
- Surrey, Military Tribunals 1915–1918

Further, the Battalion War Diaries for the Queen's Royal West Surrey and East Surrey Regiments, 1914 to 1918, have been digitised and are accessible at the Queen's Royal Surrey Regimental Museum website (**www.queensroyalsurreys.org.uk**).

SHC has produced a useful guide, 'Tracing military records' available on its website, which includes a downloadable PdF guide to 'Tracing Military Records at Surrey History Centre'.

Tudor and Stuart Muster Rolls (sixteenth and seventeenth century)

The Tudor and Stuart Muster Rolls are militia rolls of the defence forces organised locally as temporary military forces to support the permanent army in times of potential invasions. Their role was to keep the peace and defend a locality.

The rolls comprised assessments of able-bodied men between the ages of 15 and 60 who could be called on to serve. The assessment included details of the weapons and armour owned by the wealthiest. They do not include *all* 15- to 60-year-old men; those unfit for service or too poor to possess the necessary weaponry were excluded. The earliest records date from 1522, which in particular provides an in-depth valuation of property.

They are arranged by Hundred (or Wapentake etc.) and by parish. *Tudor and Stuart Muster Rolls* by Jeremy Gibson and Alan Dell notes the record office in which they can be found and those which have been published. They are mainly held at TNA (in series SP 1, 2, 10, 12, 14, 16,17 and E 101, 36 and 315), local record offices and the British Library.

For Surrey, the Tudor and Stuart Muster Rolls have been published by Surrey Record Society (Volume 3, in four parts). This provides a compilation of muster rolls and other related documents dating between

1544 and 1684 taken from the Loseley Manuscripts held at SHC (Ref: 6729 & LM (section B.1.8)).

Apart from those which are published, the largest collection for Surrey is held at TNA variously found in series E 36, SP 10, SP 12, E 101 and SP 14 covering muster rolls taken in 1539, 1548, 1569, 1600/1, and 1624, while the British Library, in its manuscript collections, holds a muster roll from 1627 titled 'A Muster of 100 footmen for the Low Counties' (BL Ref: Add. MSS. 290609B), and the TLA holds the militia records for Southwark (in series A/JM).

Militia lists and muster rolls 1757 to 1831.

Following the Militia Act of 1757, each parish was required to provide a number of able-bodied men who were conscripted into the militia by ballot. Lists were drawn up, in each parish, of able-bodied men – from which a ballot was made. Clergy, teachers, seamen, apprentices, peace officers and peers were among those excused.

Parish constables prepared an annual muster ballot list of every man aged between 18 and 50 (for years 1757–1762), and 18 to 45 (for years 1762–1831), recording their names, occupations and details of any infirmities. Those excused were also included in the lists. The lists were then organised into Hundreds or Wapentakes, with each providing one company for the county regiment of militia.

In addition to the militia lists, militia enrolment or muster rolls provide details of those who were actually chosen by ballot, or their paid substitutes (those who could afford to, could pay for a substitute to serve in their place). Again, these lists were prepared annually by the parish constable.

Where they survive, together, militia lists and rolls should provide an annual census of the male population for a parish (aged 18 to 50 (for years 1757–1762), and 18 to 45 (for years 1762–1831)), along with details of their family circumstances.

Details of what is held for each county can be found in *Militia Lists and Musters 1757–1876* by Jeremy Gibson and Mervyn Medlycott. For Surrey, they can be found at page 32; however, this is a little outdated with SHC now being the main archive for Surrey, many of the records previously held at Kingston History Centre (previously Kingston Borough Archives) have now been transferred to SHC.

The following records are now held at SHC:

- Oxted militia dated *c.*1784 (SHC Ref: P3/5/113)
- Bletchingley: Two militia lists giving names, occupations and ages of males between 18 and 45 and reasons for exemption (1819

list is incomplete – A to H only), dated 1813 and 1819 (SHC Ref: 2727/1/48/91a-b)
- Ewhurst militia list: names and occupations, dated 10 November 1810 (SHC Ref: 2132/6/17)
- Surrey Militia muster rolls: Accounts of Sir John Frederick's Company, Surrey Militia, with alphabetical list of names of members of the company and a page of accounts relating to each, including payments for clothing, 1794 (SHC Ref: 183/34/29)
- Wimbledon: Militia roll call: names as P5/20/19 but probably later. Cavalry not infantry, c.1797 (SCH Ref: P5/20/2)
- Godalming, Farnham and Blackheath Hundreds: Militia roll for the Hundreds of Godalming, Farnham and Blackheath, giving names, ages and civilian occupations, arranged by parish, 1759 (SHC Ref: LM/1330/87 published by WSFHS – see below)
- West Surrey: Names of substitutes accepted for principals at Subdivision Militia Meetings held at Guildford, but relating to several west Surrey parishes, 26 August, 23 September and 7 October 1786 (SHC Ref: G51/21/2)
- West Surrey: Militia Roll of 'Persons to serve in the Additional Army (Substitutes), 30 July 1803–September 1803 (SHC Ref: G1/1/82)
- West Surrey: Roll of Militia in West Surrey under Act of 1792, 14 November 1807–May 1808 (SHC Ref: G1/1/83)
- Transcript of Guildford militia rolls, 1793–1800 (SHC Ref: Zg/14/1)
- Subdivision of Guildford: militia muster roll, 19 January 1793–23 November 1793 (SHC Ref: 6330/8/8/6)
- Subdivision of Guildford: militia muster roll. Comprises: parish, name and name of substitute, signature or mark of attestation, 11 February 1797–29 December 1800 (SHC Ref: 6330/8/8/8)
- Guildford Sub-Division militia roll listing persons by ballot to serve in the militia under the Act of Parliament for completing the Militia of Great Britain (1808–1809). 1 vol. Enrolment details include: parish or place; names of persons drawn, names of substitutes, number of regiments, attestation of principal or substitute. Enclosure: page relating to ballot, September 1810–August 1827 (SHC Ref: 1748/2).
- Mitcham Militia, 1655–1811 (SHC Ref: LA5/8)

Records held elsewhere include:

Lambeth Archives (LA)

- The Lambeth Loyal Volunteers and the Independent Lambeth Cavalry Records, 1803–4 held at Lambeth Archives (series Ref: IV/161)
- Yeomanry Cavalry papers, Egham, 1805–1820 held at the National Army Museum (series Ref: MF 29/1)
- Militia and Voluntary muster books and pay lists both by parish militia and county militia: 1st Surrey (1780–1876), 2nd Surrey (1798–1876), 3rd Surrey 1798–99, 1853–76 held at TNA (series WO 13)

There are also a small number of published records:

- Published in *Root and Branch*, the journal of the West Surrey Family History Society, vol 8, no.3: Militia roll for the Hundreds of Godalming, Farnham and Blackheath, giving names, ages and civilian occupations, arranged by parish. 1759 (SHD Ref: LM/1330/87)
- Published by East Surrey Family History Society: Mitcham – *Indexes to Settlement Certificates 1700–1806, Bastardy Examinations 1715–1819, Apprenticeship Indentures 1700–1844, Apprentices' Registers 1802–1844 & Militia Records 1709–1811* (includes an alphabetical list of 190 names, some showing place of birth, residence and substitute information)
- Published by East Surrey Family History Society: Mortlake – *Indexes to Apprenticeship Records 1614–1915, Poor Law Records 1631–1834 & Militia Records 1801–1809* (includes eleven names only)
- Selon Index – includes Militia for Southwark St George the Martyr for 1807 (held in private hands)

Defence lists 1798 & 1803/4

Two very specific Defence lists were created in 1798, known as the *Posse Comitatus*, and in 1803/4, known as the *Levee en Masse*. They are very similar to militia ballot lists and are thus often confused with the same; however, their purpose was different. They listed those men who were not already serving in any form of military capacity and thus would be able to assist in evacuating civilians in the event of a French invasion.

The men would also be employed to gather arms held in private hands, supply and transport food to those on the front line of defence and remove cattle and crops from the path of any invaders.

Where they survive, the lists included all men between the ages of 15 and 60 not already serving. Lists were also compiled of those who could provide specific services such as millers, bakers and those who owned wagons and barges; they can, therefore, provide details of family circumstances.

For Surrey, the only surviving records appear to be Levee en Masse lists, 1803/4 for:

- Oxted: Returns of men eligible for service in army or militia, 1803 (SHC Ref: P3/11/1-44)
- Mickleham: 'Mickleham Subscription for Volunteers'. List of names, with ages and occupations noted. 1803 (SHC Ref: MIC/38/3)
- Seal and Tongham, 1803 (British Library Ref: Add.MSS.45524 ff.21–30)

H. Mental health asylums

One of the oldest and perhaps most infamous (in particular for allowing the public to pay to watch ill patients for entertainment) and first ever psychiatric institutions in Europe is Bethlem (or Bedlam) Royal Hospital now in Bromley, South London (originally part of Kent) but founded in 1247 as the Priory of the New Order of our Lady of Bethlehem near Bishopsgate just outside the City of London walls. It is not known exactly when it first began to specialise in treating the mentally ill, but it is believed that by 1377 the mentally ill accounted for the majority of Bedlam's population[2] although the first records date to 1403, being a visitation by the Charity Commission.[3]

The Madhouses Act 1774 was the first of its kind to regulate asylums. The focus was on private houses which treated those with mental health issues who, following this Act, were required to obtain an annual licence from the Justice of the Peace. Records of these institutions can therefore be found among QS records. For Surrey, these are held at SHC in series QS5/5/3–10 and QS5/5/box1–box3 between 1774 and 1933 with the following licensed private houses noted:[4]

- Great Fosters, Egham. Active c.1774–c.1866
- Lea Pale House, Stoke-next-Guildford. Active c.1774–c.1879
- Frimley Lodge, Frimley. Active from c.1799

- Weston House, Chertsey. Active from c. 1815
- Church Street, Epsom. Active c.1846–c.1933
- Timberham House, Charlwood. Active c.1856–c.1861
- Canbury House, Kingston. Active c.1879–c.1895
- Woodcote End, Epsom. Active c.1880–c.1882
- Croshams, Sutton. Active c.1881–c.1889
- Sutherland House, Surbiton. Active c.1884–c.1897
- Chalk Pit House, Sutton. Active c.1889–c.1908
- Abele Grove, Epsom. Active c.1908–1914

It was not until the nineteenth century when attitudes towards mental illness really began to change. The County Asylum Act 1808 saw the establishment of partially state-funded public mental asylums, treating patients with a variety of conditions from epilepsy to depression, cerebral palsy, learning disabilities and speech problems, among conditions such as alcoholism. Included in the records for Brookwood Hospital in Woking in the later nineteenth century, are details of William Waller, a young man I researched. He was a petty criminal and alcoholic who was admitted to Brookwood twice, his records suggesting a troubled young man with a history of excessive drinking causing quite severe mental health problems with episodes of hallucinations, tremors, confusion, sleeplessness, restlessness, memory loss, described as 'mania' and 'dementia'.

The first county asylum to open in Surrey was Springfield Asylum, Wandsworth in 1841 (and remains open today as Springfield University Hospital), followed by:

- The Royal Earlswood Asylum Redhill (formerly known as Earlswood Asylum for Idiots and Imbeciles) in 1847 (closed 1997)
- Brookwood Asylum, Woking in 1867 (closed 1994)
- Cane Hill Asylum, Coulsdon in 1883 (closed in 2008)
- Holloway Sanatorium, Egham in 1885 (private asylum) (closed 1981)
- Manor Asylum, Epsom in 1899 (by London County Council and became part of the Mid-Surrey Area Health Authority in 1973 and closed in 1996)
- St Ebba's Hospital, Epsom in 1903 (by London County Council and in now part of Surrey and Borders Partnership NHS Trust now West Park Hospital)

Extract from Brookwood Asylum Male Case Book No 18, page 106, Dated November 1897 (SHC Ref: 3043/5/9/1/23).

- Long Grove Hospital, Epsom in 1907 (administered by the Asylums Committee, later Mental Hospitals Committee, of the London County Council (closed 1992)
- Netherne Hospital, Coulsdon in 1909 (closed 1994)
- West Park Hospital, Epsom in 1924 (by London County Council merged with St Ebba's Hospital, the former site is now a housing development)

Records for these institutions are held variously between SHC and TLA. Surviving records relating to the opening, running and daily life of the county asylums (Springfield, Brookwood, Cane Hill and Netherne) can be found in the QS records held at SHC in series QS5/6 dating between 1838 and 1889. In addition, the following records are also held at SHC:

Springfield Asylum

- Case books, 1849–1887 (Ref: 6367/1/1–13)
- Indexes to case books, c.1878–1936 (Ref: 6367/1/14–16)

Brookwood Asylum

The main records for Brookwood Asylum are held in series 3043 and include, but are not limited to:

- Alphabetical registers held in 3043/5/2/1–8, transcribed and available as a PdF from the Exploring Surrey's Past website
- General indexes to case books held in 3043/5/10/1/1–5 also transcribed and available as a PdF from the Exploring Surrey's Past website
- Admission registers, 1867–1906 and 1961–1987
- Civil registers of certified, voluntary or temporary patients, 1931–1949
- Registers of admission and transfer, 1915–1958
- Registers of removal, discharge and death, 1894–1988
- Records of patients discharged, 1894–1960
- Registers of forms of notices of deaths, 1909–1961
- Post-mortem Registers, 1867–1962
- Registers of return of patients' property, 1867–1959
- Medical Superintendent's reports on admission, 1880–1963
- Medical Superintendent's case books, 1941–1957
- Case books, 1867–1921

- Case books relating to chronic patients, 1867–1901
- Case files c.1893–1980s
- Registers of Medical Treatment, 1893–1973
- Staff and Appointments: Registers, 1866–1949

Further patient case files can be found in series 7173 for the period c.1893–1980s. These are arranged in alphabetical order by surname. Additional records can also be found in series 6906 and 8056.

Netherne Hospital

The main records for Netherne Hospital are held in series 3540 and 7338/1 and include, but are not limited to, the following in relation to patients and staff:

- Burial Registers, 1909–1960 (Ref: 3540)
- Admission Registers, 1909–1996, Discharge/Transfer and Discharge/Death Registers, 1909–1996, Death Registers, 1909–1931, Notice of Death Registers, 1909–1994, Inquest Register, 1942–1991, and Post Mortem Register, 1942–1947 (Ref: 7338/1)
- Staff Records, 1905–1992 (Ref: 6376/10)

Further records can also be found in series 6376 and 6523.

The Royal Earlswood Asylum Redhill

The main records for the Royal Earlswood Asylum are held in series 392, 6523, 6817 and 7338 and include, but are not limited to, the following in relation to patients and staff:

- Visitors of Friend of Patients, 1848–1960 (Ref: 392/10/9)
- Patient records, 1849–1983 (Refs: 392/11/ and 6817/3/)
- Patient Admission Papers, 1852–1949 (Refs: 392/21/ and 6523/1)
- Staff Records, 1868–1995 (Ref: 6814/4/)

Holloway Sanatorium

The main records for Holloway Sanatorium are held in series 2620, 3237, 3473, 6864 and 7267 and include, but are not limited to, the following in relation to patients and staff:

- Patient records, 1885–1972 (Ref: 2620/4/ and 3473/3/) *
- Registers of patients, 1885–1930 (Ref: 3237/5/)
- Treatment registers, 1926–1973 (Ref: 3237/6)

- Patient case files 1889–1950 (Refs: 6864, 7267/3 and 8855)*
- Staff records, 1884–1961 (Ref: 2620/5/ and 3237/3/ and 3473/5)
- Nursing records, 1894–1980 (Ref: 3473/4/)

Manor Asylum, Epsom

The main records for Manor Asylum are held in series 2865/5, 6280, 6282, 6317, 6380, 6390, and 7329 and include, but are not limited to, the following in relation to patients and staff:

- Staff records, 1899–1974 (Ref: 2865/5, 6280/1/, 6282/10/ and 6380/2/4/)
- Patient records, 1899–1985 (Ref: 6282/13/ and 6380/2/5/)
- Case books and papers, 1899–c.1975 (Ref: 6282/14/)
- Photographs of patients and staff, c.1900–c.1930 (Ref: 6371)
- Admissions and Discharge Registers 1899–1950 (Ref: 6390/1/)

St Ebba's Hospital, Epsom

The main records for St Ebba's Hospital are held in series 6292, 6380, 6390, 7329 and 7856 and include, but are not limited to, the following in relation to patients and staff:

- Staff records, 1893–1989 (Ref: 6292/21/ and 6380/1/3/)
- Patient registers, c.1899–1977 (Ref: 6292/22/)
- Case books and papers, 1903–1960 (Ref: 6292/27/)
- Patient Index cards, 1927–2004 (Ref: 8837/3/1)

Long Grove Hospital, Epsom

The main records for Long Grove Hospital are held in series 6251, 6275, 6276, 6289, 6423, 6718 and 7422 and include, but are not limited to, the following in relation to patients and staff:

- Staff records,1905–1960 (Ref: 6251/6/, 6423/4/ and 7422)
- Patient records 1907–1961 (Ref: 6251/4/)
- Post-mortem records, 1962–1970 (Ref: 6275/2/)
- Photographs and videos of patients, c.1984–1999 (Ref: 6718)

---

* These records (excluding those held under reference 6864), have been digitised and can be accessed at the Wellcome Library's website (**https://wellcomecollection.org/collections**) free of charge. The Wellcome Library also holds nine case books for Holloway Sanatorium.

West Park Hospital, Epsom

The main records for West Park Hospital are held in series 6280, 6294, 6366, 6380, 6423, 7329, 7604 and 7856 and include, but are not limited to, the following in relation to patients and staff:

- Staff records, c.1943–c.1979 (Ref: 6280/2/ and 7604/5/)
- Patient records, 1924–1988 (Ref: 7329/1/ and 7604/4/)
- Admissions Registers 1924–1990 (Ref: 6423/7/ and 7856/3/)
- Post-mortem records, 1942–1957 (Ref: 6423/7/)

Records held elsewhere:

Springfield Asylum
Some records, including patient records, staff records, administration records, are not held at SHC but are available at TLA in series H46/SP dating between 1844 and 1990.

Cane Hill Asylum
The main patient records for Cane Hill are held at Croydon Archives. The records include management, patients, staff, and administration, among others. Patient and medical records are held in series CAN/2 and staff records are held in CAN/5.

Mental Deficiency Act 1913
This Act set out to control and certify arrangements and institutions for those who were deemed 'mentally defective': 'idiots', 'imbeciles', 'feeble-minded persons' and 'moral imbeciles' (as defined in section 1 of the Act). In other words, those who did not present the same level of mental illness as those in asylums. A Board of Control was established to grant certification to establishments, the records for which are usually found in QS records. In Surrey, these include the following institutions, for which documents can be found among QS records in series QS5/6A, and where there is a specific series of records for the institution, the SHC reference is given:

- Godstone Poor Law Institution, Bletchingley
- Clerk's Croft, Bletchingley, which was also used to house some patients from Netherne
- St Mary's Hospital, Carshalton
- St Lawrence's Hospital, Caterham (Caterham Metropolitan Asylum)

- Chertsey Poor Law Institution, Ottershaw (later Murray House) (Ref: BG1) Admission and Discharge Registers area available on CD to purchase from SHC
- Botleys Park Hospital, Chertsey (Ref: 6206 and 9853)
- St Teresa's, Dockenfield (Convent)
- Dorking Poor Law Institution (Ref: 6057)
- Royal Hostel, Elstead
- Mount Olivet Monastery, Frensham
- Farmfield State Institution and Farmfield Institution, Charlwood (Under London County Council 1898–1947) then under the management of The Royal Earlswood Hospital (see above) (Ref: 6817)
- Kingston Poor Law Institution (Ref: BG8)
- Eagle House, London Road, Mitcham
- Reigate Poor Law Institution (Later St Anne's Institution) (Ref: CC10)
- Ellen Terry Home, Reigate (Formerly Sandfield)
- Spelthorne St Mary Home, Thorpe
- St Peter's Memorial Home, Maybury, Woking (Ref: 7805/9/)

Note: there are likely to be access restrictions to patient records less than 100 years old and staff records less than 75 years old.

For more information about the history of mental illness and institutions in Surrey, including further history on the asylums themselves, visit the Exploring Surrey's Past website.

I. Nonconformity

Nonconformity is a complex subject and specialist texts should be consulted for a greater understanding of the subject; a brief overview is offered here.

Nonconformity is a term used to describe religious groups who did not conform to the beliefs, rites and practices of the Church of England, particularly following the Act of Supremacy 1534 which abolished papal authority and declared Henry VIII the Supreme Head of the Church of England. Prior to this, Catholicism was the principal Christian faith in England. One may expect, therefore, that Catholic registers and records commenced prior to this and indeed they may well have done but none survive today.

Three Nonconformist denominations established themselves over the late sixteenth and early seventeenth century: Baptists, Congregationalists (Independents), and Presbyterians (Unitarians), followed from the mid-seventeenth century by Quakers (the Society of Friends), Jews, Methodists, and Walloons (French Huguenots). This is a rather simplistic list as within each (save for the Quakers) sub-groups emerged. However, for the purposes of considering the survival of their records it is sufficient (unless otherwise stated) to detail these main denominations.

Between 1534 and the Toleration Act 1869, Nonconformists suffered persecution for failing to conform to the Church of England with various Acts of Parliament (such as the two Acts of 1559 Act of Supremacy and Act of Uniformity) imposing the Church of England on everyone without exception. The periods of reign under Mary I and Elizabeth I were arguably the worst periods of persecution with James I seemingly being more tolerant, while there was suspicion that Charles I wanted to return the country to Catholicism, which ultimately, of course, caused his downfall, the Civil War and Interregnum years.

The Puritan government of the Interregnum was 'dominated by men who were hostile to the imposition of strict religious uniformity, and who were prepared to tolerate at least orthodox dissent',[5] with Church of England ministers ejected and replaced with Presbyterian or Independent ministers. The Restoration of Charles II in 1660 saw a concerted effort to re-establish the Church of England. The Act of Uniformity 1662 (one of four Acts of Parliament which together became known as the Clarendon Code) once again required (among other things) conformity to the Church of England with all clergy being ordained by a bishop. It also introduced the new Book of Common Prayer which clergy were required to accept and preach. Nonconformists were liable to three months' imprisonment if they continued to preach in public or work as a private tutor or schoolmaster without first obtaining a licence to do so from an archbishop, bishop or ordinary of the diocese.

Nonconformists once again faced persecution; however, the Civil War and Interregnum years had enabled them to grow in numbers, in particular Quakers, described as 'the runaway success of the Interregnum'[6] gaining as many as 50,000 converts nationally by 1660 and making them the largest religious Protestant denomination in the country.

Numerous Acts of Parliament followed, enforcing varying degrees of persecution and toleration until the Act of Tolerance 1689 which allowed freedom of worship, provided Protestant Nonconformists (thus excluding Catholics) swore an oath of allegiance to the monarch, at that time being William III and Mary II following the Glorious Revolution (1688–1689) when James II was deposed in their favour. William III did, however, use his influence to restrain the continued persecution of Catholics enabling them to worship discreetly until the introduction of the Catholic Relief Acts 1778 and 1791, after which Catholic priests were formally free from persecution. They were able to establish Catholic chapels and openly maintain records, with remaining restrictions on Catholics largely ending by the introduction of the Catholic Emancipation Act 1829.

In Surrey, it has been suggested that nonconformity was perhaps 'important in the northern parishes and particularly those along the Thames because of the proximity to London, and also in the main market towns of Croydon, Dorking, Epsom, Farnham, Guildford and Kingston upon Thames'.[7] It was generally not until the later centuries (late eighteenth into the nineteenth) that nonconformity increased in popularity across the rest of Surrey. The Compton Census 1676, a census conducted by incumbents setting out the numbers of Nonconformists in their parish, revealed the second largest religious group in Surrey after the Church of England according to the number of attendees at public worship,[8] was the Independents, followed by (in order of number of attendees) Baptists, Catholics, Methodists, Quakers, then Jews. Eighteenth and nineteenth century developments in nonconformity in Surrey include:

- The creation of the Surrey Mission in 1797, originally as non-denominational, later developing into Congregational and/or Baptist churches.
- The establishment of the Surrey Congregational Union in 1863.
- The uniting, in 1972, of the Congregational Union with the Presbyterians, forming the United Reformed Church.

It is notable there were relatively few Jews in Surrey until the twentieth century. Prior to this, they were largely concentrated in the areas closer to London such as Bermondsey, Newington and Southwark, although by the nineteenth century Surrey had become the home of notable Jewish families such as the Sassoons of Ashley Park in Walton-Upon-Thames when it was purchased by David Sassoon in 1867. The family earned their wealth through cotton and opium industries.

Nationally, because of the fear of persecution, there are no Nonconformist registers until the mid-seventeenth century. Quaker (aka the Society of Friends) records are generally among the oldest surviving Nonconformist records dating from as early as 1650. They are often found in local record offices and the library of the Society of Friends in London.

SHC has some useful research guides, accessible via its website, for researching Nonconformists in Surrey, particularly useful for those researching Catholic and Jewish ancestry.

Parish registers may provide the first clue that an ancestor was a Nonconformist, for example if a marriage or burial is found but no baptism: marriages were only valid (whether by banns or licence) if conducted in a parish church, while burials were in Anglican graveyards. While Quaker meeting houses often had their own burial grounds, Catholics could not legally establish their own burial grounds until 1853, with non-denominational cemeteries opening from the early nineteenth century.

Where Nonconformists were buried in an Anglican graveyard, the burial register entry may have been annotated with 'anabaptist', 'dissenter', 'papist' or similar.

Records of recusancy, and other records which may help identify a recusant/Nonconformist, can be found locally among QS records (see earlier section), Ecclesiastical court records (see later section), parish records (see earlier section) and, from 1692, Land Tax records. There are also a number of records held nationally at TNA such as Pipe Rolls, Recusant Rolls, Oaths of Allegiance rolls, Lay Subsidy rolls, Protestation Oath rolls, among others. This section will concentrate on those held locally.

The persecution of Nonconformists, and in particular Catholics, essentially criminalised them and QS records can often contain the largest collections of documents such as:

- Indictments and Presentments – Details of Nonconformists who were fined, imprisoned, banished from the country and sentenced to execution
- Oaths of Allegiance, including lists of those refusing to take the various Oaths (may also be found among Chancery Court/ Exchequer Court or King's Bench division records if the person lived within 30 miles of London – so include some of the northern parishes of Surrey)
- Declarations against transubstantiation
- Registers of names and estates of Catholics who refused to take the Oath of Allegiance following the Papist Act 1715, arranged alphabetically by county and town
- Records of land and property seized for failing to take the Oath of Allegiance and/or registering their monies and estates
- Certificates of Roman Catholic Chapels and priests following the 1791 Catholic Relief Act

These numerous records can provide names, addresses and occupations of Nonconformists who were prosecuted, or who had land seized, or who registered themselves as required. They may include details of family members. Specific records held within the QS records for Surrey in relation to nonconformity include:

- Registration of the Estates of Roman Catholics (1717–1718) (SHC Ref: QS6/12/1 & 2)
- Certificate of Protestant Dissenting and Roman Catholic Places of Worship and related documents (1786–1853) (SCH Ref: QS6/13/1–94)

However, in Surrey some of the earliest records relating to nonconformity and recusancy in the sixteenth and seventeenth centuries can be found among one of the richest surviving collections of correspondence such as those of the More-Molyneux family of Loseley Park (SHC Ref: 6729 and Ref: LM). Sir Christopher More (c.1483–1549), Sir William More (1520–1600) and Sir George More (1553–1632), were the first three successive Mores of Loseley Park, all of whom were MPs, with Sir William and Sir George also holding several significant local and national offices.

SHC does hold registers and records for some individual churches/chapels although many continue to be retained by the churches/chapels themselves or are held by the overarching associations or other agencies. For example. many Baptist church records are held centrally by the Baptist Union that a Baptist church falls within; Congregationalist church records may be held the Congregational Union (these were set up in 1863). In particular, Jewish records are largely retained by individual synagogues.

Records held by SHC include:

- Baptist church records such as church meeting records and church membership records for churches such as those at Epsom, Godalming, Wimbledon, Merstham, Mitcham, Barnes, Richmond, Dormansland, Chertsey Street Baptist church in Guildford (records dating back to 1713)
- Godalming Unitarian church
- Godalming United Reform church (formerly Congregational church)
- Norbiton Methodist church
- Meadrow Unitarian church (formerly a general Baptist church), Godalming dating back to 1699

- Ward Street Unitarian Church, Guildford
- Redhill Congregational church
- Haslemere Congregational church (later United Reformed church)
- Guildford Methodist circuit – including Methodist churches at Cranleigh, Shalford, and Wonersh
- Effingham Methodist church
- West Croydon Methodist church
- Wimbledon Methodist church
- Surbiton Hill Methodist church
- Religious Society of Friends, Guildford (Quakers) (later Guildford and Godalming) records dating back 1668 (earlier records are deeds relating to meeting house)
- Dorking and Horsham Quaker records dating back to 1650

In relation to Catholics, SHC holds the following Roman Catholic marriage registers:

- Convent Chapel, Convent of the Sacred Heart (Woldingham School Chapel from 1989), 21 July 1984 to 29 July 1989
- Church of The Holy Family, Farnham, 20 December 1969 to 12 August 2000
- Farnham Poor Law Institution (later Farnham Hospital) House Committee Chaplains' register of baptisms, services and visits, 3 October 1926 to 21 August 1969. Includes some baptisms by the Roman Catholic chaplain.
- Church of the Assumption of Our Blessed Lady, Merton (single entry, 27 November 1982)
- Church of St Martin de Porres, Weybridge. Sixteen entries are recorded, 1971 to 1981
- St Anselm's Roman Catholic Church, Hindhead, 27 September 1965 to 19 December 1977 and 27 July 1978 to 26 September 1987
- St Oswald's Roman Catholic Church, Deepcut, Frimley, 6 July 1935 to 20 April 1985
- St Joseph's Church, Guildford, 26 June 1971 to 2 August 2008
- Church of our Lady of the Assumption, Mitcham, 28 September 1991 to 6 June 1998
- St Thomas of Canterbury Church, Whyteleafe, 5 June 1971 to 3 September 1994
- St William's Church, Mays Corner, Send, 10 August 1991 to 2 August 2002
- Greyfriars Church, Chilworth, 1998 to 2002

Following the creation of the General Register Office in 1837, the Non-Parochial Registers Act 1840 and 1857 required all Nonconformist registers, except Quakers, to be deposited with the Registrar General. These are now held at TNA:

- Series RG 4: Registers of Births, Marriages and Deaths, dating between 1567–1858, surrendered to the Non-parochial Registers Commissions of 1837 and 1857
- Series RG 5: Birth Certificates from the Presbyterian, Independent and Baptist Registry and from the Wesleyan Methodist Metropolitan Registry, dating between 1742–1840
- Series RG 6: Exclusively Quaker Registers, Notes and Certificates of Births, Marriages and Burials, dating between 1578–1841
- Series RG 8: Registers of Births, Marriages and Deaths surrendered to the Non-Parochial Registers Commission of 1857, and other registers and church records, dating between 1646–1970

All of which are available to search online at various commercial websites.

For records relating to other denominations such as the Huguenots, records were deposited with the General Registrar held at TNA in series RG 4 and RG 8 detailed above. For Huguenots in particular, contact the Huguenot Society which holds a Huguenot library housed at TNA and has published many registers. Records for these denominations are not usually found in local record offices and if not at TNA, the individual churches should be contacted.

There may also be records of Nonconformists, particularly earlier Nonconformists, found among ecclesiastical court records (see next section).

J. Ecclesiastical court records (excluding probate)

Ecclesiastical court records extend beyond wills and probate records prior to 1857, Bishops Transcripts and Marriage licences.

Ecclesiastical courts were created in 1072 when William the Conqueror separated common law from canon law. Prior to the mid-nineteenth century, the Ecclesiastical courts were responsible for the social and moral well-being of the population; this included appointing clergy, discipline, and criminal cases involving a clerk in Holy Orders as a defendant. They were also responsible, alongside criminal courts, for religious discipline. For example, anyone failing to attend church would be reported to the bishop at his visitation and brought before the court. They also had jurisdiction over marriage, probate, defamation, and tithes, among other matters. That jurisdiction was not lost until variously between 1836 and 1858. Ecclesiastical courts do continue today but are largely concerned with ecclesiastical administrative matters.

There were two types of court business:

- **Office business**, i.e. disciplinary matters concerning morality and the behaviour of the public, which could include assaults on priests, misbehaviour in a church or churchyard, working on Sunday, recusancy, rowdy drinking, operating without a licence, irregular marriage, neglecting to baptise children, usury (money lending), witchcraft, blasphemy, adultery, fornication, bearing an illegitimate child, heresy etc.
- **Instance business**, i.e. civil cases between private individuals which concerned morality and offences against religion such as sexual misconduct, defamation, marital disputes (legal separation, not divorce), pew seat disputes, non-payment of church rates, granting professional licences (midwives, schoolmasters, surgeons, apothecaries, undertakers, parish clerks) etc.

The least serious cases would be dealt with at the archdeaconry court which met frequently on an ad hoc basis, sometimes as often as every three to four weeks. More serious cases would be referred to the bishop's court often held during the bishop's visitation (bishops were required to tour their dioceses to meet church officials and make enquiries of the clergy and congregation), with the most serious being reserved to the archbishop's court.

Surviving records are held at diocesan or local record offices, with records being in Latin prior to 1733. The records can consist of:

- **Muniment books** which recorded non-controversial matters such as the granting of licences. They are therefore less use from a genealogical perspective but may provide a starting point for research, providing clues as to what other records there may be and where (dates etc.).
- **Libel/Allegation** were the records or document that commence an action, depending on the type of case. These provide the name, location and occupation of the plaintiff, the name of the defendant, the nature of the complaint and the name of the judge.
- **Citations** which were issued to the defendant to answer the libel/allegation and to those witnesses who were required to

give evidence. They set out the name, residence (parish, county, diocese) and sometimes the occupation of the defendant along with a brief description of the charge against them and date when they were to attend court.
- **Personal Responses** (personal answers) of the defendant or accused which are normally straightforward answers to the libels or articles.
- **Depositions** were sworn examinations of witnesses that can provide a great deal of useful family history information. As well as their name, age, residence and occupation, depending on the dispute, they could include their place of birth, marital status (particularly for women), and information about where they lived in the past. There may be details about the deponent's wealth because a person's prosperity was an indicator of their reliability. They may include details of complex family relationships.
- **Act or Court Books** were used to record the daily business of the court, listing those who appeared in court and summarised the decisions taken.
- **Articles of Visitation and Enquiry** were a series of questions issued prior to the visitation, which were designed to elicit replies (*detecta*) from the churchwardens, forming the basis of their presentments. Such Articles usually include only basic details such as the person's name and details of their 'offence'.
- **Churchwarden Presentments/Visitation Records** brought causes to the ecclesiastical courts. Three series of visitation books may be found:
  1. the *liber cleri*, (call book or exhibit book) containing the names of clergy, churchwardens, schoolmasters and others summoned to the visitation
  2. the *liber compertorum* containing copies of the most important presentments, that is a list of things which were wrong in the parish
  3. the *liber actorum* (act book) recording, chronologically, various stages in 'correcting' the wrong including penances and other punishments

Prior to 1936, Surrey was within the Diocese of Winchester. In 1937, the ecclesiastical jurisdiction transferred to a newly created Diocese of Guildford. Records from 1937 are held at SHC; however, those records are significantly less important to the genealogist, except where an ancestor in the twentieth century was a member of the clergy.

For records prior to 1937, the Archdeaconry of Surrey had jurisdiction over the ancient parishes of Surrey, excluding thirteen parishes within the Peculiar Court of the Deanery of Croydon. The Archdeaconry records are largely found among records of the Diocese of Winchester held at TLA in series DD cover the years 1480–1936.

The records include Bishop's Transcripts, marriage licences (including marriage bonds and allegations), clergy's licences, registry material, church consecrations and dedications, dissenters' meeting house certificates, and terriers of church property in each parish, court probate material including wills, and the records of the Commissary Court of Surrey.

The records they hold are vast, consisting of 130.41 linear metres of records and include (excluding probate records):

- Ref: DW/AB   Assignation Books
- Ref: DW/CB   Consecration Books
- Ref: DW/CP   Consecration Papers
- Ref: DW/D   Certificates for Registering Dissenters' Meeting Houses
- Ref: DW/FB   Financial Records
- Ref: DW/K   Clergy
- Ref: DW/MB   Marriage Allegations
- Ref: DW/MC   Calendars of Marriage Licences
- Ref: DW/MP   Marriage Bonds and Allegations
- Ref: DW/OB   Muniments books
- Ref: DW/OC   Orders in Council
- Ref: DW/OP   Office Papers
- Ref: DW/PAB   Personal Answers Books
- Ref: DW/S   Terriers
- Ref: DW/T   Bishops' Transcripts
- Ref: DW/VB   Visitation Books

The TLA also holds some records for the Commissary court of Surrey (excluding probate):

- Ref: DW/PC/02   Acts of Court (4 items)
- Ref: DW/PC/03   Matrimonial and Testamentary Cause Papers (13 items)
- Ref: DW/PC/04   Cause Papers (14 items)

The largest set of records is held at Hampshire Records Office (HRO) in series 21M65 dating between 1282 and 2004 and include, among others (excluding probate records):

- Bishops' registers, 1282–1684
- Act books, 1743–1963
- Visitation books, 1517–1963
- Clergy visitation returns, 1725–1936
- Consistory court office act books, 1521–1683
- Instance act books, 1513–1968
- Depositions and responsa personalia, 1532–1695
- Cause papers by case and type, sixteenth–nineteenth centuries
- Ordination papers, 1715–twentieth century
- Meeting house certificates, 1702–1844
- Tithe maps and apportionments, 1839–53

Peculiar Court of the Deanery of Croydon
The parishes of Barnes, Burstow, Charlwood, Cheam, Croydon, East Horsley, Harrow Weald chapelry, Hayes, Merstham, Mortlake, St Mary's and Trinity Church Newington, Norwood, Pinner, Putney, Roehampton, St Peter's Walworth and Wimbledon fell within the jurisdiction of the Peculiar Court of the Deanery of Croydon. These parishes were exempt from the jurisdiction of the bishop. Its records are held at Lambeth Palace Archives in series VH and include (excluding probate records):

- Licences (VH 28–33)
- Dissenters: Registers (VH 37)
- Dissenters: Certificates (VH 38)
- Visitation records (VH 52–74)
- Court Records (VH 75–86) including Act books, Cause papers, and Orders of Penance
- Many administration, official and clerical records

As with many records, ecclesiastical court records are vast but can provide invaluable information to genealogists and family historians, particularly in periods when other records, such as parish records, may be lacking.

K. Heraldry

Heraldry is a vast and complex topic in itself but is worth a brief mention because the antiquarian Robert S. Boumphrey undertook extensive research into the coats of arms of families associated with Surrey.

Heraldry has a long history dating back to medieval times when symbols were a means of identifying knights in battle and tournaments; from this, it evolved into a complex system of symbols that conveyed lineage, alliances, and personal achievements. The heraldic language, with its own terminology and grammar, which developed over centuries, allowed for the precise description and reproduction of these complex symbols.

Today, heraldic records are sources not to be overlooked in genealogical research and are a particularly valuable resource which can bridge gaps in other records, dating from the later medieval period into the twenty-first century. New coats of arms are still created today.

The principal resources are the heraldic visitations published by the Harleian Society, many of which have been published and are available at the various commercial websites such as Ancestry, along with the various sources for identifying coats of arms and armigerous families, such as Papworth's 'Ordinary of British Armorials' and Burke's 'The General Armoury', which are also available to search on Ancestry.

Surrey has a long history and strong historical ties to the monarchy, captured through the coats of arms of its various towns, families, and institutions. Many of Surrey's ancient families have distinct coats of arms that have been passed down through generations. These arms often reflect the land, titles, and historical significance of the families. The presence of royal residences and significant historical events have also influenced local heraldic designs. The county of Surrey has its own coat of arms (originally granted in 1934 and replaced in 1974 due to the boundary changes) which reflects the heraldry of the region.

Boumphrey's work has been deposited at SHC and having been checked and edited by volunteers at Surrey Heritage, the Surrey coats of arms, containing over 4,000 coats of arms, are available as free downloadable PdFs from the SHC website. They are arranged alphabetically by surname proving details of the descent of the coat of arms and a blazon (a written description using specific heraldic language and syntax) of the coat of arms. These records should therefore not be overlooked when researching in Surrey.

L. Miscellany

The records discussed above represent the main and largest records available but often underused by family historians. However, they do not provide the complete picture of records available at local archives. Among many family papers are records relating to a wide range of topics. These include records of the slave trade associated with Surrey families such as the Goulburn Family of Betchworth, among whose papers are found 'The Bishop of Jamaica to Goulburn: reporting on the "progress" of the slaves on Goulburn's estates in Jamaica' dated 19 March 1832 (SHC Ref: 304/A1/2/8/43).

In relation to women in the twentieth century, SHC holds a large collection of records for local Women's Institutes, searchable by location (SHC main Ref: 7650), along with records for the Surrey Federation of Women's Institutes. The Women's Institute in England started in 1915. Its records can provide an insight into the roles of women, particularly in rural communities. They can include records of meetings, scrapbooks, notes about local events, records or notes relating to evacuees in the First and Second world wars, recipe books, photographs and much more.

For those with relative connections to the fairgrounds of Surrey and London, SHC is also home to the Philip Bradley Fairground Collection which contains, among other '44 volumes of "Fair notes" dating from 1932 to 1999' and 30,000 photographs. There is a research guide at the SHC website with the collection held under SHC Ref: 6790.

SHC holds records relating to Gertrude Jekyll who lived at Munstead Wood, Godalming and was a renowned garden designer in the later 1800s/early 1900s and also wrote *Old West Surrey* which offers an insight into her life and rural life and homes in and around Godalming. The records are held among various collections and the SHC research guide 'Gertrude Jekyll Collection' should be referred to for more details.

One last collection to highlight is that of Charles Lutwidge Dodgson, otherwise Lewis Carroll (1832–1898) for whom SHC holds several significant archives and again its research guide 'Lewis Carroll at Surrey History Centre' provides full details and for which there is a downloadable guide.

Chapter 5

RECORDS AT THE NATIONAL ARCHIVES

A. Civil court records

The English legal system has its origins in medieval times and the principles of common law which dominated the royal courts, known as the *Curia Regis*. Anglo-Saxon laws were based on local customs but, as the feudal system developed, the legal system became increasingly centralised eventually evolving into the central London courts, which ruled common law until the introduction of County Courts (County Courts Act 1846) and the introduction of the High Court (Judicature Acts 1873 and 1875).

Common law encompasses both civil and criminal law and is the foundation of the justice system based on judicial decisions which set precedents rather than written laws. These courts were characterised by juries, sworn on oath, investigating and deliberating cases.

Over time, the common law royal courts separated into civil and criminal law courts as we know them today.

Civil law courts further evolved into common law courts which act *in rem*, i.e. deal with claims against an item or property; and equity courts which *in personam*, i.e. acts only against the conscience of a person or several persons.

The earliest courts developed in the twelfth and thirteenth centuries:

- Curia Regis/King's Council (Later King's/Queen's bench) (now a division of the High Court)
- General Eyre (to the fourteenth century)
- Assizes (from thirteenth century to 1971)

- Exchequer (to 1880)
- Common Pleas (to 1880)

From the thirteenth century, Edward I introduced the most significant legal change of the Middle Ages, adopting unwritten common law into basic statute law. This remained for centuries and was supplemented by masses of specialised statutes passed to meet temporary problems as they arose. The Statute of Westminster 1285 introduced, among other changes, the writ, creating 'off the shelf' justice. Litigants could purchase *writs de cursu* (as a matter of course), later known as *writs ex debito justitiae* (as a matter of right), which were associated with particular circumstances and led to a particular kind of judgment.

These writs produced unjust results because plaintiffs could only bring a case if there was a single form of action or prescribed writ allowing it. This lack of a legal remedy left plaintiffs only one option: to petition the king. Petitions were originally processed by the King's Council. However, as the King's Council become overworked, they began to delegate the hearing of petitions to the Lord Chancellor, known as the Keeper of the King's Conscience.

During the fourteenth century, the Lord Chancellor established the Court of Chancery providing remedies that the strict procedures of other civil law courts were unable to provide. Chancellors at this time frequently had theological and clerical training and were influenced by the Roman concept of *aequitas*, thus developed the law of equity.

Several other central law courts developed and dissolved over time, each meeting a specific need or having a specific jurisdiction.

Claims coming before the courts are akin to today: breach of contract, personal injury, libel, slander, fraud, business/trade disputes, debt, and so on, but it is those claims relating to land, such as boundary disputes, inheritance disputes, fictitious claims to record transfers of land (see section on deeds) which are of particular interest to family historians.

The records of these civil law courts are vast and are held at TNA, with the largest series being:

- King's Bench – KB
- Common Pleas – CP
- Exchequer – E
- General Eyre – KB and JUST 1
- Chancery – C
- Assize – ASSI (see separate section below)

The records of the Chancery Court should be particularly noted because from the earliest records they are all written in English. Before 1733, records of the other courts were generally written in Latin.

The records of these courts, however, are not easy to access as many are not indexed in the TNA Discovery catalogue and with records being held by type rather than bundled together per case, contemporary indexes held in IND 1 need to be consulted to find the different types of documents; these vary between courts but include:

- Writs
- Pleadings
- General Eyre/Plea Rolls
- Depositions and Affidavits
- Documents and Exhibits
- Files
- Entry Books of Decrees/Orders
- Final Concords/Feet of Fines
- Decree Rolls
- Clerk Papers
- Masters' records (Documents, Certificates and reports, Exhibits)

In addition to the indexes in IND 1, there are various finding aids available:

- Anglo American Legal Tradition (**http://aalt.law.uh.edu/Commonwealth.html**)
- Bernau index (Chancery and Exchequer) at SOG
- Coldham's Index
- Inheritance Disputes Index 1574–1714 available at the Findmypast website
- Local records offices
- The List and Index Society (Chancery)
- Newspapers
- Index to *The Times*
- Index to the Dormant Funds in Chancery
- Estate Duty Registers

Courts were generally held every law term – Michaelmas (October), Hilary (January), Easter (March) and Trinity (June) – with records arranged by law term. For general information on court records held at

TNA and the associated records and finding aids, TNA research guides for the individual courts are the best starting point.

It is not possible to determine the size of the collection within these records for Surrey residents, property and land but it is fair to say it vast. The resources and finding aids specific to Surrey include a collection of indexes produced by Cliff Webb, published by WSFHS:

- A List of Surrey Feet of Fines 1558–1706 (five volumes; Record Series (RS) 20, 22, 24, 26 and 28)
- Handlist and Index to Surrey Cases and Depositions in the Court of Requests c.1500–1624 (RS 29)
- Handlist of Surrey Cases in the Court of Star Chamber 1485–1558 and 1603–1641 (RS 32)
- Surrey Cases in the Court of Chancery 1391–1714 – A Guide and Handlist (RS 34)
- Surrey Cases and Depositions–Chancery 1714–1758 and Exchequer 1497–1603 (RS 27)

These can be purchased from WSFHS via the GenFair website. The indexes, except for those of the Feet of Fines, are also digitised in the collection 'Surrey court cases 1391–1835' at Findmypast, which can be searched by name, year and court. Each entry provides name, year, court, county, country, names of other parties involved, WSFHS source, and the TNA reference. Note, the paper indexes available from WSFHS are arranged by location/parish BUT online they cannot be searched in this way.

B. Assize courts

The assize courts ('the assizes') were established in the thirteenth century, replacing the General Eyre, to deal, originally, with property disputes and in the later thirteenth century, civil cases originating in the Westminster courts by writ of *nisi prius*. This writ ordered a trial to be held in London unless the judges of the assizes visited the county first, which in practice is what usually happened. The type of civil disputes heard at the assizes included:

- Land
- Money or debt
- Personal injury
- Negligence
- Libel

They could also deal with civil matters that would otherwise be dealt with by quarter sessions, usually when the assize was to be held before the next QS. This could, therefore, include routine administration, licensing, repairs to highways, settlement and removal proceedings, etc.

Their remit was soon widened and by the late thirteenth century the courts were dealing with serious criminal cases of homicide, theft (stolen goods were often under-valued as worth less than 12d to avoid making it a capital offence), highway robbery, rape, assault, coining, forgery, witchcraft, trespass, vagrancy, recusancy, and infanticide. They retained their jurisdiction in civil cases under the writ of *nisi prius* and in the early twentieth century their jurisdiction was extended to deal with divorce cases, which had previously been the sole jurisdiction of the central London courts post-1856, parliament having created a secular divorce court in 1857 to replace the role of the ecclesiastical court in the determination of family matters.

The assizes typically sat twice yearly at Lent (spring assizes held in March/April) and summer (summer assizes heard in July/August) when judges from Westminster travelled round the country to six circuits:

Circuit	Counties
Home	Essex, Hertfordshire, Kent, Middlesex*, Surrey, Sussex
Midland	Derbyshire, Leicestershire, Lincolnshire, Nottinghamshire, Northamptonshire, Rutland, Warwickshire
Norfolk	Bedfordshire, Buckinghamshire, Cambridgeshire, Huntingdonshire, Norfolk, Suffolk
Northern	Cumberland, Lancashire, Northumberland, Westmorland, Yorkshire
Oxford	Gloucestershire, Herefordshire, Shropshire, Staffordshire, Worcestershire
Western	Berkshire*, Cornwall, Devon, Dorset, Hampshire, Oxfordshire*, Somerset, Wiltshire

* During the sixteenth century, two major changes occurred:

- Middlesex was removed from the Home Circuit and grouped with neighbouring City of London, which was served by the Old Bailey and never part of the circuits.
- Oxfordshire and Berkshire were transferred from the Western Circuit to the Oxford Circuit.
- The Welsh County of Monmouthshire was transferred into the Oxford Circuit.

The circuits of England remained largely static for almost four centuries. Wales was not included, being served by the Court of Great Sessions. By the nineteenth century, assizes sat more regularly, with spring, summer, autumn and winter assizes with circuits further reorganised:

Circuit	Counties
South-eastern (from 1876)	Cambridgeshire, Essex, Hertfordshire, Huntingdonshire, Kent, Norfolk, Suffolk Surrey (from 1893), Sussex
Midland	Bedfordshire (from 1876), Buckinghamshire (from 1876), Derbyshire, Leicestershire (from 1876), Lincolnshire, Northamptonshire (from 1876), Nottinghamshire, Rutland (from 1876), Warwickshire, Yorkshire (1863 to 1876)
Norfolk	Bedfordshire, Buckinghamshire, Cambridgeshire, Huntingdonshire, Leicestershire (1863 to 1876), Lincolnshire, Norfolk, Northamptonshire (1863 to 1876), Rutland (1863 to 1876), Suffolk.
Northern (from 1876)	Cumberland, Lancashire, Westmorland
North-eastern (from 1876)	Northumberland, Yorkshire and Durham
Oxford	Berkshire, Gloucestershire, Herefordshire, Oxfordshire, Monmouthshire, Shropshire, Staffordshire, Worcestershire
Western	Cornwall, Devon, Dorset, Hampshire, Somerset, Wiltshire
North Wales** (1830–1945)	Anglesey, Caernarvon, Chester, Denbigh, Flint, Merioneth, Montgomery
South Wales** (1830–1945)	Brecon, Cardigan, Carmarthen, Glamorgan, Pembroke, Radnor
Wales and Chester (from 1945)	Anglesey, Brecon, Caernarvon, Cardigan, Carmarthen, Chester, Denbigh, Flint, Glamorgan, Merioneth, Montgomery, Pembroke, Radnor

** replacing the Welsh Court of Great Sessions

The jurisdiction of the Old Bailey extended into parts of the counties of Essex, Kent and Surrey from 1834 when it was renamed the Central Criminal Court, although is still more commonly known as the Old Bailey.

Assizes records are held at TNA in series ASSI arranged by county, surviving from 1559 to 1971. The survival rate varies between counties.

Surrey assizes were usually held at Kingston upon Thames (usually the Lent assizes), and either Guildford or Croydon (usually summer assizes).

The main records for the civil side include:

- Minute books recording brief details of trials including the names of the parties, the type of case and the judgement order, including any made-on appeal
- Pleadings which set out the details of the claim brought and any defence
- Judgement orders
- Correspondence (largely administrative concerning the running of the court)
- Financial records providing details of the costs of a case

Surviving records for Surrey include and can be found in:

Record Type	Years covered	Series
Minute Books	1792–1971	ASSI 32
	1870–1890	ASSI 37
Other	1672–1970	ASSI 34*
	1754–1872	ASSI 38**
	c.1674–1908	ASSI 39***

* Includes civil cause books, 1673 to 1768; certificate books, 1876 to 1890; cost and account books, 1791 to 1890; clerk of indictments entry books, 1774 to 1827; postea books, 1769 to 1862; a presentment book, 1768 to 1804; process books, 1773 to 1863; judges' calendars, 1887 to 1923; costs books, 1959–1970; and a rule book, 1737 to 1741, being a record of *nisi prius* cases referred to arbitration.
** Estreats (records of fines and forfeits)
*** include posteas from 1694 and orders etc. and *nisi prius* from 1790. The series also includes papers of the lords' commissioners of appeal in prize causes, 1798 to 1799; and documents concerning appeal cases taken to the House of Lords, 1824 to 1855.

The main records for the criminal side include:

- **Crown and Gaol** (delivery) books (also known as minute or agenda books) which detailed the prisoners delivered from gaol to the court on a particular date, usually included the names of the accused, their charge(s), their plea, the verdict and sentence.

- **Indictments** which were the formal records of charges against a person and usually included the person's name and any aliases, their occupation, parish, date and details of the alleged offence, and a list of prosecution witnesses. They could also include the person's plea, the verdict and sentence.
- **Depositions** which were pre-trial witness statements; the survival rate is poor, with those for capital offence trials, such as murder and riot, being the most likely to survive.
- Other records: pleadings, statements of claim, defence and counterclaim, draft minutes of trials, correspondence of the assize clerks, mostly administrative, coroners' inquisitions, jury lists, financial business including fees and costs, and estreats (records of fines and forfeits).

Surviving records for Surrey include and can be found in:

Record Type	Years covered	Series
Crown & Gaol Books	1734–1943	ASSI 31
	1826–1971	ASSI 32
Indictments	1559–1688	ASSI 35
	1689–1850	ASSI 94
	1851–1971	ASSI 95
Depositions	1820–1971	ASSI 36
Other	1672–1970	ASSI 34
	1754–1872	ASSI 38
	c.1674–1908	ASSI 39
	1944–1957	ASSI 90

Records before 1559

- Plea rolls recording proceedings before itinerant justices sitting in various courts including the General Eyre (which was superseded by the assizes in the late thirteenth century), the early assizes, the Oyer and Terminer and some keepers of the peace (superseded by the justices of the peace), which are held at TNA in series JUST 1 dating variously between 1198 and 1528. These can be searched by county and year.
- Gaol Delivery Rolls and Files dating between 1271 and 1476 are held in series JUST 3 which again can be searched by county and year.
- Most files (including writs) of the justices in Eyre and of assizes for the period 1248–c.1450 are held in series JUST 4.

Some of these early records have been digitised and the images are available through the Anglo-American Legal Tradition website (AALT) (**http://aalt.law.uh.edu/AALT.html**).

Surrey Record Society has published the following records of the General Eyre:

- Volume XXXI. *The 1235 Surrey Eyre. Part I* Introduction and Biographia edited by C.A.F. Meekings and prepared for press by D. Crook (1979)
- Volume XXXII. The 1235 S*urrey Eyre. Part II* Text and Translation edited by C.A.F. Meekings and prepared for press by D. Crook (1983)
- Volume XXXVII. *Index to the 1235 Surrey Eyre* prepared by S. Neal and edited by D. Robinson (2002)
- Volume XXXVIII. *The 1258 to 1259 Special Eyre of Surrey and Kent* edited with an introduction by Andrew Hershey (2004)
- Volume XL. *The 1263 Surrey Eyre* edited with an introduction by Susan Stewart (2006)
- Volume XLV. *Royal Justice in Surrey, 1258 to 1269* edited by Susan Stewart (2013)

C. Land records

Inquisitions Post Mortem

Inquisitions Post Mortem (IPMs) were enquiries, commenced by writ in Chancery, by the Crown on the death of a tenant-in-chief from the thirteenth century until 1660. Their purpose was to identify a deceased tenant's heir, ensure they took possession of the property and swore fealty to the monarchy. IPMs were initiated when a deceased person was believed to be a tenant-in-chief. However, it was sometimes discovered that this was not the case, so IPMs do survive for those who were not tenants-in-chief.

A report on the inquisition was made to Chancery and there are two types of documents: the IPM itself and the entries in the Fine Rolls, both of which are in Latin. They date from 1235 to 1649 and the original records are held by TNA in C 132 to C 142, and E 149 to 150. In the series C 132 to C 142 there are almost 1,400 IPMs for Surrey.

IPMs include the name of the deceased, details of their land and property including value and services due, date of death, age and relationship of their heir. They may include details of other family members and/or a family history. Many other people may also be mentioned incidentally in the inquisitions as sub-tenants, trustees, jurors or witnesses, all of whom may have been called to corroborate events from their own knowledge.

Calendars of IMPs have been published covering 1236 to 1447 and 1485 to 1509, which are available at TNA and have been digitised and made available at the British History Online website (**www.britishhistory.ac.uk/series/inquisitions-post-mortem**) where abstracts (in English) of IPMs for the City of London between 1485 to 1561 and 1577 to 1603 are also available.

For IPMs between 1418 and 1447, Calendars have also been translated and digitised at the 'Mapping the Medieval Countryside' website (**https://inquisitionspostmortem.ac.uk**). Copies of Calendars may also be found at various websites such as the 'Internet Archive' website (**https://archive.org**) and in local archives.

SHC holds several records relating to IPMs, such as:

- Extracts from the Calendars of Inquisitions Post Mortem, thirteenth and fourteenth centuries, relating to Reigate (SHC Ref: 2277/7/6)
- Notes on Inquisitions Post Mortem for several Bletchingley families, 1273–1501 (LK90) (SHC Ref: 3924/11/21)
- Extracts from mediaeval records (including Inquisitions Post Mortem) relating to Albury manor. seventeenth century copies (SHC Ref: 1322/4/56–57)
- Copies (*c*.1502) of Inquisitions Post Mortem on William Sydney of Stoke D'Abernon, 17 June 1477, and Thomasina Hopton, 9 March 1499, with copies of deeds, 1476, relating to the Sydney estate. Two paper rolls, damaged (SHC Ref: LM/1620/1–2)
- Transcript (early twentieth century) of an Inquisition Post Mortem into the ownership of the lands of John Gaynesford, gent, deceased, made on 22 May 1560. Manor of Crowhurst, etc. Manor of Newlondes and lands called Darelondes and Motelonds, with a parcel of land called Blackgrove. Also parcels of land called Powlyns and Estlondes in Tandridge and Godstone. Anne Gaynesford was his sister and sole heir Document reference: PRO Chancery Inquisitions Post Mortem II. Vol 128 No 78 (LK 69) (SHC Ref: 3924/11/56)
- Paper endorsed 'Mr Wight's record' being an abstract of deeds, Inquisitions Post Mortem and court roll entries relating to the manor of Artington, 19 Hen III-1639, with marginal comments concerning encroachments, Mr Wight's claim to Harmans and disputed title to Longis Downes and Foote Meade, once in

possession of Sir Richard Pexall. Includes two small pedigrees of descendants of Radolphus de Brooke (Ralph de Broc) and Robert Loxley. (HMC p.599a; see also LM/COR/6/7–8, dated 1654) (SHC Ref: 6729/7/1–2)
- Transcripts of Chancery Inquisitions Post Mortem: John de Berewyco, 3 April 1314 (Ref: Edw II File 29 No 10) John de Crouhurst, 19 June 1323 (Ref: Edw II File 76 No 7) John le Latymer, 8 April 1336 (Ref: Edw III File 46 (14) John de Sancto, 27 April 1349 (Ref: Edw III File 104 (23) John de Warblyngton, 27 March 1351 (Ref: Edw III File 113 (4) Roger de Sancto Johanne, 4 May 1353 (Ref: Edw III File 121 No 2) William at Lee, 30 May 1499 (Ref: H VII Vol II 186 (124) With covering letters from Ethel Stokes who undertook some of the transcription (1924) (LK76) (SHC Ref: 3924/11/121)

IPMs between 1447 to 1485 and 1509 to about 1640 have not been calendared or digitised so the original records held at TNA need to be consulted. These can be searched in the TNA Discovery catalogue by name and county.

If an heir was a minor (under the age of 21) the king would claim wardship on the property. In such cases, after 1540, duplicates of IPMs can also be found in the Court of Wards and Liveries which administered and heard disputes relating to such property between 1540 and 1645. These can be found in series C 142, E 150, and WARD 7 which again can be searched by name and county.

National Farm Survey

With concern over food availability, in particular the reduced capacity to import food, in the midst of the Second World War, the National Farm Survey was taken between 1941 and 1943 to ensure every bit of available land was used for food production and farmed as efficiently as possible. It was a survey of around 300,000 farms of 5 acres or more (around 85 per cent of agricultural land). Each farm record consists of four forms: the first three being mailed to the farmer as part of the return for the farm census held on 4 June 1941, the fourth being the actual farm survey, or the 'primary survey'.

The records are held at TNA in series MAF 73 (Ordnance Survey maps) and MAF 32 (primary survey) and are arranged by county and parish. The information they provide includes:

- Maps showing the farm's boundaries and fields
- Details of the farmland

- Names of farmers and farm owners (where the farmer was a tenant)
- Terms of occupancy
- Details of life on a farm – conditions, crops, livestock, number of workers
- Details of the wider community within the parish where a farm was located

The records for Surrey are found in:

- Maps: MAF 73/40/1 to MAF 73/40/47
- Survey: MAF 32/ 1044 to MAF 32/1052

D. Tax records

Throughout the centuries, whenever the Crown has needed to raise money, be it to fund military causes, defence or other reason, taxes have been imposed to varying degrees. These tax records offer varying information.

Lay Subsidies

The Lay Subsidy was a tax levied on movable property rather than land, with the poor (paupers) and clerical property being exempt. It was first levied in the early thirteenth century at one-tenth of the value of property in towns, boroughs and the royal demesne, and one-fifteenth of the value of property elsewhere. It therefore became commonly known as the fifteenth and tenth. Lay subsidies continued to be raised as and when required until 1624 when they were abolished. Their usefulness for family history research is really from 1523 onwards. Between 1334 and 1524, only village totals are given because fixed sums were required from each village or township, so names were rarely recorded.

From 1523, 'the Great Subsidy' was levied for four years, based on the value of the person's moveable goods worth more than £2 per annum, wages of more than £1 a year or income from land, whichever was greater. The records provide the names of those paying tax along with the amount paid. It applied to everybody over the age of 16 at a rate of 4d in the pound (which varied over the years) with Roman Catholics and other Nonconformists being forced to pay double. Because the thresholds were low, many taxpayers were recorded.

While they do not provide any family history information, where an ancestor is listed, they can provide supporting evidence of their existence in that place at that time.

They are available at TNA in series E 179 and E359, county record offices and may have been indexed or calendared by local family history societies.

Searching the TNA E 179 database (**www.nationalarchives.gov.uk/e179**) for Surrey, identifies the first surviving lay subsidy to be that of 1332 for Kingston Hundred only. The majority of surviving records for Surrey are for the sixteenth and seventeenth centuries.

The following record series (RS) are available from WSFHS:

- MS 22: Calendar of Surrey Lay Subsidies, Western Surrey (1585–1603) (available to download)
- Calendar of Miscellaneous Elizabethan Lay Subsidies, Surrey (1570–1600) (RS 12)
- Calendar of Late Elizabethan and Stuart Lay Subsidies, Central and South-Eastern Surrey (1593–1641) (RS 31)
- Calendar of Surrey Lay Subsidies (1543–1547) (RS 37)
- Calendar of Surrey Lay Subsidies, Miscellaneous (1549–1561) (RS 39)

WSFHS has also produced a guide to the *Surrey Lay Subsidies 1500–1654* which can be downloaded from its website.

The calendars provide the names and amount paid arranged by Hundred and parish. They have also been digitised and are available to search by name, year, parish and Hundred at Findmypast in its collection 'Surrey lay subsidies 1524–1645'.

SHC also holds copies of some lay subsidies:

- Lay subsidy roll dated 1334 for the Hundred of Tandridge (SHC Ref: 2575/1/)
- Lay subsidy roll dated 9 April 1611 for the Hundreds of Tandridge and Reigate (SHC Ref: 3924/7/2)
- List entitled 'The book of the xvth for Bramley' dated 1526/1540 (SHC Ref: 5410/1/30)

Poll Tax

Poll Tax was first introduced in England in 1377 as a tax on individuals rather than land, property or wealth and was levied in 1377/8, 1379/80, 1381/2, 1513/4, 1641/2, 1660/1, 1677/8, 1694/5 and 1698/9 (although the records may be dated shortly after these dates).

Parish officials collected and compiled lists of residents over the age of 15 or 16, depending on which year the tax was levied, although they sometimes listed the entire household including children. It is thought that up to a third of the population who were liable evaded payment, even so, the records do include a high percentage of the population. Clergy only paid poll taxes in 1377, 1379, 1380, and 1381.

The records provide information about people who are rarely, if ever, mentioned in other documents and include names, occupations, parish addresses and family relationships. Again, these will not provide any genealogical information but can be used as supporting documentary evidence of an ancestor's presence in a parish at that time.

The original records are held by TNA in series E 179 and details of what survives for each county can be found in the guide created by Jeremy Gibson, *The Hearth Tax, other Later Stuart Tax Lists and the Association Oath Rolls*, in which the only surviving poll tax for the whole county of Surrey is stated to be that of 1677/8.

Searching the E 179 database, the earliest surviving poll tax is that of 1377. Other surviving poll tax records in E 179 for Surrey include poll taxes with documents dated 1514/5, 1517, 1641, 1667, 1678 and 1696. These records do not include the whole county, and in many cases, there are several for each year, each covering different Hundreds and parishes. The database should be consulted as to which Hundreds and parishes are included.

SHC also holds several records of, and relating to, poll tax:

- Poll Tax 1667, a transcript of accounts in E179/188/491(SHC Ref: Z/104)
- Transcript of the poll tax assessment of Walton-on-Thames, 1666 prepared by Walton and Weybridge Local History Society (SHC Ref: 7441/Box7)
- Notebook headed 'Poll tax assessments Walton-on-Thames 1666' (SHC Ref: 10201/Box5/6)

Hearth Tax
The Hearth Tax was a tax, imposed half yearly between 1662 and 1689, at the rate of 1 shilling on each hearth or stove in a building. Those exempt included paupers and those in houses worth less than 20 shillings a year, with only one or two hearths and chattels worth less than £10. The tax was paid by the occupier, but if a property was empty the house owner was liable, and from May 1664, landlords of exempt occupiers were liable for paying the tax.

Also exempt were charitable institutions such as hospitals and almshouses, and buildings with industrial hearths, except those businesses with ovens, such as bakeries or forges, had to pay.

The assessments provide a list of names. Occupations are rarely given; however, descriptions sometimes were, from which an occupation may be deduced, particularly if other records can also be found to support that deduction.

They provide little, if any, genealogical information, other than who the head of the household was at a certain date. However, as they were undertaken every half year the disappearance of an individual may indicate their death or that they have moved elsewhere.

Assessments dating from 1662 to 1666 and 1669 to 1674 are held in the Subsidy Rolls in series E 179 at TNA. However, there is an ongoing project to digitise and transcribe Hearth Tax records being undertaken by the University of Roehampton. Its database can be accessed and searched online for free at **https://gams.uni-graz.at/context:htx**. These include the Hearth Tax for Surrey taken in 1664, which has also been indexed and can be searched at the My Heritage website, and are available in Volume XVII, Surrey Hearth Tax 1664 edited by C.A.F. Meekings (1940) from Surrey Record Society.

Hearth Tax records also survive in varying degrees and for varying Hundreds and parishes for assessment conducted in Surrey in 1662, 1663, 1665, 1666, 1667, 1669, 1670, 1672, 1673, and 1674. Jeremy Gibson's *The Hearth Tax, other Later Stuart Tax Lists and the Association Oath Rolls* includes details of the parishes for which records survive; however, the E 179 database should also be consulted.

SHC also holds several records of and relating to Hearth Tax:

- Notes on persons chargeable for the Hearth Tax for the Borough of Bletchingley, 1663 (SHC Ref: 3924/11/44)
- Notes of names taken from the Horne Hearth Tax records, 1662 (SHC Ref: 3924/11/99)
- Note on the Surrey Hearth Tax, 1662–3, for Godstone and Tandridge along with a brief note on undated lay subsidy for the village of Tandridge (SHC Ref: 3924/11/91)
- Receipts for Hearth Tax paid on Loseley (thirty-three hearths) and two other properties in St Nicholas parish (three hearths; two hearths) (SHC Ref: LM/2179)
- Copies of warrants, 1675–1677, relating to the hearing of appeals against distraints for refusals to pay Hearth Tax by the Hospital of the Holy Trinity, Guildford (Abbot's Hospital), and Thomas Bignold of Chiddingfold (SHC Ref: LM/1047/36)

Free and Voluntary Present to Charles II 1661/2

This was an attempt to raise money for Charles II following his restoration to the throne. The payment was voluntary; however, the wealthier did subscribe. Those for Surrey are held at TNA in E 179/257/28 (excludes Brixton and Southwark) and for which a Calendar is available from WSFHS (MS 8) via the GenFair website.

Association Oath Rolls 1695

These include those who refused to swear the Solemn Association Oath introduced following the attempted assignation of William III under the 'Act for the Better Security of His Majesties' Royal Person and Government'. This would, in particular, include Catholics. Many of the records contain original signatures, but they also include marks and listings made by clerks.

The records survive for the county of Surrey and for individual parishes: Bletchingley, Gatton, Kingston upon Thames, Reigate, and Southwark. They are held at TNA in series C 213/269 to C 213/274, C 213/415–416.

SHC holds a manuscript extract of the Association Oath Roll for Merrow (SHC Ref: 5015/5/6) and a transcript is available from WSFHS to download via the GenFair website.

Chapter 6

DIRECTORY OF ARCHIVES, LIBRARIES AND SOCIETIES

In alphabetical order

Royal Berkshire Archives
9 Coley Ave, Reading RG1 6AF
Tel: 0118 937 5123
www.royalberkshirearchives.org.uk

British Library
96 Euston Road, London, NW1 2DB
Boston Spa, Wetherby, West Yorkshire, LS23 7BQ.
Email: customer@bl.uk
www.bl.uk

British Telecommunications Archive
BT Group Archives, Third Floor, Holborn Telephone Exchange, 268–270 High Holborn, London, WC1V 7EE
Email: archives@bt.com
www.bt.com/about/bt/our-history/bt-archives

Croydon Local Studies & Archives Service
Central Library, Croydon Clocktower, Katharine St, Croydon, CR9 1ET.
Tel: 020 8726 6900 Ext. 61112
Email: localstudies @ croydon.gov.uk
www.croydon.gov.uk/leisure/archives/lslibrary

East Surrey Family History Society
www.eastsurreyfhs.org.uk
www.eastsurreyfhs.org.uk/index.php/about-us/contact-us

Guildhall Library
Aldermanbury, London EC2V 7HH
Telephone: 020 7332 1868/1870
Email: guildhall.library@cityoflondon.gov.uk
www.cityoflondon.gov.uk/things-to-do/history-and-heritage/ guildhall-library

Hampshire Archives and Local Studies
Sussex Street, Winchester, SO23 8TH
Tel: 01962 846154
Email: Culture.InformationServices@hants.gov.uk
www.hants.gov.uk/librariesandarchives/archives

Kingston Heritage Centre
Guildhall, High Street, Kingston upon Thames, KT1 1EU
Tel: 020 8547 6738
www.kingstonheritage.org.uk

The London Archive (latterly the London Metropolitan Archives and formerly Greater London Records Office or GLRO)
40 Northampton Road, London, EC1R 0HB
Tel: 020 7332 3820
Email: TLA @ ms.corpoflondon.gov.uk
www.cityoflondon.gov.uk/things-to-do/history-and-heritage/london metropolitan-archives

Lambeth Archives
Minet Library, 52 Knatchbull Rd, London SE5 9QY
www.lambeth.gov.uk/libraries-0/minet-library
Tel: 020 7926 6076

Lambeth Palace Archives
15 Lambeth Palace Road, London, SE1 7JT
Phone: 020 7898 1400
Email: archives@churchofengland.org
www.lambethpalacelibrary.info

Society of Genealogists
40 Wharf Road, London, N1 7GS
Tel: 020 7251 8799
Email: hello@sog.org.uk
www.sog.org.uk

Southwark Local History Library
211 Borough High St, London SE1 1JA
Tel: 020 7525 0232
Email: local.history.library @ southwark.gov.uk
www.southwark.gov.uk/Sutton archives

Surrey History Centre
130 Goldsworth Rd, Woking, Surrey GU21 1ND
Tel: 01483 518737
Email: shs@surreycc.gov.uk
www.surreycc.gov.uk/culture-and-leisure/history-centre

Surrey Record Society
c/o Surrey History Centre (see above)

The National Archives
Bessant Drive, Kew, Richmond, TW9 4DU
Live chat Tuesday to Saturday (excluding bank holiday weekends) 09:00 to 17:00 and online enquiry form
www.nationalarchives.gov.uk

West Surrey Family History Society
https://wsfhs.co.uk
For any general queries about the Society, please email us at: secretary@wsfhs.org

NOTES

Introduction
1. Peter Brandon, *A History of Surrey*, p.11
2. The county of Sussex was not separated into two distinct county councils until 1888.
3. Walter De Gray Birch, *Cartularium Saxonicum*, p.55
4. Birch ibid p.106
5. Birch ibid p.64
6. Also known as Suthriea, Suthereia Sutherie Suthereye Suderige and Sudrei
7. *The Anglo-Saxon Chronicle*, Part 2: AD 750–919 as transcribed and digitised at The Medieval & Classical Literature Library **http://mcllibrary.org/Anglo/part2.html**
8. The Anglo-Saxons **www.theanglosaxons.com/the-will-of-king-alfred**
9. Simon Keynes, *Kingston-upon-Thames, The Blackwell Encyclopaedia of Anglo-Saxon England*.
10. *Domesday Book, A Complete Translation*, p.71
11. Surrey County Council www.surreycc.gov.uk/culture-and-leisure/countryside/what-to-see/woodlands
12. Martin Tupper, *Stephen Langton, or, The days of King John*
13. Rev. Owen Manning and William Bray, *The History and Antiquities of the County of Surrey* Volume 1, p.i
14. Surrey County Council *Count me in Census 2001: 200 years of the Census in ... Surrey*; 1801 census return, TNA, Kew, London, Reference: HO 107 and 1881 census returns, TNA, Kew, London, Reference: RG 11.
15. Ibid; 1891 census return, TNA, Kew, London, Reference: RG 12
16. Ibid
17. Ibid
18. *Count me in Census 2021*: Office of National Statistics **www.ons.gov.uk**

Chapter 1
1. Surrey County Council 'Count me in Census 2001: 200 years of the Census in...Surrey'
2. **www.surreyhillssociety.org/surrey-a-county-of-rural-peasants**

3. Brayley Hodgetts, E.A., *The Rise and Progress of the British Explosives Industry: History of Gunpowder* (1909) p.18
4. **https://wandle.org/aboutus/displays/wandle**

Chapter 2
1. SHC Reference HORS/1/1
2. SHC Reference COB/1/1

Chapter 4
1. As noted in the 'The borough of Guildford: Borough, manors, churches and charities' section of *A History of the County of Surrey*: Volume 3 published at British History Online (**www.british-history.ac.uk/vch/surrey/vol3/pp560-570#fnn5**)
2. Porter, Roy, *Madmen: A Social History of Madhouses, Mad-Doctors & Lunatics*, p.156 and Whittaker, Duncan, *The 700th Anniversary of Bethlem. Journal of Mental Science*, p.742
3. Andrews, Jonathan; Briggs, Asa; Porter, Roy; Tucker, Penny; and Waddington, Keir, *The History of Bethlem*
4. Early Mental Health Records – Quarter Sessions and Private Asylums, Exploring Surrey's Past **www.exploringsurreyspast.org.uk/themes/subjects/mental_hospital_records/early_mental_health_records_quarter_sessions_and_private_asylums/** (22 May 2024)
5. John Coffey, *Persecution and toleration in Protestant England, 1558–1689* p.147
6. Coffey ibid p.151
7. David L. Wykes, *Early Religious Dissent in Surrey after the Restoration*, Southern History Society volume 33 (2011) p.54
8. As published in *The 1851 Religious Census Surrey* transcribed by Cliff Webb, edited by David Robinson, published by Surrey Record Society at p.lxv

BIBLIOGRAPHY

Books

Andrews, Jonathan, Briggs, Asa, Porter, Roy, Tucker, Penny, and Waddington, Keir, *The History of Bethlem* (1997, London & New York: Routledge)

Aubrey, John, *The Natural History and Antiquities of the County of Surrey* (Five volumes, 1719, London)

Birch, Walter De Gray, *Cartularium Saxonicum* (1885, Whiting & Company (Ltd), London)

Brandon, Peter, *A History of Surrey* (1998, The History Press, 2nd Edition)

Coffey, John, *Persecution and Toleration in Protestant England, 1558–1689* (2000, Longman, Pearson Education Press)

De La Bedoyere, Guy, *Diary of John Evelyn* (2004, Boydell Press)

Gibson, Jeremy and Dell, Alan, *Tudor and Stuart Muster Rolls* (1989, Federation of Family History Societies)

Gibson, Jeremy and Medlycott, Mervyn, *Militia Lists and Muster 1757–1876* (1994 (3rd edition) Federation of Family History Societies))

Gibson, Jeremy, *The Hearth Tax, Other Later Stuart Tax Lists and the Association Oath Rolls* (1987, Federation of Family History Societies)

Janaway, John, *Surrey: A County History* (1994, Countryside Books)

Keynes, Simon, *Kingston-upon-Thames in The Blackwell Encyclopaedia of Anglo-Saxon England* (2001, Blackwell Publishing)

Lapidge, Michael, Blair, John, Keynes, Simon, and Scragg, Donald, *The Blackwell Encyclopaedia of Anglo-Saxon England* (2001, Blackwell Publishing)

Malden, Henry Elliot, *Victoria County History: Surrey* (Four volumes, 1902–1912, Westminster, Archibald Constable and Company Limited)

Malden, Henry Elliot, *A History of Surrey* (first edition 1900, republished 1977, E.P. Publishing Ltd)

Manning, Rev. Owen and Bray, William, *The History and Antiquities of the County of Surrey* Volume 1 (1804, John White, London)

Members of The Cranleigh and District U3A, *Cranleigh Life and Times: Two Centuries of Everyday Life in a Village* (1999, The Cranleigh and District U3A, Cranleigh, Surrey)

Porter, Roy, *Madmen: A Social History of Madhouses, Mad-Doctors & Lunatics* (2006 revised ed., Stroud Tempus)

Seymour, B. & Warrington, M., *Bygone Cranleigh* (1984, Phillimore)

Surrey Record Society, *Surrey Musters* (Volume 3 (originally Number 2) in four volumes, 1914 to 1920, Surrey Record Society) (available to download for free from https://archaeologydataservice.ac.uk/)

Surrey Record Society, *The 1851 Religious Census Surrey* (1997, transcribed by Cliff Webb, edited by David Robinson, published by Surrey Record Society)

Tupper, Martin, *Stephen Langton, or, The Days of King John* (1880, Frank Lasham, Guildford)

Williams, Dr Ann and Martin, Professor G.H., *Domesday Book: A Complete Translation* (1992, Penguin Books),

Academic papers

Brayley Hodgetts, E.A., 'The Rise and Progress of the British Explosives Industry: History of Gunpowder', (1909, Published under the Auspices of the VIIth International Congress of Applied Chemistry and its Explosives Section by Whittaker & Co, London)

Crocker, A.G., Crocker, G.M., Fairclough, K.R., and Wilks, M.J., 'Gunpowder Mills: Documents of the 17th and 18th Centuries', (2000, Surrey Record Society, Vol XXXVI)

Crocker, A., 'The Paper Mills of Surrey', (3 parts) (Surrey Local History Council, 1889–90 Vol IV, Nos. 1, and 4; Vol V, No. 1 published by Phillimore p.49)

Crocker, G., 'The Godalming Framework Knitting Industry', (Surrey Local History Council, 1889-90 Vol IV, No. 1 published by Phillimore, p.3)

Hodgkinson, J., 'Iron Production in Surrey', (2004 *Aspects of archaeology and history in Surrey: towards a research framework for the county* Surrey Archaeological Society, Chapter 17, pp. 233–44)

Parton, A.G., 'Parliamentary Enclosure in Nineteenth-Century Surrey: Some Perspectives on the Evaluation of Land Potential', (British Agricultural History Society, *The Agricultural History Review*, Vol 33, 1985, p.51)

Priestley, M., 'Gunpowder', (2006, The RH7 History Group, Fact Sheet 37, https://www.rh7.org/)

Surrey County Council, *Count me in Census 2001: 200 years of the Census in... Surrey* (PDF: **surre_tcm77-181790 at www.surreyi.gov.uk**)

Whittaker, Duncan, 'The 700th Anniversary of Bethlem', *Journal of Mental Science* (1947, Vol 93, issue 393, published online by Cambridge University Press: 8 February 2018)

Wykes, David L., 'Early Religious Dissent in Surrey after the Restoration', *Southern History Society*, Volume 33, 2011 p.54

Websites

Ancestry **www.ancestry.co.uk**

Exploring Surrey's Past **www.exploringsurreyspast.org.uk** (as of 8 November 2023)

Family Search **www.familysearch.org**

Findmypast **www.findmypast.co.uk**

Free BMD **www.freebmd.org.uk**

The Genealogist **www.thegenealogist.co.uk**
GenFair **https://genfair.co.uk**
General Registration Office **www.gro.gov.uk**
My Heritage **www.myheritage.com**
Hitchhikers Guide to the Galaxy **https://h2g2.com/approved_entry/A1745 1047** (as of 22 November 2023)
Probate Service **https://probatesearch.service.gov.uk/#wills**
Surrey Hills Society **www.surreyhillssociety.org** (as of 8 November 2023)
Surrey Hills **https://surreyhills.org**
The Anglo-Saxons **www.theanglosaxons.com/the-will-of-king-alfred** (as of 8 November 2023)
The Fourth Reserve **https://fourthreserve.org/railway** (as of 8 November 2023)
The Medieval & Classical Literature Library **http://mcllibrary.org** (as of 8 November 2023)
UKBMD **www.ukbmd.org.uk**
The Wey River **www.weyriver.co.uk/theriver**
Wonersh History Society **www.wonershhistory.co.uk**

INDEX

Abinger, xvi, 11, 23, 63, 107
Addington, xxi, 31, 34, 39, 63, 118
Addlestone, 4, 50, 52
Administration, 38–39, 41–47, 65, 66, 82, 92, 110–11, 141, 152, 159
Admon, 41–43
 see also Administration
Agricultural, x, 1–2, 10, 43, 52, 110, 165, 177
Agricultural Labourer, 1–3, 12, 22, 70
Agriculture, v, xviii, 1, 3, 12, 20, 120, 128
Albury, xii, xvi, 4, 10–11, 23, 63, 125, 164
Alfold, 13, 23, 63, 107
Allegation, 27–29, 149, 151
Almshouses, xviii, 78, 168
 see also Poorhouses; Workhouse
Anabaptist, 145
Ancestry, vii, 16, 19, 26, 28–29, 32, 40–44, 47, 54–58, 81, 89, 123–124, 130, 145, 153, 177
Apportionment, 61–62, 152
Apprentice, 124–125, 130, 132
Apprenticed, 74, 82, 123–124, 126–129
Apprenticeship, 3, 82, 119–120, 124–129, 134
Apprenticeship Indentures, vi, 123–127, 134
Archbishop, xv–xvi, 27, 38, 41, 115, 143, 149
Archdeacon, 38, 68
Archdeaconry, 28, 38, 151
Archdeaconry Court, 28, 39–46, 149
Arches, 38
Artington, 164
Arun, xx

Arundel, xix
Ash, 23, 62
Ashford, xxi, 25, 50–51, 62, 106
Ashtead, 25, 34, 60, 63, 123
Assize, 85–86, 90, 158–162
Assize Court, vi, 85, 158
Association Oath Rolls, 127, 168–170, 176
Asylum, 22, 85, 89, 135–136, 138, 140–142, 175
Award, 61, 105–106, 109

Banns, 19, 24, 26, 29, 145
Banstead, xii, xix, 2, 18, 34, 51–52, 63
Baptised, 25, 122
Baptism, 19, 23–26, 28–32, 79, 82, 145, 147
Baptist, 35, 142, 144, 146, 148
Barnes, xxi, 39, 63, 107, 146, 152
Basingstoke, xiii, xx
Bastard, 81–82
Bastardy, 82, 86, 127, 134
Bastardy Bonds, 81, 129
Battersea, xxi, 25, 34, 66, 104, 123
Beckingham, 122
Beddington, xii, xvi, xxi, 18, 25, 34, 57, 63, 66, 87, 120, 123
Bedfordshire, 159–160
Bedlam, 133
 see also Bethlem
Berkshire, x, xiii, 18, 55, 66, 159–160
Bermondsey, xxi, 10, 17, 25, 31, 66, 79, 123, 144
Betchworth, 34, 63, 107, 116, 153
Bethlem, 135, 175–177
 see also Bedlam

Bexley, 92
Birth, ii, 15–17, 19, 23–24, 29–30, 36, 48, 64, 77, 79, 81–82, 134, 148, 150
Bishop, v, xv, 23, 27–28, 31, 38–43, 115, 143, 148–149, 150–153
Bishops Transcripts, 148
Bisley, 23
Blackheath, 7, 133–134
Blacksmith, 3, 11–12
Bletchingley, xvi, 20, 34–35, 39, 56, 63, 106, 141, 164, 169–170
Borough, vii, xiii, xv–xvi, xviii, xxi, 7, 17–19, 25, 32, 51–53, 55–57, 62, 65, 82, 84, 87, 90–92, 95–96, 99, 106, 118, 122–123, 127, 132, 166, 169, 173, 175
Boundary, vii, x–xi, xx–xxii, 5, 10, 17–18, 61, 65, 77, 79, 105, 110–112, 114, 117–118, 153, 156, 165
Bramley, 23, 34, 63, 97, 107, 167
Brickmaking, 13–14
Brickworks, 13–14
Bridewell, 93
Brighton, xx, 14
British Library, iv, 50, 114, 131–132, 135, 171
British Newspaper Archive, 50
Brixton, 34, 92, 96, 170
Brockham, 117
Bromley, 92, 135
Brookwood, xx, 136, 138
Brookwood Asylum, 136–138
Buckinghamshire, 159–160
Buckland, 5, 63, 107
Burial, xviii, 19, 23–26, 28–32, 35, 139, 145, 148
Byfleet, xii, xvii, 10, 13, 23, 34, 52, 106

Camberley, 50–51
Camberwell, xix, xxi, 17, 25, 34, 66, 79, 123
Cambridge, 119, 123, 177
Cambridgeshire, ii, 159–160
Canal, ii, xx, 85
Cane Hill Asylum, 136, 141
Canon, xii, 24, 115, 148
Cantabrigienses, 123
Canterbury, xii, xvi, 24, 31, 38, 41, 114–115, 119, 147
Capel, 14, 23, 63, 107, 116
Carshalton, xii, xvi, xxi, 7, 11, 13, 18, 25, 34, 57, 61, 63, 66, 118, 141
Caterham, 18, 31, 34, 50–51, 63, 141

Catholic, ii, 9, 59, 142–147, 166, 170
Catholicism, 142–143
Catteshall, 10
Cemetery, 32, 145
Census, ii, 14, 20–23, 79, 109, 119–121, 132, 144, 165, 174–175, 177
Census Returns, v, 3, 19–23, 53, 79, 120, 174
Certificate, 15, 19, 60–61, 70, 74–75, 92, 127, 134, 145–146, 148, 151–152, 157, 161
Chaldon, xii, 34, 63, 107, 117
Chancery, 102, 105, 112, 156–158, 163–165
Chancery Court, 102, 145, 157
Chapel, 26, 31–32, 35, 144–147
Charlwood, 34–35, 39, 63, 107, 136, 142, 152
Charterhouse, 121, 123
Cheam, xii, xxi, 18, 25, 34, 39, 57, 61, 66, 106, 118, 152
Chelsham, 34, 63
Chepstede, xii
Chertsey, xii, xvii, 1, 13, 17–18, 23, 30, 50, 52, 64, 79, 81, 106, 114, 116, 118, 136, 142, 146
Chessington, xxi, 34, 63
Chester, 160
Chichester, x, xix
Chiddingfold, 12–13, 23, 63, 107, 169
Chilworth, xvi, 6–7, 10, 13, 147
Chipstead, xii, 34, 63
Chobham, 14, 20–21, 23
Christchurch, 114
Church, ii, iv, 2, 16, 19, 26–27, 29, 31–35, 38–39, 48, 61, 65–66, 68, 70, 95, 104, 114–115, 119–120, 122–123, 136, 142–149, 151–152, 175
Churchwarden, 20, 66, 68–70, 74, 77, 128, 150
Churchyard, 149
Civil, vi, xviii, 7, 22, 24–25, 38, 48, 84–88, 111, 138, 143, 149, 155–156, 158–159, 161
Civil Registration, 15, 19, 22–23, 28
Clandestine, 26, 67
Clandon, xii, 23, 63, 117
Clapham, xix, xxi, 25, 66, 123
Clay, xv, 1, 3, 13–14
Claygate, 60
Clergy, xvii, 9, 24, 27, 61, 132, 143, 148–152, 168

Clergyman, 16
Clerical, 152, 156, 166
Clerk, 20, 55, 66, 84, 87, 100, 141, 148–149, 157, 161–162, 170
Clerkenwell, 65
Cobham, xii, 11, 13, 23, 25, 50, 60, 65, 106, 108–109
Coldharbour, 12, 14
Commissary Court, 28, 38–42, 44–45, 151
Commission, 5, 61, 84, 92, 95, 135, 148
Commissioned, 84
Commissioner, 60, 105, 161
Common, xviii, 1–2, 9, 14, 25–26, 34–35, 37, 62, 85–86, 99, 101–102, 104–105, 112, 121, 143, 148, 155–156
Common Pleas, 100, 102, 106, 156
Compton, xii, 23, 63, 144
Congregational, 32, 35, 144, 146–147
Congregationalist, 142, 146
Consistory Court, 38–43, 45, 152
Constable, 66, 71, 77, 79, 82, 84, 132, 176
Copyhold, 36, 101, 1010–112
Copyhold Land, 55, 101, 110–111
Copyholders, 57, 89
Cordwainers, 3, 9
Coulsdon, xii, xxi, 18, 31, 63, 136, 138
Court, xvi–xvii, xix, 36–42, 44, 46–48, 64, 66, 68, 77, 84–87, 90–92, 94, 100, 102, 105, 109–114, 117–118, 145, 148–151, 155–162, 164–165
Court Baron, 111–112
Court Records, vi, 39, 102, 110–112, 116, 118, 145, 148, 152, 155, 157
Craftsmen, v, 3, 124
Cranleigh, 11–12, 18, 23, 26–28, 50, 58, 63, 67, 69, 72–73, 82–83, 98, 107, 113, 120–122, 147, 176–177
Crowhurst, 9–10, 14, 35, 63, 108–109, 164
Croydon, iv, xvi, xviii, xx–xxi, 17–18, 30–32, 34–35, 39, 44, 50, 53–54, 63, 79, 87, 92, 95, 122–123, 141, 144, 147, 151–152, 160, 171
Cuddington, xii, 2, 5, 63, 118

Deanery, 38–39, 44, 151–152
Death, ii, xvii, 15–17, 19, 29–30, 32, 36–37, 41, 43, 46–47, 64, 70–71, 79, 81, 85, 111–112, 115, 138–139, 148, 163, 169

Death Duty Wills, 46
Deed, ii, 36, 39, 96–103, 105, 112, 114, 116, 147, 156, 164
Demonstrating, 25
Deptford, xxi, 66, 123
Diocesan, 38, 45, 61, 149
Diocese, 24, 28, 32, 38, 61, 143, 149–151
Ditton, 23, 60, 63
Dockenfield, 23, 62, 107, 115, 142
Dorking, xiii, xvi, 5, 14, 17–18, 23, 30, 50, 64, 79, 81, 107, 129, 142, 144, 147
Dormansland, 14, 146
Dunsfold, 12, 23, 107

Earlswood, 136, 142
Eashing, xiii, 10
East Surrey Family History Society, viii–ix, 31, 34, 127, 134, 172
Ecclesiastical, vi, 22, 26, 37–39, 42, 46, 68, 110, 145, 148–150, 152, 159
Ecclesiastical Court Records, vi, 39, 145, 148, 152
Education, 119–120, 122–123, 176
  see also School
Effingham, xii, 23, 60, 63, 104, 107, 147
Egham, 18, 23, 50–52, 106, 134–136
Electoral Registers, v, 56–58, 88–89
Elmbridge, xv, 30, 50, 52, 60
Elstead, 23, 34, 63, 107, 142
Enclosure, 2, 84, 105–106, 109, 133, 177
Enclosure Awards, 2, 89, 104–106
Enfranchisement, 101–102, 110, 112
Epsom, xii, xix, 2, 17–18, 32, 34–35, 50–52, 62, 78, 118, 136, 138, 140–141, 144, 146
Esfhs, ix, 23, 31, 34
  see also East Surrey Family History Society
Esher, xii, xvii, xix–xx, 11–12, 18, 23, 51–52, 60, 63, 117–118
Essex, ii, 48, 54, 159–160
Establishment, xviii, 8, 96, 136, 141, 144
Estate, xviii–xix, 3, 32, 39, 41, 43, 46–47, 57–61, 87, 100, 102–103, 105–106, 108–109, 116, 145–146, 154, 157, 164
Estreat, 90, 112, 160–161
Exchequer, 102, 105, 145, 156–158

Familysearch, 16, 177
Farleigh, xxi, 35, 62, 107, 117
Farley, 118

Farm, xii, 2–3, 9–10, 12, 116, 165–166
Farmed, 165
Farmer, xiii, xviii–xix, 1–3, 9, 13, 105, 165–166
Farming, 1–3, 13, 105
Farncombe, 10
Farnham, xii–xiii, xvii–xviii, 2, 7–8, 17–18, 23, 34, 51–52, 56, 129, 133–134, 144, 147
Fetcham, 5, 23, 62
Feudal, xv, xvii, 109–110, 155
Findagrave, 32
Findmypast, 16, 19, 21, 26, 29, 32, 40–41, 44–47, 50, 54, 90, 123–124, 127, 131, 157–158, 167, 175, 177
Forge, 11–12, 168
Freebmd, 16, 177
Freehold, 55–56, 62, 100–101, 110–111
Freeholders, 56–57, 84–85, 88–89, 111, 118
Freemason, ii, 89, 92
Freemen, 55–56, 127–128
Frensham, 23, 107, 115, 117, 141
Frimley, 18, 23, 63, 135, 147

Gaol, 22, 64, 71, 84, 93–96, 161–163
Gatton, 56, 63, 170
Gatwick, xvi, 51
Genealogist, 55, 62, 64, 150, 152, 178
General Eyre, 155–158, 162–163
General Registration Office, v, 15, 178
Glassmaking, 3, 13
Godalming, xiii, xv, xix–xx, 8, 10, 18, 23, 39, 50–52, 60, 63, 121, 133–134, 146–147, 154, 177
Godley, 60
Godstone, 5, 7, 14, 17–18, 63–64, 79, 81, 107, 117, 141, 164, 169
Goldsmith, 124–126
Gomshall, xvi, 10
Graveney, xxi, 25, 35, 66, 117, 123
Graves, 33
Graveyard, 145
Grinstead, 17, 79
Guild, 119, 124
Guildford, xiii–xv, xvii–xviii, xx, 7–8, 10, 14, 17–18, 20, 23, 30, 50–52, 56, 63–64, 79, 81–82, 86–87, 90–91, 95–96, 116, 118, 121, 125–127, 133, 135, 144, 146–147, 150, 161, 169, 175, 177
Guildhall Library, 53, 172

Guldford, 121
Gunpowder, 3, 5–7, 13, 175, 177

Ham, 35, 60, 63
Hambledon, 13, 17–18, 23, 30, 63, 79, 107
Hampshire Archives and Local Studies, 172
Harrow, 107, 152
Hascombe, 23, 63, 107
Haslemere, xviii, xx, 12, 18, 23, 56, 63, 147
Hastings, xiii
Headley, 34–35, 107
Hearth Tax, 168–169, 176
Heraldry, vi, 151–153
Herefordshire, 159–160
Hersham, 21, 52
Hershey, 163
Hertford, 10
Hertfordshire, 54, 56, 159–160
Hindhead, 145
Holloway Sanatorium, 136, 139–140
Hook, 60, 123
Horley, 18, 51, 63, 107
Horne, 35, 63, 106, 169
Horsell, 23–24, 63, 109, 116, 118
Horsemonger, 95–96
Horsham, 147
Horsley, 23, 39, 62, 106, 152
Horton, 32
Hospital, xviii, 32, 64, 93, 135–136, 138, 141–142, 147, 168–169, 175
Houses of Correction, 79, 84, 93
  see also Prison
Huguenot, ii, 9, 13, 143, 148
Huntingdonshire, 159–160

Ifield, 63
Illegitimate, 74, 81–82, 149
Inclosure Awards, 104
  see also Enclosure Awards
Incumbent, 26, 31, 66, 68, 144
Indenture, 124–126, 127–128
Independent, 35, 51, 53, 134, 142–144, 148
Inheritance, 111–112, 115, 155–156
Inherited, 36, 110
Inland Revenue Valuation Records, v
Inquest, 48, 139
Inquisitions Post Mortem, 163–165
Inventory, 42–45, 122

Ireland, iv, 50, 123
Irish, ii
Iron, xx, 3, 11–13, 177
Ironforging, 5
Ironmaking, 3
Ironmasters, 12
Ironmongers, 3
Ironworks, 11–12

Jewish, ii, 144–146
Jews, 26, 143–144
Jurisdiction, 38–39, 44, 46, 84–85, 88, 92, 149–151, 156, 159–160

Kennington, 35
Kent, x, xii–xiii, xv, 48, 50, 54–55, 92, 115, 135, 159–160, 163
Kew, xxi, 35, 60, 173–174
Kingston, xiii, xxi, 17–19, 30, 35, 52, 56, 60, 63, 81, 86–87, 91, 95, 121, 126, 132, 136, 142, 144, 161, 167, 170, 172, 174, 176
Kingston Heritage Centre, 50, 52, 91, 172
Kingswood, 35, 63
Kirdford, 13
Knaphill, xx

Labourers, 2, 12, 14, 86
Laleham, xxi, 25, 62, 106
Lambeth, xix, xxi, 17, 25, 41, 44, 66, 81, 115, 123, 134, 172
Lambeth Archives, 134, 172
Lambeth Palace Archives, 152, 172
Land, v, x, xii–xiii, xv, xvii–xx, 1–3, 7, 22, 35–36, 38, 43, 55–56, 58, 61–63, 71, 85, 89, 99–102, 104–106, 109–113, 115–118, 145–146, 153, 156, 158, 163–167, 177
Land Ownership, vi, 96
Land Records, vi, 163
Land Tax, v, 55–56, 59–61, 85, 88–89, 104, 145
Landholder, xvii, 104–105, 112, 115
Landholdings, 104
Landlord, 103, 168
Landowner, xvi, 2, 20, 59, 61–64, 105, 113
Landowning, 12
Lay Subsidies, 166–167
Lease, 57, 97, 99–102
Leased, 12

Leasehold, 101, 111
Leaseholders, 57, 62, 111
Leatherhead, xiii, 18, 39, 50–51, 63, 118
Lingfield, 9–10, 12, 14, 63, 106
Livery, 99–100, 124, 127–128, 165
Lloyd George Domesday Survey, v, 61
London, ii, vii–x, xii–xiii, xv–xvi, xviii–1, 3, 5–7, 10, 12, 14–15, 17–19, 25–26, 28–30, 32, 38, 40, 52–55, 57, 62, 65, 92–93, 115, 121, 123–127, 131, 135–136, 138, 142, 144–145, 154–155, 158–159, 164, 171–174, 176–177
Long Grove Hospital, 138, 140
Loseley, xviii, 87, 106, 115, 132, 146, 169
Lunatic, 85, 175–176

Magistrate, 86, 90
Malden, xvii, xx–xxi, 21, 35, 52–53, 60–61, 63, 104, 118, 176
Manor, vi, xii, xvii–xviii, 2, 5, 7, 36, 39, 100–101, 103, 108–118, 164, 175
Manor Asylum, 136, 140
Manorial, xvii, 36, 39, 43, 59–60, 64, 66, 100–103, 105–106, 108–110, 112–114, 116, 118
Manorial Court Rolls, 111, 117
Manorial Records, vi, viii, 100–101, 109, 112–114, 116
Marriage, ii, 15–17, 19, 23–32, 36, 48, 68, 77, 102, 144, 146–148, 150
Married, 27, 36, 41, 120
Marry, 27, 82, 125
Marrying, 74
Marshalsea, 94
Matrimonial, 151
Maybury, 125, 142
Mayford, 64
Mental Deficiency Act, 141
Mental Health Asylums, vi, 135
Merchant, ii, xix, 2, 12, 53, 128
Merstham, xii, 5, 23, 31, 35, 39, 63, 107, 114, 146, 152
Merton, xvi, xxi, 8, 11, 18–19, 32, 34–35, 61, 118, 147
Mestham, xii
Methodist, 143–144, 146–148
Micham, xii
Mickleham, 23, 107, 135
Middlesex, x, xxi, 18–19, 25, 30, 34, 39, 48, 51–52, 54, 62, 106, 124, 129, 159
Military, vi, 32, 36, 85, 96, 109–110, 120, 129–130, 134, 166

Military Records, 63, 129–131
Militia, vi, xviii, 82, 127, 130–135
Militia Lists, 132, 176
Mill, v, 3–7, 9–13, 23, 177
Millers, 9, 135
Molesey, xii, xvii, 7, 12, 23, 60, 63, 109, 117
Monastery, xii, xvii, 99–100, 113–115, 119, 121, 142
Monmouthshire, 159–160
Monumental Inscriptions, v, 30, 32–35
Morden, xxi, 11, 32, 34, 61, 129
Mortlake, xxi, 5, 20, 39, 63, 104, 106, 127, 134, 152
Munstead, 154
Muster Rolls, 131–133, 176
Myheritage, 178
Mytchett, xx

National Archives, 115, 169, 175
National Farm Survey, 167
National Probate Calendar, 46
Netherne Hospital, 140–141
Newdigate, 14, 23, 35, 64, 105, 108
Newington, xxi, 17, 25, 39, 67, 82, 87, 93, 96, 124, 128, 146, 154
Newspaper, v, 10, 48, 50–53, 125, 159
Nonconformist, 85, 144–148, 150, 168
Nonconformity, 144, 146, 148
Nondenominational, 144
Nonparochial, 148
Nonsuch, xvii–xviii, 2, 5
Norbiton, 146
Norfolk, ii, 159–160
Northampton, 29, 172
Northamptonshire, 159–160
Northumberland, 6, 158–160
Northumbria, xiii
Norwood, 152
Nottingham, 84
Nottinghamshire, 159–160
Nutfield, 35, 39, 63

Oatlands, xvii
Occupation, v–vi, 1–3, 5, 7, 9, 11, 13, 27, 32, 37, 41, 47, 56, 90, 96, 98, 111, 120–122, 124, 127, 132–135, 146, 149–150, 162, 168–169
Occupier, x, 20, 57–64, 71, 98, 103, 168
Ockham, 23, 63, 118
Oglethorpe, xix
Ottershaw, 116, 142

Overseer, 20, 70–71, 74, 75, 79, 82, 127–128
Overseers of the Poor, 66, 70, 72–73
Owner, xix, 13, 20, 56–57, 60–64, 99, 101, 103, 166, 168
Ownership, 61, 64, 99, 164
Oxford, 118–119, 159–160
Oxfordshire, ii, xiii, 159–160
Oxonienses, 123
Oxted, 14, 21, 63, 132, 135

Paper, 3, 10–13, 19–21, 24, 31, 39, 43, 48, 56, 59–61, 77, 86–87, 90, 92, 102–103, 106, 112, 134, 139–140, 151–153, 157–158, 161, 164, 177
Papermaking, 5, 10–11, 48
Papist, 84, 145
Parish, vi, xi, xviii–xix, xxi, 2, 13–14, 17, 19–26, 28–32, 34, 38–39, 41, 43, 57–58, 60–68, 70–71, 74–78, 81–83, 90, 102, 104–108, 110, 114–115, 118, 120, 122, 126–128, 131–134, 144–145, 149–152, 158, 162, 165–170
Parish Apprenticeships, 128–129
Parish Records, 28, 30, 58, 77, 79, 82–83, 106, 129, 145, 152
Parish Registers, v, 23–24, 26, 28–32, 65, 109, 145
Patient, 64, 82, 135–136, 138–142
Pauper, ii, 166, 168
Peculiar Court, 38–39, 44–45, 151–152
Peculiars, 45
Pedigrees, 165
Peperharow, 23
Petersham, xii, xxi, 60
Petty, xii, 92–93, 136
Petty Sessions, vi, 84–86, 90–92
Pirbright, 23
Polesden, xix
Poll, xvii, 57, 168
Poll Books, v, 55–56
Poll Tax, xvii, 167–169
Pollingfold, 115
Poor, xviii–xix, 1, 15, 24, 64–68, 70–71, 74, 79–82, 86, 92, 104, 106–107, 119–120, 127–129, 131, 134, 141–142, 147, 162, 166
Poor Relief, 68, 70–74, 79, 81, 128
Poorhouses, 71
Population, xv, xvii–xviii, xx–3, 19–21, 48, 99, 110, 121, 132, 135, 148, 168
Portsmouth, xx

Prerogative Court of Canterbury, 40–44
Presbyterian, 142–144, 148
Presentment, 86, 91, 145, 150, 161
Press, 11, 51, 85, 163, 176–177
Prison, 26, 79, 82, 90, 93–96
Prisoner, ii, 64, 86, 89–90, 92–96, 160
Private Apprenticeships, 124–127
Probate, vi, 35–47, 148–149, 151–152, 178
Protestant, 143, 146, 175–176
Protestation, 145
Putney, xx–xxi, 25, 35, 39, 66, 122, 152
Puttenham, 23
Pyrford, 23, 63–64, 118

Quaker, 26, 120, 143–145, 147–148
Quarter Sessions, vi, ix, 77, 82, 84, 90, 92–94, 111, 124, 159, 175

Railway, ii, xx–xxi, 14, 84, 176
Rate, xix, 2, 32, 58, 64–67, 69–72, 76, 80, 85, 102–103, 105–106, 112, 118, 147, 158, 160, 164, 166
Recusancy, 143–144, 147, 157
Regiment, 93, 128–131
Regimental, 129
Registration Districts, 15, 17–19, 22
Registry, 46–47, 146, 149
Reigate, xvi–xvii, 5, 17–18, 35, 56, 62, 80, 85, 106, 125, 140, 162, 165, 168
Removal, 9, 76–78, 85, 88, 136
Richmond, xvii, xix, xxi, 17–19, 59, 62–63, 80, 144, 171
Ripley, 23, 115
River, vii, x, xiii–xvi, xix–xx, 3–5, 7, 9–13, 176
Roehampton, 39, 150, 167
Rotherhithe, xxi, 5, 17, 25, 65, 78, 122
Royal Berkshire Archives, ix, 55, 169
Royal Earlswood Asylum, 134, 137
Runnymede, xv–xvi, 18
Rural, ii, x, xviii, 1, 30, 106–108, 154, 174

Saxon, xii–xiii, 99, 109–110, 155, 174, 176, 178
School, vi, xvii, 48, 64, 119–123, 147
Schoolmaster, 120, 143, 149–150
Settlement and Removal, 70, 74, 77, 159
Shalford, xvi, 23, 39, 107, 147

Shepperton, xxi, 25, 50–51, 62
Shere, xvi, 23, 63, 104, 113
Shottermill, 106
Shropshire, 159–160
Society of Genealogists, 33–34, 44, 123–124, 173
Soldier, 36, 38, 129
Southwark, x, xxi, 17, 25, 29–30, 56, 66, 81, 87, 91–92, 94–96, 117, 123, 127, 132, 134, 144, 170, 173
Southwark Local History Library, 173
Spelthorne, xxi, 106, 142
Springfield Asylum, 136, 138, 141
St Ebba's Hospital, 136, 138, 140
Stanwell, xxi, 39, 62
Stoke, 10, 23, 60, 116, 135, 164–165
Streatham, xii, xxi, 25, 66, 123
Subsidy, 119, 145, 166–167, 169
Surbiton, xviii, 35, 52–53, 60, 63, 136, 147
Surrey History Centre, v, viii–ix, 29, 64–65, 113, 125, 131, 154, 173
Survey, 61–63, 105–106, 108, 112, 114, 118, 165–166
Sussex, x, xiii, xv–xvi, xviii, xx, 11, 13, 17, 48, 51–52, 54–55, 60, 61, 159–161, 172, 174
Sutton, xii–xiii, xvi, xxi, 18–19, 25–26, 29, 34, 51, 53, 57, 61, 63, 66, 121, 136, 173
Sutton Local History and Archive Centre, 53

Tadworth, xii, xix, 5
Tandridge, xvii, 35, 63, 164, 167, 169
Tax, 56, 59–62, 71, 84, 103–104, 166–169, 176
Tax Records, v–vi, xvii, 58, 89, 145, 166, 168–169
Teddington, 63
Tenant, xv, xvii, 2, 57, 64, 99, 101, 104–105, 110–112, 118, 163–164, 166
Tenement, 116–117
Tenure, 36, 57, 110
Testator, 36–37, 41
Thames, vii, x, xii–xiii, xv, xvii, xix–xx, 5, 12, 19, 21, 23, 59, 63, 86–87, 91, 95, 106, 126, 144, 161, 168, 170, 172, 174, 176
the National Archives, vi, viii–ix, 65, 155, 157, 159, 161, 163, 165, 167, 169, 173

Thorpe, xii, 23, 39, 106, 109, 142
Thursley, 12, 23, 63, 104, 107
Tilford, 106
Tillingbourne, xvi, 4–5, 7, 10
Tithe, 61–62, 71, 85, 149, 152
Tithe Records, v, 60, 82
Tolworth, 5, 7, 63
Tongham, 116, 135
Tooting, xii, xxi, 25, 35, 66, 123
Trade, ii, v, 1, 3, 5, 7, 9, 11, 13–14, 20, 36, 41, 53, 124, 127, 153, 156
Trade Directories, 53
Tudor and Stuart Muster Rolls, 129, 174
Twickenham, 62

Urban and Rural District Council, 106, 108
Useful Indexes, v, 63

Vauxhall, xix, 35
Vestry, 20, 66–68, 71, 77, 79, 82, 104, 129
Visitation, 68, 135, 148–153

Waddington, xii, 175–176
Wales, 15, 38, 40, 47, 60, 93, 110, 119, 160
Walkhampstead, 117
Wallingford, xiii
Wallington, 11, 57, 60, 63, 92
Walliswood, 14
Walloons, 143
Walworth, 39, 152
Wanborough, 23, 63
Wandle, xv–xvi, 3–4, 7, 9, 11, 175
Wandsworth, xvi, xx–xxi, 7, 9, 11, 13, 17, 25, 29, 51, 66, 81, 95–96, 123, 136
Warlingham, 107
Watermills, 4–5, 11
Waverley, xvii–xviii, 7
Way, 5, 16, 29, 66, 74, 79, 82, 86, 99–103, 115, 158

Weald, xii, xv, 11, 13, 152
Weavers, 9
Wesleyan, 148
West Park Hospital, 136, 138, 141
West Surrey Family History Society, viii–ix, 30, 34, 127, 134, 173
Westminster, 7, 100, 156, 158–159, 176
Westmoreland, 6
Westmorland, 159–160
Wey, xv, xx, 3–4, 7–10, 12–13, 178
Weybridge, xii, xv, xvii, xx, 13, 21, 23, 50–52, 61, 106, 147, 168
Wills and Probate, v, 35, 38–40, 42–44, 148
Wiltshire, 159–160
Wimbledon, xx–xxi, 5, 18, 34, 39, 51, 53, 123, 126, 133, 146–147, 152
Winchester, 28, 32, 38–43, 45, 115, 118, 150–151, 172
Winchfield, xii
Windlesham, 23, 29, 106
Window Tax, 103–104
Windsor, 17–18, 52, 66, 81
Wisley, xx, 23, 117
Witchcraft, 149, 159
Woking, xv, xx, 1, 10, 14, 18, 23, 29, 50–52, 63–65, 96, 109, 125, 136, 142, 173
Woldingham, 35, 63, 147
Wonersh, 8–9, 23, 107, 147, 178
Wonham, 105
Woodmansterne, 31, 35, 63
Worcester, 48
Worcestershire, 159–160
Workhouse, 22, 64, 71, 79, 81, 120
Worplesdon, 23
Wotton, xviii, 5, 7, 23, 63, 107

Yeoman, 120, 125
York, 6, 38, 176
Yorkshire, ii, iv, 125, 159–160, 171